THE
gastro
pub
COOKBOOK

PUDDINGS

Sticky Toffee Pudding
Treacle Tart
Bread + Butter Pudding
Vanilla creme terrine with a fruit coulis
Lemon creme brulee
Meringues with clotted cream

Dark Rich chocolate torte
Fruit crumble

Cheese Board
Pudding wine

THE gastro pub

COOKBOOK

with a guide to more than
150 of the best dining
pubs in Britain and Ireland

DIANA HENRY

photographs by Jason Lowe

MITCHELL BEAZLEY

For everyone who helped with the research for this book — my sister, Lesley, my mum and dad and, most of all, my husband Iain — with love and thanks.

The Gastropub Cookbook
by Diana Henry

First published in Great Britain in 2003 by Mitchell Beazley,
an imprint of Octopus Publishing Group Limited, 2–4 Heron Quays,
London E14 4JP.
© Octopus Publishing Group Limited 2003
Text © Diana Henry 2003
Reprinted in 2003
First published in paperback 2005

ISBN 1 84533 194 X
A CIP catalogue record for this book is available from the British Library.

While all reasonable care has been taken during the preparation of this edition, neither the publisher, editors, nor the authors can accept responsibility for any consequences arising from the use thereof or from the information contained therein.

Commissioning Editor:
Rebecca Spry

Executive Editor:
Kate John

Executive Art Editors:
Yasia Williams, Christine Keilty

Design:
Miranda Harvey

Photography:
Jason Lowe

Editor:
Hattie Ellis

Recipe Editor:
Diona Gregory

Production:
Sarah Rogers

Index:
John Noble

Typeset in Spectrum and Vectora

Printed and bound by Toppan Printing Company in China

Acknowledgements
I would like to thank all the chefs and owners of the pubs in this book for sharing their recipes and their knowledge, and for talking to me about their aims and philosophies – they have been an inspiration. Thanks also to Glenda Davies at the Welsh Tourist Board, the Irish Tourist Board, Sally and John McKenna of *The Bridgestone Food Lover's Guide to Ireland* and Caroline Workman of *The Bridgestone Food Lover's Guide to Northern Ireland*, for giving invaluable help, advice and support.

The creative team behind the book has been a joy to work with. Miranda Harvey has done a stunning design job, Hattie Ellis has been a constant guiding hand and an extremely sensitive editor, and Jason Lowe has produced thrilling and brilliant photographs. The commissioning editor, Rebecca Spry, showed so much dedication and devotion to the project you'd have thought this was the only book on her list. Thanks also to Diona Gregory for editing the recipes so carefully and to Yasia Williams for overseeing the design.

Putting *The Gastropub Cookbook* together has been a huge project – bigger than any of us realized at the outset – and turned into something of a labour of love. Friends and family have looked after children, eaten both wonderful and terrible meals and acted as unofficial scouts, coming up with recommendations for pubs all over the country. I would particularly like to thank Phillipa and Andy Thomas, Eleanor Logan, Bernadette Brewster and Penny Marr. My greatest debt, though, is to my sister Lesley, who came up with the idea for this book in the first place, my parents, Joan and Robin Henry and, most of all, my husband Iain. They have considered recipes, looked at designs, put up with my terrible working hours and driven thousands of miles to find the best dining pubs in the country. Here is the fruit of your labours...

contents

In 1991 David Eyre and Mike Belben, who had worked together in restaurants, decided to open their own eating place. They didn't have enough money to open a restaurant and besides they were, as they put it, 'sick of the ponciness' of them, so they bought a run-down pub in London's Farringdon Road. Mike kitted the place out with mismatched china, battered furniture, sagging sofas and a few lamps with wobbly shades; David produced gutsy, no-nonsense food. 'We didn't want anything artificially aged or pretentious,' says Belben. 'The day we opened, David brought in his cookbooks and put them on the shelves. It felt like a home. It was real. I knew we'd got it right.'

The Eagle was an instant hit. Since then 'gastropubs', as they have come to be known, have opened all over London, and everywhere else, too. They have evolved so much — many of the newest models eschewing the shabby-chic and no-nonsense cooking of the original concept in favour of sleeker furnishings and food — that Belben feels The Eagle can no longer be regarded as a 'gastropub'. The original vision, he argues, has been lost.

Of course, the Eagle wasn't the first pub in Britain to serve good food. The cooking in some country pubs is legendary: the Walnut Tree Inn in Abergavenny in Wales is now a restaurant, but when Franco Taruschio opened it in 1963 it was a pub, where you could have a pint as well as great Italian food. The Angel in Hetton was transformed 20 years later by a Yorkshireman, Denis Watkins, who thought that putting good food in one of our greatest

introduction

national assets was an obvious thing to do. Both places have had a huge influence on country pubs. But The Eagle was the first pub to serve good food with such idiosyncratic style in a city where a trend could be set. This was the kind of cooking that depended on good ingredients, but that didn't require a battalion of chefs to prepare it. It was elevated domestic cooking; the kind of stuff that could be done well in a pub.

Chefs had been talking about the importance of sourcing ingredients for a long time, then BSE emphasized that this wasn't just a fad, but something important for health. We became more interested in where our food had come from and what was going on in the countryside. We started to visit farmers' markets and to buy directly from small producers. The number of artisan food producers shot up and, even if people didn't live in the countryside, they wanted to be linked to it. Many chefs who had trained in London decided to go back to their rural roots and cook in pubs. They didn't even have to buy a pub — enterprising breweries, whose pubs were seriously under-performing,

saw the financial potential in selling pub leases to driven young chefs who would put the place on the map and therefore increase alcohol sales.

Some of the most successful gastropub chefs have had little training, and cooking in a pub has allowed them to develop at their own pace. But many city born-and-bred chefs, trained in Michelin-starred restaurants, are also choosing to cook simpler food in the country instead of chasing accolades. For numerous chefs, working in a pub means freedom. For most of them, it is also important to be part of a rural community. Steve Reynolds, who gained the first gastropub Michelin star at the Stagg in Titley, Herefordshire, made a firm decision to source locally and to provide a home-from-home for locals where good food could be an everyday experience. I have lost count of how many chefs in dining pubs have said this was part of their motivation.

This commitment to local produce is good business for farmers and food producers. In many places, chefs in dining pubs have had a direct effect on what is grown and produced around them. Andrew Pern at the Star in Yorkshire, for example, helped a farmer start a business producing free-range chickens. There is a satisfying connectedness about this that goes beyond just serving food that tastes good. As Andrew looks round his bar, he says: 'Over there I can see the farmer who raises my beef, the man who shoots a lot of my game and a local cheese-maker. They provide for me; I feed them; their produce is eaten by everyone who lives round here: it's the way it should be.'

Some people argue the food should always be simple, but dining pubs are as different from each other as restaurants are. There are pubs in this book in which hardly any cooking goes on. At O'Sullivans, on the southwest tip of Ireland, you'll find only poached wild salmon, dressed crab and seafood chowder, but it's some of the freshest fish you will ever eat. At the other end of the scale are pubs with Michelin stars, such as The Stagg Inn in Herefordshire or The Star Inn in north Yorkshire. In Scotland I also looked at hotel bars, as they often serve the function of a pub there. A gastropub is simply a place in which you can have a drink, but which also serves great food. Whether the cooking is sophisticated or simple, the food should be true to itself, not straining after fashion or too elaborate for the kitchen to pull off.

Gastropubs are not a fad. They are our brasseries, our bistros, and they are here to stay. In the introduction to his book *Great British Chefs*, published in 1989, Kit Chapman paid tribute to the service done by Franco Taruschio at the Walnut Tree Inn in Abergavenny by providing great food in the place in which British people feel most at home: the pub. He concluded that the battle for an improvement in British dining would be won or lost in pubs. 'What is needed', he said, 'is more chefs of the order of Franco Taruschio to take up popular feeding with the same passion and enthusiasm as their confrères in the glitzier places.' He could not have imagined how prophetic this would be.

the west country

If the West Country didn't exist we would have to invent it. More than perhaps any other region, it is the essence of our idealized view of England. There's Devon, with its slumberous hills, sunken leafy lanes and snug villages, their very names – Butterleigh, Appledore – evoking the fat of the land and the scent of fruit blossom; Wiltshire, with its stone circles and sense of mystery and paganism; and Cornwall, a place of crooked houses tumbling down to the sea, cobbled streets and mesmerizing alleyways.

The region's cooking is synonymous with richness. Even the sound of a West Country burr is thick with the texture of butter and cream – and this isn't just a flight of fancy. The whole area has superb cheeses such as Beenleigh Blue, Cornish Yarg and, of course, farmhouse Cheddar. Then there's clotted cream, so lusciously fat that a buttery yellow crust sits on its surface. Wiltshire produces succulent, traditionally cured hams and smoked bacon. Devon has great beef (some of the country's best organic meat producers are in the West Country). Apples and pears are used to make cider, cider brandy and perry, and berries and plums find their way into fruit liqueurs.

And the greatest bounty of all? It's in the sea. Fish from the coast and rivers of Devon, Cornwall and Dorset are transported all over the country, but here they are at their freshest: John Dory, turbot, brill,

mackerel, crab, lobster and prawns, and fish with Mediterranean warmth – red mullet, bream and squid. The wide range is the result of west Cornwall's unique position, jutting out into the Atlantic towards the Bay of Biscay and benefiting from the warm gulf stream. There's plenty of wild food too: game from the woods and moors; blackberries, sloes and elderflowers from the hedgerows and trees.

Much of the cooking is robust, homely, and uniquely suited to pubs: think of ham hock and wild mushroom pie, fish cooked in cream and cider or baked black cap apples. Some chefs produce more refined, contemporary dishes, that still retain a strong regionality. For instance, at The Dartmoor Inn in Lydford you'll find mussel and saffron tart and Dittisham plum sorbet. There's plenty of modern seafood cookery, too, with foreign influences deftly incorporated without leaving local flavours out in the cold. You'll find menus listing first-class Cornish John Dory, with capers and anchovies beside creamy fish pie with saffron.

Not everything in the garden is rosy. Many chefs find there aren't enough small, quality producers to supply them. Others despair about disappearing apple varieties, and want the region's cherry and plum orchards to be revitalized. But on the whole the West Country has the best of all worlds. The diversity of its landscape – from undulating, fertile hills to granite-flecked moors, from stretches of balmy, Riviera-like coast to boiling seas of cream and grey froth – means it produces a tremendous range of foods. The area's relative isolation has helped it to retain its regional identity, and the effect of chefs such as Rick Stein, who champion and respect what is unique to the area while bringing in new ideas and ingredients, has influenced both cooks and eaters. It's very good news.

Moorside

Lydford

Okehampton

Devon

01822 820221

serves lunch and dinner tues to sun

lunch; bookings advised; children

welcome (although no under fives on

fri and sat night); courtyard garden

the dartmoor inn

Karen and Philip Burgess are having a meeting in the cosy office above their pub. Karen, a small, energetic blonde, is sewing antique buttons onto felt Christmas trees. Philip, a big man with the kind of exhausted face only chefs and junior doctors have, is drinking copious amounts of espresso, batting around ideas for a 'Flavours of Burgundy' dinner and wondering aloud which single-variety apple juices to put behind the bar. The Burgesses don't just run a pub; they manage a powerhouse of creativity.

When the Burgesses bought the Dartmoor Inn five years ago it had a juke box, four deep-fat fryers and eight microwaves. Karen, who had spent childhood holidays here, barely recognized the place. They set about transforming a run-down boozer into a country inn that would stop Martha Stewart in her tracks. It's old England meets New England. A small bar, with a roaring fire, gleaming copper and a huge vase of flowers, is at the centre of a network of dining rooms furnished with colour-washed dressers, ladder-backed Goldilocks chairs and plants in aged terracotta pots. Karen, who has never quite decided whether she is really a chef or a painter (she has worked as both), has done everything herself, from the wood panelling to the hand-sewn quilts on the walls.

The food is a touch American too, though in style rather than flavour. The Burgess's favourite restaurant is Chez Panisse in San Francisco, the birthplace of modern Californian cooking, and you can see its influence. Like Chez Panisse's founding chef, Alice Waters, they've used French attitudes to food to invigorate the cooking of their own area. The 'Flavours of Burgundy' dinner could just as well be celebrating the produce of Devon and Cornwall, with dishes such as mussel and saffron tart and Devon beef cooked in Burgundy with baby onions.

Also like Waters, the Burgesses spend a lot of time sourcing ingredients and forging links with small-scale producers who can provide them with the quality they want. With their butcher, they decide which breed of cattle, South Devon or Ruby Red, has the best meat for a particular dish. Fish — John Dory, scallops, crab and Cornish sea-bass — comes daily from the market at Brixham or from fishermen Philip knows at Looe. Fruit and veg come from hand-picked local growers, and the cheeses are a changing selection of the West Country's finest.

The Burgesses want to offer their food to the widest range of people and believe a pub is the best place to do that. They're as happy to serve you fish and chips with half a pint of ale as they are to bring on a three-course dinner and a £40 bottle of wine. And they don't just want to feed you; they want you to taste the countryside and to be surrounded by pictures and artefacts that will help you enjoy the food even more. It works: there are few places, anywhere, with as much heart and soul as the Dartmoor Inn.

squash and radicchio risotto

This is a great autumnal dish — the sweetness of the squash and slight bitterness of the radicchio match each other perfectly. It's one of the Dartmoor Inn's most popular vegetarian dishes, though you could also cook it with the addition of chunks of pancetta and use chicken instead of vegetable stock.

serves 4

for the cream sauce (optional)

20g (3/4oz) cold unsalted butter

200ml (7fl oz) double cream

20g (3/4oz) Parmesan cheese, freshly grated

salt and pepper

for the risotto

400g (14oz) squash flesh (Crown Prince or butternut)

55g (2oz) unsalted butter

60ml (4tbsp) olive oil

2 large shallots, finely chopped

1 red onion, finely chopped

6 cloves garlic, finely chopped

1.2 litres (2 pints) veg stock

325g (11 1/2oz) arborio rice

120ml (4fl oz) dry white wine

60g (2 1/4oz) Parmesan cheese, freshly grated

1 small head radicchio, core removed, leaves finely sliced

200g (7oz) hazelnuts, roasted and skinned, finely chopped

to serve

8 slices squash, cut about 1.5cm (½ inch) thick and/or 4 wedges radicchio (optional)

olive oil

Parmesan cheese shavings

4 sprigs parsley

1 To make the cream sauce (optional), cut the butter into small cubes. Put the double cream and grated Parmesan cheese in a pan. Whisk together and bring to the boil, then whisk in the butter. Remove from the heat and season.

2 If you want to garnish the risotto with pumpkin slices and/or radicchio wedges, brush both with olive oil and roast the pumpkin at 180°C/350°F/gas mark 4 until lightly brown and tender and grill the radicchio under a medium heat until coloured and slightly wilted. Keep them warm in a low oven.

3 To make the risotto, cut the squash into 1.5cm (½inch) cubes. Melt half the butter with half the olive oil in a heavy-based pan and gently cook the shallots, red onion and garlic on a low heat for 5 minutes.

4 In a separate pan, bring the stock to the boil.

5 Add the rice, white wine and half the Parmesan cheese to the shallot mixture, stir well and season. Add the squash, followed by one-third of the boiling stock. Stirring constantly, simmer until all the stock has been absorbed by the rice — approximately 5 minutes.

6 Repeat the process with another third of the boiling stock. Finally, add the remaining stock. You must stir all the time. The rice is cooked when it is soft, with a slightly chewy centre. The stock should be used up just at the point that the rice is cooked, so add the final third slowly to ensure you don't add too much.

7 If you're serving the cream sauce, when the rice is nearly cooked, very gently reheat the sauce in the pan — it must not boil.

8 Stir the finely sliced radicchio into the risotto with the toasted hazelnuts and the remainder of the olive oil, butter and Parmesan cheese. Check the seasoning.

9 Take 4 warm plates. Serve a mound of the risotto on each and pour around the cream sauce. Place pumpkin and/or radicchio slices on top of each plate of risotto, if using, with some Parmesan shavings and a sprig of parsley.

braised beef short ribs with pickled walnut relish

Short ribs, or 'tip of rib', as they are known in England, is a very flavourful cut of beef that certainly proves the saying, 'the nearer the bone, the sweeter the meat'. You should be able to get this cut from a good butcher.

serves 4

1.8kg (4lb) beef short ribs

salt and pepper

55g (2oz) plain flour

olive oil

4 large shallots, roughly chopped

1 medium leek, white and pale green parts only, roughly chopped

1 medium carrot, peeled and roughly chopped

2 plum tomatoes, roughly chopped

4 cloves garlic, smashed

6 sprigs thyme

3 bay leaves

285ml (1/2 pint) red wine

710ml–1.2 litres (1 1/4–2 pints) hot beef stock

for the pickled walnut relish

good handful parsley, finely chopped

zest of 1/2 lemon

1 large clove garlic, finely chopped

115g (4oz) pickled walnuts, finely chopped

20ml (4tsp) olive oil

1 Cut the short ribs into 5cm (2 inch) pieces, roughly square, so that each piece includes a bone. Trim off any excess fat. Season generously with salt and pepper and dust lightly with the flour.

2 Preheat the oven to 220°C/425°F/gas mark 7. Heat a little olive oil in a large, heavy-bottomed pan and sear the short ribs until lightly browned all over.

3 In another heavy-bottomed pan, heat a little olive oil and sauté the shallots until lightly coloured. Stir in the leek and carrot, and cook gently until softened, then add the tomatoes, garlic, thyme and bay leaves and cook for a few more minutes.

4 Pour the vegetables into a large baking dish – big enough to hold the short ribs – and spread them out. Arrange the ribs on top, bone side up, then pour on the red wine and add enough hot beef stock to just cover them.

5 Cover the dish tightly with foil and place in the oven. After 15 minutes, reduce the heat to 180°C/350°F/gas mark 4 and cook slowly for approximately 2–2½ hours, until the meat is tender but not falling off the bone.

6 When the beef is ready, pour off the cooking juices and vegetables into a bowl and turn the ribs over so that the bone side is down. Increase the oven temperature to 220°C/425°F/gas mark 7 and, once the oven is ready, cook the meat for 10 more minutes.

7 Meanwhile, strain the cooking juices, reserving the vegetables, then carefully spoon off any grease from the top. Pour the juices into a saucepan, then boil to reduce the liquid by half to intensify the flavour and thicken it a bit. Purée the vegetables and add them to the sauce. Check the seasoning.

8 Mix all the pickled walnut relish ingredients together.

9 Just before serving spread the walnut relish over the beef and serve it with the sauce and some mashed potatoes.

casserole of sea fish with saffron and cream

Simple but luxurious. You can substitute other fish – haddock, sea-bass, turbot or brill – for the Dover sole, monkfish and red mullet if that happens to be what is freshest at your local fishmonger's.

serves 4

2 whole 340–400g (12–14oz) Dover sole or lemon sole, skinned and filleted

225g (8oz) monkfish fillet

225g (8oz) red mullet, filleted

8 scallops, cleaned, in the half shell

285ml (1/2 pint) good fish stock

40ml (2½tbsp) white wine

1 medium leek, white and pale green parts only,. washed and finely sliced

2 bay leaves

good pinch of saffron threads

salt and pepper

285ml (1/2 pint) double cream

85g (3oz) cold unsalted butter, cut into small cubes

to serve

1 courgette, finely sliced lengthways (optional), and brushed with oilive oil

40ml (2½tbsp) finely chopped parsley

1 Preheat the oven to 180°C/350°F/gas mark 4. Prepare all the fish. Fold over one-third of each sole fillet, then fold the other end over the top, to make a little parcel. Cut the monkfish into 2.5cm (1 inch) chunks and each of the red mullet fillets into 2 or 3 pieces. Place all the fish together with the scallops in a heavy-bottomed pan. Add the fish stock, wine, leek, bay leaves and saffron. Season.

2 Bring gently to the boil on a medium heat. Cover with buttered greaseproof paper, place in the oven, and cook for 8–10 minutes. Meanwhile, if serving with courgette, grill under a medium heat for 5 minutes or until just coloured. Carefully remove the fish from the pan and keep warm, with the courgette, covered with foil.

3 Strain the cooking liquor into a saucepan and boil rapidly to reduce by two-thirds. Stir in the cream and bring back to the boil. Simmer for 2 minutes, then whisk in the butter to thicken the sauce. Take off the heat and check the seasoning.

4 Put the fish on a large, warmed serving dish, or on individual plates. Pour the sauce over the top, garnish with parsley and serve immediately with the grilled courgette slices.

bramley apple custard and honey tart

At The Dartmoor they add a little saffron, thought by some to have come to the West Country via the Phoenicians and their tin trade with Cornwall, to the custard filling for this tart

serves 4–6

for the pastry

225g (8oz) plain flour

50g (1³/₄oz) caster sugar

125g (4¹/₄oz) unsalted butter, slightly softened

1 medium whole egg

1 medium egg yolk

for the filling

2 large Bramley apples

caster sugar, to taste

1 large Cox's apple

20g (³/₄oz) unsalted butter

4 medium egg yolks

1 medium whole egg

15ml (1tbsp) clear honey

600ml (22fl oz) double cream

pinch of saffron threads (optional)

to serve (optional)

1 large Cox's apple

icing sugar

a little whipped cream

1 Rub the flour, sugar and butter together gently with your finger tips until they resemble breadcrumbs (or whizz in a food processor). Lightly beat the whole egg and pour it onto the flour mix. Stir in with a spoon, then bring everything together with your hands to form a dough. Rest in the fridge for 30 minutes.

2 Preheat the oven to 180°C/350°F/gas mark 4. Lightly grease a 20cm (8 inch) loose-bottomed tart tin. Roll out the pastry into a circle 3mm (⅛ inch) thick and 5–7.5cm (2–3 inches) wider than the tin. Line the tin, gently easing the pastry down into the corners. Leave 2.5cm (1 inch) pastry overhanging the edge. Chill for 10 minutes. Place a baking sheet in the oven, on the middle shelf.

3 Line the pastry case with greaseproof paper and fill with dried beans or rice. Put the tin onto the preheated baking sheet and bake for 8 minutes. Remove the paper with the beans and bake the pastry case for a further 5 minutes, so the pastry no longer looks glassy. Carefully trim off the overhanging pastry edge level with the top of the tin, then brush the inside of the case with the egg yolk to seal the pastry. Put the pastry case back into the oven for a further 3 minutes to cook the yolk, then remove from the oven.

4 Reduce the oven temperature to 170°C/325°F/gas mark 3. Peel, core and roughly slice the Bramleys. Place in a pan with 15ml (1 tbsp) water. Cook over a medium heat for 5–10 minutes, until soft. Sweeten with sugar to taste and beat to a purée.

5 Peel and core the Cox's apple, and cut it into neat 6mm (¼ inch) slices. Fry gently in the unsalted butter until softened and lightly coloured. Place the apple purée in the bottom of the pastry case and overlap the apple slices on top.

6 In a bowl, beat together the 4 egg yolks, 1 whole egg and honey. Place the cream and saffron (if using) in a small pan and bring to the boil. When boiling, whisk the cream into the egg mix, beating all the time. Pour into the pastry case, over the apple, and bake for 20 minutes, until the mixture has set and is golden brown.

7 If you want to garnish with caramelized apple, peel and core the Cox's apple and cut it into half-moon shaped slices, 3cm (1¼ inches) thick. Sprinkle with icing sugar and toast under a hot grill until caramelized. Serve the tart warm with a few pieces of caramelized apple and a dollop of cream on each slice.

Broadhembury

Devon

01404 841267

serves lunch and dinner mon
to sun; bookings advised;
children welcome; garden

the drewe arms

You could spend ages just examining the objects here — little flags, old baskets, a teetering ceramic clock, even a big antique wooden horse on wheels — and looking at the walls, which are covered in Beryl Cook prints, modern seascapes, and fish in every material under the sun. Wood, iron, pottery, papier mâché: you name it and a sea creature fashioned from it will swim into view.

Owner Kerstin Burge is Swedish, and the Drewe Arms feels more like a Scandinavian country restaurant than a British boozer, despite the snug bar and beer from the nearby Otter Brewery. The menu is as fish-focused as the décor. They offer Scandinavian classics such as grav lax, cured herring and Jansson's temptation, as well as Mediterranean, French and British fish dishes such as seared salmon with samphire, sea bream with orange and chilli, or turbot with hollandaise.

The Swedish recipes come from Kerstin's mother, who Kerstin describes as Sweden's equivalent to Fanny Cradock. After 18 years, Kerstin no longer works in the kitchen, but The Drewe is still a family affair. Kerstin's husband Nigel makes the puds — English dishes such as bread pudding — and their son Andrew cooks everything else. The food here is unfussy, but few places can turn out a perfectly cooked bit of Dover sole or mouth-puckering herring with a glass of ice-cold aquavit like they do at the Drewe Arms.

jansson's temptation

A great Swedish classic and a very good lunch or supper dish – perfect with a green salad. It's also a good accompaniment to grilled salmon.

serves 10–12 as a starter or side dish, 6-8 as a supper dish

1kg (2lb 3oz) large floury potatoes, such as King Edward, peeled

255g (9oz) anchovies in brine, preferably Swedish Abba or Marina brand, or anchovies in oil

unsalted butter

1kg (2lb 3oz) onions, thinly sliced

salt and pepper

710ml (1¼ pints) double cream

full-fat milk

1 Preheat the oven to 200°C/400°F/gas mark 6. Cut the potatoes into matchstick shaped strips.

2 In a small bowl, lightly mash the anchovies with their salty liquid. If you're using anchovies in oil, drain and chop finely.

3 Place half the potatoes in a layer in a buttered earthenware dish, followed by a layer of half the sliced onion. Then add all the anchovies in a thin layer and season (remember that the anchovies will be very salty). Add another layer of onions, and top with a layer of potatoes.

4 Carefully pour over the cream, then add milk to come up to about 2.5cm (1 inch) below the surface level of the mixture.

5 Cover with foil and bake for 45 minutes, then remove the foil and cook for another 30 minutes.

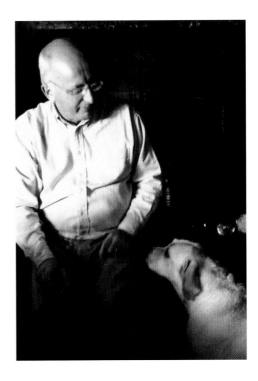

grav lax

This is a Swedish recipe for grav lax, used by Kerstin's mother and grandmother. 'Grav' means 'buried' and 'lax' means 'salmon'. The spelling is different from the more common Danish spelling, 'gravadlax'. Slotts Senap mustard is available from www.scandelicious.co.uk.

serves 10–12

for the salmon

1kg (2lb 3oz) fresh salmon, scaled and filleted, with the skin left on, in two matching 500g (1lb 2oz) pieces

good shot of brandy

85g (3oz) granulated sugar

85g (3oz) coarse sea salt

large bunch dill, roughly chopped (including stalks)

for the sauce

200g (7oz) sweet mustard, hot dog mustard or Slotts Senap

50g (1¾oz) granulated sugar

140g (5oz) mayonnaise

50ml (1¾fl oz) white wine vinegar

small bunch of dill, leaves only, chopped

to serve

10-12 sprigs dill

1 Check that there are no little bones left in the salmon by running your hand over the flesh. Remove any remaining bones with tweezers.

2 Take a large sheet of cooking foil and lay one of the salmon pieces on it, skin side down. Rub half of the brandy into the flesh. Mix the sugar and salt together and sprinkle half of the mixture onto the salmon. Put the roughly chopped dill on top, stalks and all, and then sprinkle over the rest of the salt and sugar mixture.

3 Rub the remaining brandy into the other piece of salmon. Lay this on top of the salmon in the foil, flesh side down. Seal the salmon into a parcel by crimping the edges of the foil securely together.

4 Lift the parcel carefully onto a deep tray or very large plate. Cover with a plate or board and put a heavy weight on top, then leave in the fridge for 3 days, turning the package on the second day. You can eat the salmon after one day, but it's much better after marinating for 3 days.

5 To make the sauce, mix all the ingredients together in a plastic bowl. Store in the refrigerator.

6 When the salmon has marinated, remove it from the foil package. Scrape both fillets fairly clean.

7 Use a very sharp knife to cut the salmon into 3mm (⅛ inch) thick slices. Serve with a sprig of fresh dill and the dill and mustard sauce.

'many of the recipes we use come from my mother, the swedish fanny cradock of her day.' kerstin

john dory with anchovies and capers

Made with good fresh John Dory, this is a fantastic dish – easy to make and full of the taste of the sea.

serves 4

1kg (2lb 3oz) John Dory fillets

olive oil, for frying

unsalted butter, for frying

30ml (2tbsp) finely chopped parsley

200g (7oz) butter

50g (1¾oz) French anchovies in brine, or cured anchovies in olive oil, soaked in a little milk and drained

50g (1¾oz) capers, rinsed of salt or brine

1 In a large frying pan, heat a little olive oil and butter, then pan-fry the John Dory fillets skin side up until golden brown on the flesh side (about 2–3 minutes).

2 Turn the fish over and fry on the other side until cooked through.

3 Meanwhile, roughly chop the anchovies. Melt the butter in a small saucepan and stir in the anchovies and capers.

4 Place the John Dory on warmed plates and pour over the anchovy and caper butter. Sprinkle with chopped parsley and serve immediately.

'we love fish, and we like to cook it simply. a wonderful bit of john dory, some capers and anchovies – what more could you want?' kerstin

lemon posset

A simple, old-fashioned English pudding. You could pile some raspberries or small hulled strawberries on top and sprinkle with icing sugar if you want to make a bit more of it.

serves 6

500ml (18fl oz) double cream

140g (5oz) caster sugar

juice of 2 large lemons

to serve

grated zest of 1 unwaxed lemon

1 Put the double cream in a large pan and stir in the sugar.

2 Bring slowly to the boil. Boil for precisely 3 minutes, then remove from the heat.

3 Add the lemon juice and whisk well.

4 Pour into 6 tall serving glasses. Refrigerate for 3 hours, then sprinkle a little lemon zest on each one before serving.

Corscombe

Dorset

01935 891330

serves lunch and dinner mon to
sun; bookings advised;
children welcome; garden

The Fox Inn looks too pretty to be real. Thatch snuggles down onto its clotted-cream coloured walls, lupins and hollyhocks grow along the front, and there are, indeed, roses round the door. Inside, you find stuffed owls in glass cases, old watercolours and shelves lined with demi-johns of home-made damson gin. The Fox Inn is, without a doubt, one of the loveliest pubs in England.

When the place gets busy, diners can spread into two rooms: the conservatory, a glorious room filled with just one huge, rough-hewn table, or the kitchen, with its Aga, old kettles and newspapers. As treacle tarts and braised lamb shanks are whipped out of the Aga, you feel you're eating in someone's home.

The food, from young chef George Marsh, is unfussy country cooking and just right for the place: braised venison with juniper and redcurrant jelly, smoked ham and mushroom pie, and bread and butter pudding. They're the kind of old-fashioned dishes you wish would turn up more often. The more contemporary fish dishes, such as roast sea bream with chilli and coriander butter, are based on sound ingredients and are wonderfully fresh and unadorned. But the food is only part of the Fox Inn experience. The place is genuinely rural, picture-book pretty and confers a great sense of ease. Definitely worth a detour.

the fox inn

trout tartare with anchovy mayo

Make sure you get good well-flavoured tomatoes, such as vine tomatoes, for this.
The anchovy mayo is great with other foods too, such as deep-fried squid or
whitebait and hard-boiled quails' eggs.

serves 4

450g (1lb) trout fillet, skinned

225g (8oz) coarse sea salt

1/2 medium cucumber

6 ripe tomatoes

6 fresh asparagus spears

to serve

*salad leaves, such as
watercress or lamb's lettuce*

1 The trout needs to be prepared 24 hours in advance. On a small tray covered
with clingfilm, sprinkle half the coarse sea salt, then lay the trout on top. Sprinkle
the remaining sea salt onto the trout and cover with another sheet of clingfilm.
Place a heavy weight on top of the fish and refrigerate for 24 hours.

2 Remove the seeds from the cucumber and tomatoes and chop into 3mm
(1/8 inch) fine dice. Trim the asparagus and cook it in boiling water for 3–4 minutes,
or until just tender. Cool under cold water and chop into 3mm (1/8 inch) dice. Mix
the cucumber, tomatoes and asparagus together in a bowl and set aside.

3 Remove the trout from the fridge and wash off all the salt under a cold tap.
Dry. Chop the trout into 3mm (1/8 inch) dice.

4 Put the trout and the cucumber mixture into a large bowl together and add
half the anchovy mayonnaise. Stir well and then add more anchovy mayonnaise to
taste. Mix and check the seasoning. Divide the mixture between 4 plates and
garnish with a few salad leaves.

anchovy mayo

2 medium egg yolks

*4 anchovy fillets in oil,
drained*

2 cloves garlic

10ml (2tsp) Dijon mustard

*30ml (1fl oz) white wine
vinegar*

250ml (9fl oz) mild olive oil

250ml (9fl oz) groundnut oil

salt and pepper

1 Put the egg yolks, anchovy fillets, garlic, mustard
and white wine vinegar into a food processor.
Alternatively, finely chop the anchovy fillets and
garlic, then mix with the yolks, mustard and white
wine vinegar.

2 Start to blend the ingredients, then very slowly
add the oils drip by drip, until the mixture comes
together to look like a thick mayonnaise.

3 To loosen the mayo, add 30ml (1fl oz) of warm
water, then season to taste. The anchovies are very
salty, so you may not need to add salt.

braised rabbit with cider, rosemary and cream

You can use chicken joints instead of rabbit if you prefer, but if you do you should reduce the cooking time to about 40 minutes. You may have to remove the chicken and reduce the sauce to thicken it, adding it back to warm through.

serves 4

2 rabbits, cut into joints, ie legs removed, ribcage discarded and body chopped into 2 pieces

sunflower oil, for frying

unsalted butter, for frying

3 cloves garlic, thinly sliced

2 medium onions, thinly sliced

425ml (¾ pint) Blackthorn cider

450ml (16fl oz) double cream

4 sprigs rosemary

30ml (2tbsp) wholegrain mustard

2 bay leaves

30ml (2tbsp) finely chopped parsley

salt and pepper

to serve

4 deep-fried bay leaves or parsley sprigs (optional)

1 In a frying pan, heat a little oil and a knob of butter. Fry the joints of rabbit until golden brown. Remove from the pan and set aside.

2 In the same pan, add the garlic and onions and fry until softened but not coloured. Transfer the onion mix to a heavy-bottomed pan, add the rabbit, cover with the cider and cream, then add the rosemary, wholegrain mustard and bay leaves and bring to the boil. Turn the heat down, cover and, stirring occasionally, cook on a very low heat for about 1½ hours, or until the rabbit is tender. Just before serving add the parsley, and season to taste.

3 Serve a front and back leg and half of the body to each person. Garnish with a sprig of parsley or a bay leaf quickly deep-fried in vegetable oil, until dark green but not brown.

'there are mediterranean and thai influences on the menu, but i like cooking with typical west country produce – cider, cream, apples and cheese.' george

treacle tart

Wicked and calorific but easy to make and always popular. You can add a bit more zest and lemon juice if you don't want such a sweet tart.

serves 10

for the pastry

225g (8oz) plain flour

115g (4oz) unsalted butter, chilled and diced

1 medium egg yolk

40ml (2¹/2tbsp) cold water

for the tart filling

1.25 litres (just under 2¹/4 pints) golden syrup

1 unwaxed lemon, zest and juice

1 medium egg

225g (8oz) coarse white breadcrumbs

1 First make the pastry. Put the flour and butter in the food processor and whizz quickly until it looks like breadcrumbs. Alternatively, in a large bowl rub the butter into the flour using the tips of your fingers.

2 Mix in the egg yolk with a knife and enough cold water to make a stiff dough. Wrap in clingfilm and refrigerate for half an hour.

3 Preheat the oven to 170°C/325°F/gas mark 3. Warm the tin of golden syrup in a saucepan of hot water to make the syrup easier to measure. Spoon the syrup into a bowl. Add the remaining ingredients for the tart filling and stir well. The lemon juice stops the tart being too sweet.

4 Lightly butter a 30cm (12 inch) tart dish. Roll out the pastry into a circle 3mm (⅛ inch) thick and 5cm (2 inches) bigger than the dish. Lift the pastry into the dish and press it gently to fit.

5 Add the tart mixture and trim off any extra pastry. Bake in the preheated oven for half an hour, or until the tart is golden brown. Serve hot or warm with thick cream.

'the waitress, sue, makes all the puddings. everybody loves her treacle tart.' george

the best of the rest

the museum inn

Farnham

Dorset

01725 516261

www.museuminn.co.uk

themuseuminn@supernet.
com; serves lunch and
dinner mon to sun;
bookings advised
fri-sun restaurant only;
no children; garden

This red-brick, 17th-century inn, on a corner right opposite the park, was owned by General Pitt Rivers and used to accommodate and feed visitors to the nearby Pitt Rivers Museum, now defunct. The inn itself was bought several years ago and refurbished, with considerable panache, to make a spacious, contemporary pub with a sense of history.

The bar-room has retained the elements of warmth and age that make a place a pub rather than a bar – massive flagstones, handsome oak tables, sparsely adorned antique dressers and a huge pile of logs for the fire – while remaining uncluttered. Its restaurant, 'The Shed', meanwhile, is more Californian in feel. A big high-ceilinged barn with sisal carpeting, cream tongue-and-groove and prints of Victorian cookbook illustrations, it shows just how soothing and untwee 'modern country' can be.

The food, too, is a blend of the modern and the traditional. There's a rich pigeon-and-ham-knuckle terrine with spiced apples, a delicious turret of Parma ham and wild mushrooms with poached egg and hollandaise, and a fine treacle tart with custard. The flavours are honest, with no gimmickry or tricks of presentation, and the kitchen aims high.

The place is thronged with the smart set – well-off locals and Londoners down for a bit of country air – and the service is supremely professional, friendly and intelligent. There are some bedrooms upstairs, modern-country in style, should you want to make a weekend of it.

george and dragon

Rowde

Wiltshire

01380 723053

gdrowde@tiscali.co.uk

serves lunch and dinner
tues to sat;
bookings advised;
children welcome; garden

You could easily drive past the George and Dragon. It has an unprepossessing exterior, sitting snug to a bend in the road, where it is battered by spray from cars in wet weather, and its front door is hidden around the far side. But in two pretty, unfussy little dining rooms by the bar, you'll get spectacular fish, fresh every day from Cornwall.

The fish specials, chalked up on a blackboard, take you on a gastronomic world tour: hake with roasted peppers and aïoli, Thai fish curry, monkfish with tzatziki, grilled Dover sole. A printed menu has the beefy stuff – skirt steak with garlic butter, or fillet with Gorgonzola – and fishy starters. There's a pungent Provençal soup with Gruyère and a good, spicy rouille, freshwater crayfish with green mayonnaise, and oysters from the River Exe. Classic dishes, such as turbot with hollandaise sauce, are exemplary, and puddings, such as strawberries in Muscat jelly or banana and cardamom ice-cream, are more interesting than the usual offerings.

The furnishings have obviously evolved over the years. There's the usual motley collection of old tables, chairs and settles, all softened with earthy-coloured fabrics. Small windows and big fires make the rooms cosy and comfy, and it's a good place to eavesdrop: the retired colonels, ladies-who-lunch and whispering couples all seem to be buoyed up by domestic scandals and local gossip. If you closed your eyes, you'd think you were in a Jane Austen novel.

the roseland inn

Philleigh
Cornwall
01872 580254
serves lunch and dinner
mon to sun;
bookings advised;
children welcome; garden

This white-washed 16th-century inn is hidden among winding hedgerows in the sleepy Roseland peninsula. On a summer evening, punters sit outside by the ancient well, partially illuminated by strings of coloured lights and basking in the scent of roses and honeysuckle. It's what you dream of finding. A higgledy-piggledy warren of low-beamed rooms spans out from a tiny central bar and a crammed notice board indicates that it's a real village local. It's pleasantly shabby, stuffed with oddities such as driftwood sconces and hunting paraphernalia.

The food is superior pub grub: melting Philleigh shank of lamb braised in orange and rosemary, good Cornish pasties baked on the premises, local smoked haddock topped with Cornish Yarg cheese, and what they call 'proper job ham': a thick slice of home-baked ham served with mustard mash. Fish specials, according to the catch of the day, are on the blackboard. It's not ambitious cooking, but good, wholesome stuff served by young, chatty staff, and the location is unbeatable.

the acorn inn

Fore Street
Evershot
Dorset
01935 83228
www.acorn-inn.co.uk
serves lunch and dinner
mon to sun;
bookings advised;
children welcome;
patio garden

If you're in the mood for a bit of Hardyesque brooding, seek out the village of Evershot. A quiet, untouristy place, full of terraced stone cottages, it appeared in Hardy's novels as 'Evershead', and its 16th-century inn, The Acorn, was 'The Sow and Acorn' in *Tess of the D'Urbevilles*.

The Acorn is meticulously well run and friendly – they even offer printed sheets with suggestions for local walks – and the food is simple and prepared with care. You can eat in the Swedish-style dining room, with its handsome stone fireplace, or in any of the eating areas round the bar, with their warm ochre walls, old oak tables and spindle-backed chairs. There are stuffed fish in glass cases and old prints of country scenes on the walls but it's genuine and restrained.

There's a mixture of old-fashioned dishes, such as chicken and ham pie, and more modern ones, such as sea-bass with fennel and chilli salsa. Plenty of West Country produce is on offer, such as Capricorn goats' cheese from Crewkerne in Somerset, grilled and served with beetroot relish, and there's a daily changing fish menu, based on what's available at the market. Desserts are solidly hearty; the clientele is similar.

the victory inn

Victory Hill
St. Mawes
Cornwall
01326 270324
serves lunch and dinner
mon to sun; bookings
advised; children welcome;
patio garden

The Victory Inn is a little, white-washed terraced pub on a hill by the harbour in St. Mawes. An old sign depicting Nelson's Victory and a profusion of flower baskets suggest that everything inside will be neat, comfortable and old-fashioned. But you get two distinct experiences here.

The upstairs room, where you can book, is as contemporary a dining room as you will find. It's colourful, with modern paintings, while uncurtained windows and white walls make the most of the Cornish light. The menu is mostly fishy and fresh: sweet, pearly-fleshed sea-bass with crème fraîche and chilli sauce, tender grilled squid with salsa verde, and simple sole with beurre noisette.

Downstairs is as old-fashioned as the upstairs is modern: dark and cosy with standard-issue dark pub furniture and more red than you'd find in a brothel. Carpet, curtains, banquettes and stools are all deep scarlet. The bar food is simpler and cheaper than the food served upstairs, but standards are just as high in dishes such as crab and spring onion omelette, salmon fishcakes with mayo, and a 'fish of the day' with extra virgin olive oil and lemon, which is superb in its simplicity.

the angel inn

Angel Lane
Hindon
Wiltshire
01747 820696
eat@theangelinn.co.uk
serves lunch and dinner
mon to sat, lunch only on
sun; bookings advised;
children welcome;
courtyard garden

A Georgian coach house, with a cobbled courtyard where fairy lights are strung through the trees, the Angel is so pretty you could eat it. Inside, the bar-room is bold and beautiful, with a flagstone floor, blood-red walls and brass candlesticks. You can either dine here, from the blackboard menu, or in the restaurant, which is 'modern country' in style, with sage-green walls, Roman blinds, large black-and-white photographs of the surrounding countryside and cream lamps.

The cooking is sophisticated but not pretentious, interesting and bold. A salad of chickpeas and warm new potatoes, with cured anchovies, preserved lemon and a creamy garlic dressing, is one of the best dishes you'll eat anywhere. There's also a delicious spin on chowder, with roast cod on a stew of potato, clams, corn and Toulouse sausage, and good puds such as prunes in orange and tea with vanilla ice-cream. The bar has slightly more down-to-earth fare, such as excellent beer-battered fish with chips and crushed peas, or rabbit braised with mushrooms and bacon. Vegetables, such as carrots with orange and cumin or buttery peas with button onions and lettuce, are first-rate.

They really care about their raw ingredients here. Much of the produce is organic; the fish comes from Brixham; the beef from Aubrey Allen in Stratford (who also supplies Rick Stein), and the cheeses from Neal's Yard. If you want a smart pub, rather than a laid-back one, and savvy, superior food, this is your place.

the white hart

Dartington Hall
Dartington
Devon
01803 847101
serves lunch and dinner
mon to sun;
bookings advised;
children welcome; garden

The White Hart, tucked away in the corner of a medieval courtyard in the grounds of Dartington Hall, is a real find. The interior is in the spirit of the Arts and Craft movement: contemporary honey-coloured wooden beams, old blond stone, a mixture of pale modern and antique furniture and wall lights in the shape of halved ceramic bowls. There are wild flowers on every table. Brushed steel fire irons and a bleached basket of logs sit beside the fireplace. Everything is light, bright and the very model of civility.

Dartington Hall often has concerts in the grounds and an international music school takes up residence in the summer, so the White Hart's clientele is correspondingly arty. The two small dining areas by the long, pine bar (which also dispenses coffee and cakes) are awash with copies of the *Times Literary Supplement* and the *Guardian Review*, and you have to negotiate violin and lute cases on the way to your table.

You're welcome to stop by for a pint of ale and a roll-up, but book a table in advance and you can enjoy the food, which is spot-on. Served on big white plates, it's mostly Mediterranean in influence, with a little of the East thrown in – mozzarella-stuffed chicken wrapped in Parma ham with roast vegetables, or fillets of sea-bass with sweet potatoes and tomato-chilli jam. The kitchen uses organic produce wherever possible and you can tell: everything, down to the big perfumed leaves of basil which garnish Mediterranean dishes, is full of flavour and zingily fresh.

Desserts – interesting offerings such as gypsy tart and raspberry marquise – are polished and the home-made ice-creams and sorbets (usually about nine on the menu) are worth a trip in their own right.

trengilly wartha

Nancenoy
Constantine
Cornwall
01326 340332
www.trengilly.co.uk
serves lunch in the bar
only and dinner mon to
sun; bookings advised for
the restaurant;
children welcome; garden

Trengilly Wartha is part of a simple country hotel, hidden among trees at the end of a single-track road, perched on a hillside by a river and a lovely garden. There are plenty of wooden tables outside and inside it's homely, scruffy and delightful. There's a brown swirly carpet, a bar made partly of beer barrels, a piano piled high with dog-eared paperbacks and old school paraphernalia.

The food is just as laidback. A blackboard lists the specials, many of which are fishy. As much of the produce as possible is local and organic. There are simple salads, such as local feta cheese, beans and cherry tomatoes and an excellent ploughman's with West Country cheeses, homemade breads and chutneys, and top-notch versions of 'pub regulars': fresh wholetail scampi with tartare sauce, Cornish pasties from the Lizard Pasty Shop and fillet steaks from the Brian Etherington Meat Company. There are also modern brasserie dishes: crab cakes, risotto and Thai pork with noodles.

There are about 300 wines, and you can browse the 'wine library' at the end of the bar, which houses individual bottles. There are also 50 whiskies, and guest ales from small West Country breweries. Trengilly Wartha has a separate restaurant, but the chilled-out bar can't be beaten.

hop pole

Upper Bristol Road
Royal Victoria Park
Bath
01225 446327
www.bathales.com
hoppole@bathales.co.uk
serves lunch and dinner
mon to sun;
bookings advised;
children welcome; garden

Bath is packed with locals who love to dine out and tourists in search of the places the locals love to dine out in. Yet great food pubs are thin on the ground. One of the city's best-kept secrets is the Hop Pole, a Bath Ales pub that looks so run of the mill from the outside that you'll almost certainly drive past it, and then curse as you search for somewhere to turn the car around. But once inside there's enough good food and local ales to soothe the most irritated soul.

The menu changes a little with the seasons and has a British feel. Typical fare ranges from seared Scottish scallops with rocket and Parmesan salad and cullen skink – a Scottish soup made with smoked haddock – to grilled local trout with toasted almonds and belly of pork with mash and red wine sauce. The food is prepared well by chef Barry Wallace, whose training included a stint with top chef Nico Ladenis, and is served by friendly and helpful staff.

the rising sun

Harbourside
Lynmouth
01598 753223
risingsunlynmouth@
easynet.co.uk
serves lunch (bar only)
and dinner mon to sun;
bookings advised;
children welcome; garden

The Victorians likened Lynmouth to the Black Forest, and were fond of its tidiness, its conifers and cliffs. The Rising Sun, on a steep slope down by the harbour, stretches over three ivy-covered 14th-century cottages. Byron spent his honeymoon in one and thought Lynmouth would be a good place to set up a commune.

The disintegrating thatch gives the pub a beguilingly run-down feel. At twilight, with candles burning in its leaded windows and tiny coloured lights under the eaves, it glows. Inside, a sense of easy-going gentility prevails. As well as a dark, cosy bar with booths and settles, there's a small dining room with wood-panelled walls, antique plates and a Victorian fireplace. It's proper in an old-fashioned way, with flowers, candles and silver condiments on every table, but not grand.

The food is simple, mostly modern, with clean, fresh flavours: there's exemplary grilled vegetables with marinated mozzarella; salmon and monkfish brochette on a tomato and fennel salad; and grilled poussin with an orange and cinnamon glaze on baby leaves. Puddings, such as bread and butter pudding with clotted cream or rhubarb crème brûlée, are spot-on.

the south

With five motorways crossing the three counties of Berkshire, Buckinghamshire and Oxfordshire, it is difficult to feel that you are in deep countryside here, but there are areas of real beauty in the south of England. Get off the main roads and drive round the Chilterns' wooded chalk hills and neat, rolling farmland; go to the Berkshire village of Cookham, which the painter Stanley Spencer equated with some kind of earthly paradise; or enjoy the manicured grace of riverside towns such as Henley and Marlow, where acres of velvet lawns run down to the Thames. There are plenty of small, pretty villages which seem enticingly private, almost secretive.

A lot of the produce used in the home counties comes via the London wholesale markets, and chefs can get their hands on anything they want. But there are plenty of fruit and vegetable growers in the area too, providing the food we most associate with English summers – asparagus, peas, broad beans, gooseberries and, of course, strawberries, ready for the hordes at Henley regatta and endless bowls of Eton mess. There are dessert cherries too; people in Buckinghamshire used to celebrate 'Cherry Pie Sunday' at the beginning of August, after the harvest of Black Bucks cherries. You should also scan menus here for cheeses from the outstanding Berkshire cheese-maker, Anne Wigmore, who makes a tangy, hard sheep's

cheese called Spenwood, a semi-soft sheep's cheese called Wigmore, and Waterloo, a luscious, creamy semi-soft cow's cheese made in the same way as French Coulommiers.

Further away from London, Hampshire has a very different tone. The New Forest, an ancient enclosure of heather and gorse, birch and Scots pine, ancient oak and beech, has 150 miles of car-free gravel roads. It feels unknowable, as if it were owned by the animals — ponies, deer, ducks, pheasant and partridge — who live here. It was requisitioned by William the Conqueror in the 11th century as a game reserve and nothing much has changed. Misty autumn mornings are synonymous with the phut of gun shot. All this makes the place seem further away from urban living than it actually is.

Most chefs don't do their own shooting (though Marco Pierre White is a regular here) — they generally source either from butchers or directly from game-keepers and local shooters. Venison crops up a lot on menus in the area, and Michael Womersely from The Three Lions at Stuckton even does a dish with three varieties of duck when it's in season.

The New Forest is paradise, too, for the silent hunt of mushroom foraging. The moisture-retaining woodland and lack of agricultural chemicals make it the best place in the country for wild fungis and intrepid mycologists come here from all over Britain to go on secret, early morning searches. There's also good fish and excellent local producers of organic pork.

Hampshire now has some superlative dining pubs and is attracting quite a few of the good chefs who are leaving London for the country. It's an area to watch.

58 Middlebridge Street
Romsey
Hampshire
01794 512639
serves lunch and dinner mon to
sun lunch; bookings advised;
children welcome; patio garden

This is the kind of eatery you might have lunch in after a morning's shopping in Avignon or Bayeux — the classic, unfussy food; simple but elegant surroundings; service that makes you feel good and a bill that won't break the bank.

The manager, who used to do front of house at St Martin's Lane Hotel in London, brings you the short, daily-changing menu. It warms your soul: pork rillettes with crudités and cornichons, braised shoulder of lamb with onion gravy and potato purée, and seared scallops with black pudding and red wine *jus*. It's mostly French, though risotto appears sometimes, as do British classics. The cooking is careful, exact and full of flavour.

Chef Billy Reid, who had Michelin stars at both The Vineyard in Stockcross and L'Escargot in London, set the style and Damien Brown executes it. They both moved to Hampshire for a better life — houses in the country, shorter working hours, and a clientele that would appreciate simple food. 'When you're cooking in a Michelin-starred restaurant you are striving to keep everything as swish as the luxury décor,' explains Billy. 'It is hard to wow people with your cooking in that kind of environment, so I decided I wanted to work in a simple, neighbourhood place.' He is definitely wowing them in Romsey, and you'd be wowed by the Three Tuns even if you had to drive 40 miles to get there.

three
tuns

pea soup with parma ham and basil oil

As chef Billy Reid says, cooking doesn't get much simpler than this.

serves 4

115g (4oz) unsalted butter

1 large onion, roughly sliced

salt and pepper

450g (1lb) frozen peas

140ml (1/4 pint) double cream

4 slices Parma ham, finely shredded

to serve

basil oil

15ml (1tbsp) snipped chives

1 Melt the butter in a heavy-bottomed saucepan and sweat the onion until opaque. Add a little salt and pepper.

2 Add the peas and sweat again for 4–5 minutes. Add 850ml (1½ pints) water to cover. Bring to the boil and simmer for 5 minutes. Check the seasoning.

3 Purée in a liquidizer, then push through a sieve and return to the saucepan.

4 Bring the soup to the boil and add two-thirds of the cream. Bring back to the boil and pour into 4 hot soup bowls. Top with the shredded ham.

5 Drizzle the soup with the remaining cream. Mix a little basil oil with the chopped chives and spoon into each soup; it should form small puddles.

basil oil

30g (1oz) basil

155ml (5 1/2fl oz) olive oil

1 Plunge the basil into boiling water, remove immediately and refresh in cold water. Drain and pat dry with kitchen paper. Liquidize, adding the olive oil a little at a time.

2 Strain through muslin and store in the refrigerator.

'when you're cooking in a michelin-starred restaurant you are striving to keep everything as swish as the luxury décor. it is hard to wow people with your cooking.' billy

duck confit with french beans, rissole potatoes and haricot bean dressing

This much-loved dish harks back to the days when meat was commonly salted in order to preserve it. Be sure to plan a good while in advance as, although this is not a hugely complicated dish, there is a long curing and cooking time.

for the duck confit

4 x 255g (9oz) duck legs

115g (4oz) sea salt

1kg (2lb 3oz) duck fat or lard

for the haricot bean dressing

115g (4oz) dried haricot beans

1 sprig thyme

425ml (3/4 pint) veal or chicken stock

sea salt

40ml (2½tbsp) vinaigrette

for the rissole potatoes

12 small potatoes

sea salt

small bunch each of thyme and rosemary

4 cloves garlic, halved

40ml (2½tbsp) olive oil

fat, from duck confit

to serve

couple of handfuls of French beans, topped and tailed

knob of unsalted butter

4 sprigs chervil

1 For the duck confit, dust the duck legs with the sea salt, put them on a plate, cover and leave for 8–10 hours, or overnight, in a cool place.

2 Preheat the oven to 180°C/350°F/gas mark 4. Wash the salt off the duck legs with cold water. Dry the meat.

3 Melt the lard or duck fat in a heavy-bottomed pan, then submerge the duck legs in the fat. Cover with a lid, place in the oven and cook for 2–2½ hours, until the meat is tender (it is ready if you can twist out the thigh bone easily). Remove the duck legs from the fat and leave both fat and meat to cool. Once the fat is tepid, strain through a fine sieve into a clean saucepan, bring up to the boil and skim. Cool again and re-strain. Put the duck's legs in a clean container, cover with the fat (ensuring there are no air holes), cover and refrigerate for up to 3 days.

4 To make the haricot dressing, soak the beans in cold water for 8 hours, or overnight, then rinse. Place the beans in a saucepan of water with the thyme, and boil until tender (about 2 hours). Drain. In a pan, bring the stock to the boil and reduce by half. Add the cooked beans and bring back to the boil. Add a pinch of salt and the vinaigrette. Remove from the heat.

5 To serve, remove the duck legs from the container and fry them in a non-stick dry pan until the fat turns crispy. Then heat through in an oven preheated to 180°C/350°F/gas mark 4, for 15 minutes.

6 Meanwhile, make the rissole potatoes. Boil the potatoes in water with all the other ingredients except the fat. Cool in the liquid. Half the potatoes lengthways, and sauté, cut face down, using a little of the fat in which the duck was cooked.

7 Cook the beans in boiling salted water for 1½ minutes, drain, then add the butter. To serve, divide the hot potatoes between 4 large shallow bowls, put the confit on top, skin side up, then put the warm French beans on top of the confit. Spoon over the haricot bean dressing, garnish with chervil and serve.

beef and mushroom pie

Yes Billy Reid, Michelin-starred chef, does add Bisto to this – he believes it makes a superior pie – and he uses Oxo cubes instead of homemade stock too. Once you've tasted it, you won't argue.

serves 4–6

1.4kg (3lb) beef skirt, cut into 2.5cm (1 inch) cubes

2 large onions, finely diced

2.75 litres (4 pints) beef stock, homemade or with 2 Oxo cubes

salt and pepper

1 sheet ready-made puff pastry

1 medium egg, beaten

255g (9oz) button mushrooms, as small as possible

a good dash of Lea & Perrins Worcestershire sauce

15ml (1tbsp) Bisto granules

to serve

4-6 sprigs chervil

mashed potatoes

roasted root vegetables

1 Place the beef cubes and diced onion in a large heavy-bottomed pan. Cover with beef stock and season.

2 Bring to the boil, then reduce the heat to a simmer, skimming off any scum that might appear. Cook for about 2 hours, checking the level of the liquid and topping up with water if necessary.

3 About 1¼ hours into the beef's cooking time, preheat the oven to 180°C/350°F/gas mark 4. Roll out the puff pastry in a rectangle 20 x 10cm (8 x 4 inches) and 3mm (⅛ inch) thick. Brush with the beaten egg and pattern the top with a fork. Cut into 4 x 10 x 5cm (4 x 2 inch) rectangles. Place the pastries on a dampened non-stick baking sheet and cover with a sheet of silicone paper. Bake in the oven for 20 minutes, until well risen and golden brown. Reduce the oven temperature to 130°C/250°F/gas mark ½ and bake for 10 more minutes to dry the pastry.

4 To finish the beef, add the mushrooms and cook for a few minutes. Then add the Worcestershire sauce and the Bisto granules and stir – this will thicken it. Check the seasoning.

5 Split each of the pastry cases in half horizontally and place the bottom halves on 4 warmed plates or shallow bowls. Spoon the beef and mushroom mixture on top of the bases and cover with the pastry tops.

6 Garnish with chervil and serve with mashed potato and roasted root vegetables.

steamed syrup pudding with chantilly cream

Few puddings bring back happier memories for the British than suet pudding with golden syrup. The vanilla cream adds a stylish note.

serves 6

unsalted butter, for greasing

500g (1lb 2oz) self-raising flour, plus extra for dusting

90ml (6tbsp) golden syrup

255g (9oz) suet, grated

150g (5½oz) caster sugar

cold water

to serve

90ml (6tbsp) Chantilly cream

6 sprigs mint

icing sugar, to dust

1 Grease 6 x 9cm (3½ inch) ramekins or small pudding dishes well with butter, then dust the insides lightly but thoroughly with flour. Place 15ml (1tbsp) golden syrup in the bottom of each dish.

2 Put the flour, suet and caster sugar in a bowl, stir and add enough cold water to create a wet paste of dropping consistency. Pour into the prepared ramekins.

3 Cover in cling-film and rest for about 1 hour.

4 Remove the cling-film and steam over boiling water for ¾–1 hour (do not let the pan boil dry).

5 To turn out each pudding, run a knife around the edge of the ramekin, place a plate over it, then quickly turn them over together. Lift off the ramekin and the suet pudding should be on the plate.

6 Using a warm spoon, place a large spoonful of Chantilly cream to one side of the pudding. Put a sprig of mint in the cream and dust with icing sugar.

chantilly cream

½ vanilla pod

285ml (½ pint) double cream

10ml (2tsp) icing sugar

1 Cut the vanilla pod in half lengthways and scrape out the seeds.

2 Place the cream, vanilla seeds and icing sugar into a chilled bowl and whisk steadily until the cream thickens, becomes fluffy and forms soft peaks. Be careful not to overwhip it.

31 High Street
Stockbridge
Hampshire
01264 810833
serves lunch and dinner mon to
sun lunch; bookings advised;
children welcome

The chef here, Darron Bunn, came from London and was quite prepared for his romantic notions of cooking in the country to be dashed, 'But it's the best move I ever made,' he says. 'When I've had enough of the kitchen here I can go for a walk by the river. In the game season, I have a kitchen porter sitting by the back door plucking pheasants all day long. This is country living and I love it.'

Darron and the owner, Barry Skarin, both have frighteningly impressive cvs - a veritable roll call of Nicos and Marcos and Schragers – but got fed up with the tortuous hours and the sameness of luxury London restaurants, and so opted to work in a simpler environment. Not that eating at The Greyhound is slumming it. On the outside it looks like an ordinary pub, but inside it's all chunky wooden tables, leather-backed chairs, and halogen lights. The gastropub originators would choke at the linen napkins, Riedel glassware and white Villeroy and Bosch plates. This is about as smart as a pub can get, but the place is nevertheless relaxed. And the food is brilliant. Risotto of Dorset crab with palourde clams, beetroot and goat's cheese tart, and Romney Marsh lamb with a navarin of vegetables, are all intensely flavoured, perfectly executed and served without any *fol-de-rol*. It's a class act. And a bargain. I'd get there quickly.

the
greyhound

home-smoked venison salad with quince vinaigrette

Darron Bunn, chef at the Greyhound, serves this with a shallot tarte tatin, but the venison is very good on its own. Use conference pears (you'll need 6 of them) for the vinaigrette if you can't get hold of quinces.

serves 4

200g (7oz) venison loin

vegetable oil, for frying

unsalted butter

150–200g (5½–7oz) oak sawdust or chippings

to serve

200g (7oz) mixed salad leaves

1 Remove any sinew from the venison.

2 Place a heavy-duty cast-iron pan over the heat and leave it to get really hot.

3 Heat a little vegetable oil in a frying pan and sear the venison until it is golden brown on all sides, adding 2 knobs of butter towards the end.

4 Put the venison in a steamer that will fit inside the cast-iron pan. Sprinkle the oak sawdust into the hot pan, then place the steamer on top. Cover with a tight-fitting lid; if necessary, improve the seal with foil. Turn off the heat and leave until cool.

5 When cool, roll the venison into a sausage shape and wrap in 4 layers of cling-film. Knot both ends and place in the refrigerator to chill.

5 To serve, slice the venison as thinly as possible. Dress the salad leaves with a little quince vinaigrette, and pour a small ladleful over the venison.

quince vinaigrette

unsalted butter

2 shallots, finely chopped

4 quinces, peeled and finely diced

100g (3¾oz) caster sugar

1 sprig thyme

½ bottle red wine

40ml (2½tbsp) redcurrant jelly

salt and pepper

100ml (3½fl oz) Spanish extra virgin olive oil

1 In a heavy-bottomed pan, melt 2 knobs of butter and sweat the shallots for 2–3 minutes, stirring constantly. Add the quinces, sugar and thyme and sweat gently for a further 2 minutes.

2 Cover with the wine, bring to the boil and reduce by 75 per cent, until nearly all the liquid has gone and a thick syrup is left.

3 Stir in the redcurrant jelly and season.

4 Stir in the olive oil – the dressing will look split. Keep in a warm place, but not over a direct heat.

crab risotto with clams

This is, quite simply, one of the best dishes I have ever eaten. It does take time, but you can make the acid butter in advance. Use mussels if you can't get clams.

serves 6

unsalted butter, for frying

1 medium Spanish onion, roughly chopped

1 medium leek, trimmed and roughly chopped

2 celery sticks, roughly chopped

500g (1lb 2oz) clams, cleaned

100ml (3¹/₂fl oz) dry white wine

500ml (18fl oz) fish stock

1 small shallot, finely chopped

small sprig of thyme

500g (1lb 2oz) arborio rice

salt and pepper

100g (3¹/₂oz) Parmesan cheese, finely grated

255g (9oz) fresh brown cooked crab meat, puréed and sieved

50g (1³/₄oz) acid butter

2-3tbsp whipped double cream

255g (9oz) fresh white cooked crab meat, flaked

lemon juice, to taste

to serve

6 sprigs flat-leaf parsley

1 Melt 2 good knobs of butter in a heavy-bottomed pan and fry the roughly chopped onion, leek and celery until slightly coloured.

2 Add the clams in their shells and half the wine. Cover with a lid and cook on full heat for 4–5 minutes, until the clams have opened.

3 Drain the cooked clams, retaining the cooking liquour. Discard any clams that remain closed and remove the meat from the others. Strain the cooking liquor through a sieve.

4 Heat the fish stock in a saucepan and keep it simmering.

5 Melt 2 knobs of butter in a heavy-bottomed pan and heat until the butter foams. Add the chopped shallot and the thyme and sweat gently. Add the rice and sweat for 2–3 minutes, stirring constantly.

6 Season, add the rest of the wine and cook, stirring constantly, until the wine has evaporated.

7 Add a ladleful of the hot stock, stir constantly until the liquid is absorbed, then add another ladleful. Continue like this until the rice is *al dente* and all the stock has been added. It should take about 15 minutes.

8 Mix in the Parmesan cheese, puréed brown crab meat, a few knobs of the acid butter and the whipped cream to achieve a rich consistency.

9 Quickly reheat the clams in the reserved cooking liquor with the white crab meat. Season with salt, pepper and lemon juice and spoon over the finished risotto. Serve immediately, garnished with a sprig of parsley.

acid butter

1 medium Spanish onion, finely sliced

155ml (5¹/₂fl oz) white wine vinegar

285ml (10fl oz) white wine

255g (9oz) unsalted butter, at room temperature, diced

1 Place the onion, vinegar and wine in a small pan. Bring to the boil and reduce to a syrup.

2 Slowly whisk in the butter, then pour through a fine strainer into a bowl and chill in the refrigerator.

roast best end of lamb with a root vegetable and rosemary navarin

A refined version of a French country dish. If you don't want to 'turn' the vegetables – cutting them into little barrel shapes – just cut them into neat pieces of equal size.

serves 4

4 x two-bone baby racks of lamb (ask the butcher for all the bones and trimmings)

unsalted butter

10 large carrots

1 medium Spanish onion, roughly chopped

2 sprigs rosemary

1 bulb garlic, halved

salt and pepper

½ bottle Madeira

1 small swede, peeled

12 new potatoes

vegetable oil, for frying

200g (7oz) baby button onions

1 Preheat the oven to 220°C/425°F/gas mark 7. Finely chop the lamb bones, put them into a heavy-bottomed small roasting pan with 150g (5½oz) butter, and roast for 30–40 minutes, until golden brown.

2 Strain the bones through a colander and reserve the juices. Put the roasting pan on the hob over a medium heat. Place the bones back in the pan. Roughly chop 2 of the carrots and add to the bones with the onion, a good sprig of rosemary, the garlic and seasoning. Brown the vegetables a little.

3 Deglaze the pan by stirring the Madeira into the vegetables. Bring to the boil and reduce by 75 per cent. Strain through a fine sieve, add the reserved roasting juices, and simmer gently for 30 minutes.

4 While this is cooking, prepare the rest of the carrots, the swede and the potatoes. Cut into 3–4cm (1¼–1½ inch) lengths and turn them barrel-shaped. Par-cook the carrots for 4–5 minutes and the swede and potatoes for 3–4 minutes in boiling salted water. Refresh in cold water and drain.

5 Season the joints of lamb individually. Seal the meat in a little vegetable oil in a hot frying pan, until golden brown. Put in a roasting tin and roast in the hot oven for 6–7 minutes. Rest for 10 minutes on a wire rack.

6 In a hot frying pan, add a knob of butter and brown the lamb meat trimmings and button onions. Remove all the meat trimmings. Add the turned vegetables and some chopped rosemary leaves. Cover with the sauce and cook until the vegetables are tender and the sauce has a thick consistency. Finish by whisking in 20g (¾oz) unsalted butter. Serve with the lamb.

'in the game season i have a kitchen porter sitting by the back door plucking pheasants all day long. this is country living and i love it.' darron

caramel-poached pears with sablé biscuits and poire william chantilly

At The Greyhound they present this dessert in smart restaurant style, the pear flesh layered with the cream and sablé biscuits. I like a more down-home approach. Take your pick.

serves 6

400g (14oz) caster sugar

1/2 cinnamon stick

1 star anise

6 Williams pears, peeled

juice of 1/2 lemon

icing sugar, to dust

1 In a heavy-bottomed pan, cook the sugar with a splash of water until it caramelizes. Carefully add 375ml (13fl oz) water – it will spit – and spices, then bring to the boil. Add the pears and lemon juice. Cover the pan with greaseproof paper set on top of the pears, and simmer until the fruit is tender. Leave in the liquor to cool.

2 Pour half of the cool liquor into a small heavy-bottomed saucepan, bring to the boil and reduce to a thick syrup. Remove the pears from the pan and slice in half lengthways. Scoop out the pear pips and cut the flesh into slices.

3 To serve, layer a few pear slices with 3 or 4 sablé biscuits and the cream. Sift over a little icing sugar and serve with a little caramel syrup drizzled around each one. Alternatively, just serve the pear halves simply with a little caramel sauce, a dollop of the Poire William cream and a few sablé biscuits.

poire william chantilly cream

250ml (9fl oz) double cream

150g (5¹/₂oz) icing sugar

1 vanilla pod, split lengthways and seeds scraped out

35ml (2¹/₃tbsp) Poire William liqueur

1 In a medium bowl, whip the cream until thick. Sift the icing sugar onto the cream and add the vanilla seeds.

2 Fold in carefully with the spatula (do not use the whisk as it will whip the cream too much). Fold in the Poire William liqueur and chill.

sablé biscuits

400g (14oz) unsalted butter

500g (1lb 2oz) plain flour

200g (7oz) caster sugar

1 medium egg yolk

25ml (1fl oz) double cream

1 Cream the butter, flour and the sugar together in a bowl. Stir in the egg yolk, then the cream, and mix to a smooth paste. Wrap in clingfilm and rest in the refrigerator for at least 2 hours.

2 Preheat the oven to 170°C/325°F/gas mark 3. On a lightly floured surface, roll out the dough to a 5mm (1/5 inch) thick square and cut into 30 x 8cm (3¼ inch) squares. Bake in the moderately slow oven for 8–10 minutes. Cool on a wire rack. The biscuits will keep in an airtight container for up to 2 days.

the best of the rest

the three lions

Stuckton

near Fordingbridge

Hampshire

01425 652489

www.thethreelionsrestaurant.co.uk

serves lunch and dinner tues to sun

lunch; bookings advised;

children welcome; garden

The Three Lions looks unassuming: it's a white-painted two-storey inn, with a large car park, on the edge of the New Forest. Inside, it's homely rather than stylish, with little china figurines and bits of brass. You sit at highly polished tables and order from a daily-changing blackboard menu that modestly understates almost every dish. Forest Salad turns out to be an earthy mixture of ceps, ducks' livers that have been marinated in port and Madeira, pan-fried pigeon, duck breast and roasted shallots; beef tournedos – rich, tender, marbled meat – comes with a port and oxtail sauce and a little cake of oxtail meat, sweetbreads, foie gras and apricots.

The chef and owner, Michael Womersley, has worked with some of the best chefs – Raymond Blanc in Britain and Marc Meneau and Michel Guérard in France – but when he bought the Three Lions and moved to the countryside he says he 're-learnt how to cook', developing a style that was less complicated and labour-intensive than Michelin-starred cooking, but that could still deliver exceptional flavours. He loves country pursuits and foods, making his own preserves, chutneys and pickles, collecting wild fungi and using local game. The result is stunning food that is sophisticated yet simple – sophisticated because Michael has the skill to extract maximum flavour from ingredients; simple because he doesn't overwork them. His food is light, even when the ingredients are rich, and there aren't too many flavours on one plate. This is refined cooking with its roots in the local landscape. The Three Lions is definitely a dining destination; not many people come in just for a drink. But its inherent pubbiness and the warmth of service from Michael's wife Jayne make it an easy-going, approachable place in which to eat great food.

the red house

Marsh Benham

Newbury

Berkshire

01635 582017

serves lunch mon to sun,

dinner tues to sat;

bookings advised;

children welcome; garden

Deep in horse country, not far from Newbury (there are plenty of paddocks and stables roundabout), The Red House is a good-looking, red-brick thatched pub. Inside, it's smartly traditional. There's a long, elegant bar with a brass rail, dark dining furniture, ox-blood coloured walls and equine prints. The punters aren't short of a bob or two – there's a huge ice-bucket filled with Champagne that you can enjoy by the glass, and cravats and Ralph Lauren shirts abound – but it isn't stuffy.

The French manager thinks of the Red House as a bistro, but it feels much too English for that. Wine, though, is taken more seriously than beer; there are even six dessert wines on offer. And this is definitely a dining destination, even though locals do drop in just to drink.

The cooking is accomplished and complex dishes, such as watercress soup with white truffle oil and a lobster ravioli, are done with a sure, light touch. There are plenty of simpler dishes, such as rillettes of salmon with horseradish dressing and poulet basquaise, and the set-lunch menu is terrific value.

east end arms

Main Road

East End

Lymington

Hampshire

01590 626223

**serves lunch and dinner tues
to sun lunch;**

bookings advised;

children welcomed at lunch;

garden

Secreted away on the edge of the New Forest, this cream, four-square pub was bought by John Ilsley, a founder member of Dire Straits, to save it from being turned into a theme pub. Good job, as the bar is one of the most unpretentious you'll find, a real unspoilt old boozer with low ceilings, wood-panelled walls, a stone floor and embers spilling untidily out of the fire. Beers are from Ringwood, a small regional brewery, and eating is done in the dining room. It's a down-home kind of place, with an old-fashioned carpet, tongue-and-groove walls and chunky candles. One wall, more glamorously, is covered in old black and white photos of the likes of Peter Sellers and Jean Shrimpton.

The blackboard menu is short at lunchtime and the dishes homely: butter-fried flounder, smoked gammon and eggs and excellent Dublin coddle. There are no starters. Dinner goes up several gears with dill-marinated salmon and crème fraîche, grilled halibut with salt, olive oil and lemon, and chicken with cream and wild mushrooms. Fresh fish dominates. The food is well cooked, and everyone seems to appreciate it as the place is always thronged.

the royal oak

The Square

Yattendon

Berkshire

01635 201325

**serves lunch and dinner mon to
sun; bookings advised;**

children welcome; garden

The Royal Oak, a wisteria-covered, red-brick hostelry right on Yattendon's main street, has a restaurant and bedrooms as well as its old-fashioned bar. The whole place is neat, gracious and smart. As soon as you enter you get a whiff of fresh flowers – there are big vases and jugs of them all over the place – and you know you're in for a good bit of r-and-r.

The bar is traditional, with oak panelling, deep ochre walls, big fireplaces and highly polished old oak tables, and the clientele is made up of smartly-dressed locals and the odd townie on a day-trip to the country. The menu tells you that the chef, Jason Gladwin, has his 'finger on the pulse', which is often a worrying indication that the food will be fashionable rather than good, but the modern brasserie fare is well done. You might find a coarse, well-seasoned terrine with pear and ginger chutney, a hefty plate of black pudding and white pudding with Guinness on mustard mash, and beautifully cooked brill with mussel and pancetta chowder.

Service is tops – friendly and personal – and drinking a post-dinner coffee ensconced in the plump cushions in the lounge is a treat.

the trout at tadpole bridge

Tadpole Bridge

Buckland Marsh

Oxfordshire

01367 870382

www.trout-inn.co.uk

**serves lunch and dinner
mon to sun lunch;**

bookings accepted;

children welcome; garden

A good solid place this, with a good story behind it too. The Green family, who had worked in farming for two generations, sold their dairy herd in 1995. In 1996 they bought the Trout, a 17th-century building by the tow path along the Thames near Faringdon. Son Christopher took the reins, joined soon after by another farmers' son, and they have maintained the Trout's reputation as a homely, unpretentious local, while smartening the place up and hiring a great chef.

The menu is modern and interesting without being faddy, and ranges across dishes from the East and the Mediterranean. There's duck with ginger and chilli and seared tuna nicoise as well as American and French brasserie classics such as Caesar salad and lamb with white beans.

The interior has been refurbished but, with its farmhouse chairs, old wooden tables, flagstone floors and candles, still feels old-fashioned. You can get Archers Village, Fuller's London Pride and a guest ale or two as well as 10 wines by the glass and a good range of dessert wines.

the five bells

Five Bells Lane

Nether Wallop

Hampshire

01264 781572

serves lunch and dinner

mon to sun lunch;

bookings advised;

children welcome; garden

Pitch up at the Five Bells, a village pub the colour of Bird's custard, and you'll think that you've got the wrong place. The bar, with its ancient piano and swirly patterned carpet, displays no signs of a gastropub makeover. The owner is adamant that it should remain a true village pub, and it has. Hearty greetings ring out, plenty of back-slapping goes on, and drinkers come and go in a steady stream.

The dining room, in a former skittles alley, doesn't have a great deal of character: decoration is limited to an antique clock and a few framed prints of fruit. But when you learn that the Five Bells is the brain-child of the team behind the Three Tuns in Romsey (see page 40), you understand why it's packed with happy diners.

The food, under the direction of chef Billy Reid and cooked by Matt Appelton, is very similar to that at the Three Tuns. Slow-roasted chicken with potato purée and braised carrots, skate with capers and rib-eye of beef with woodland mushrooms are all delivered with the same skill and polish as its sister pub. Owner Nick Geany is a beer-lover, as well as a wine-lover, so drinkers fare just as well as diners.

the lamb at buckland

Lamb Lane

Buckland

Oxfordshire

01367 870484

serves lunch and dinner tues

to sun lunch;

bookings advised;

children welcome; garden

This 18th-century pub, hidden away in a calm, meandering Cotswold village, is at the end of a country road that stops abruptly by the front door. It's a square block of Cotswold stone, plainly pretty, with pots of ivy trailed on frames and a big, solid door.

The Lamb is a relaxing, good-natured place. The staff are chatty and engaging and have a sense of humour. They're keen on the lamb theme: there are pictures of fluffy lambs woven into the carpet, a cuddly lamb on top of the old piano, lambs as ornaments and lamb on the menu.

The blackboard lists dishes that pubs have been serving since the 1970s: chicken pâté, prawns with garlic butter, seafood pancakes and steak and kidney pie. But don't let that put you off. When these dishes are well done, you remember why they became popular in the first place. There are also daubes, risottos and pasta dishes, and comforting puddings such as apple and blackberry pie. Don't expect fireworks here, just straightforward, well-cooked food.

the white hart hotel

High Street

Nettlebed

Oxfordshire

01491 641245

www.whitehartnettlebed.com

serves lunch and dinner

mon to sun; bookings advised;

children welcome

I think snazzy is the word here. Cool grey tables with wood-and-chrome chairs, graphic blocks of carpet, citrussy watercolours, linen blinds and down-lighters: the White Hart is not totally 'out there', but it is still not what you'd expect in a 17th-century inn near Henley.

The whole building has been contemporized and is now a hotel with swish rooms and a restaurant, as well as a bar. The result is a little cold and rather at odds with the building in which it is housed. This is a real pity because the food here, from chef Chris Barber (who used to run the fine pub, the Goose in Britwell Salome) is very good indeed. Fishcakes, which are properly fishy, with chive sauce were the best I found while researching this book. Chicken with wild mushroom risotto and cep juice is rich and earthy, and rib-eye steak with pepper sauce is spot-on. This is exemplary modern brasserie cooking. If cool surroundings are up your street, or you can manage to ignore them, you'll love it.

the wykeham arms

75 Kingsgate Street
Winchester
Hampshire
01962 853834
serves lunch and dinner
mon to sun lunch;
bookings advised;
over 14s only; garden

Swing through the beautiful doors of this corner pub near Winchester College and your mind will go into overdrive. The place is so full of artefacts, richly dark colours and glowing pools of light from candles and lamps that it's difficult to take it all in. Oil paintings, flags, a collection of walking sticks, tankards, helmets and bugles all vie for space, and are reflected and re-reflected in mirrors.

An ancient wooden bar stretches round the whole central area and is always busy with plenty of drinkers. The food here is good, but the Wykeham Arms is first and foremost a proper pub, and you're not obliged to go for the full works; plenty of people just have a bowl of soup. The simplest dishes are the best, so beware those that have too many components. You'll find dishes such as rack of lamb with potato and celeriac gratin and fillet of sea-bass with basil mash and roasted vegetables, and lunchtime dishes such as big salads and tarts hit the spot. Elderly county types, teachers and eco-warriors all rub along happily together.

the chequers inn

Kiln Lane
Wooburn Common
Buckinghamshire
01628 529575
www.chequers-inn.com
serves lunch and dinner
mon to sun;
bookings advised;
children welcome; garden

The Chequers is homely and traditional. There are comfy tapestry sofas and small stools, oak posts, beams and a red-brick fire place. The walls are covered with old advertising posters and country prints, not many of them hung straight, and a plant sits on every one of the low tables.

Reading the blackboard menu, you think the food will be pretty ordinary; prawns with avocado and marie-rose sauce is never inspiring. But the cooking is exceptional. Fish cakes served with a poached egg and hollandaise are a triumph, and calves' liver comes with superb, well-seasoned, rich and buttery mash. Puds are down-home – syrup sponge and rhubarb and plum crumble – and well executed. Locals love the place. It's always full of blazered businessmen, home-counties ladies and mummies with toddlers. There's a chintzy restaurant, too, with more complicated cooking.

the alford arms

Frithsden
near Hemel Hempstead
Hertfordshire
01442 864480
serves lunch and dinner
mon to sun;
bookings advised;
children welcome; terrace

A cream-painted pub in a cute village, the Alford Arms is an easy-going, feel-good place where bank managers and sulky teenagers seem equally at home. There's a printed menu, which lets you know that as much of the food as possible is free-range or organic, and a board with daily specials. One section is sensibly headed 'small plates', presumably so you can feel free to order one or two of these rather than a starter and main course. The food is mouth-watering stuff; largely modern European, with a little Eastern influence creeping in. Butternut squash risotto, crab and coriander cakes with chilli relish and cod with chorizo are all well executed and plainly served. There's usually a big choice of desserts, which are neither too homely nor too complicated: elderflower crème brûlée and Marsala-roasted figs with mascarpone are both first-rate.

the plough

Winchmore Hill
near Beaconsfield
Buckinghamshire
01494 721001

As this book goes to press, the team behind The Greyhound in Stockbridge (see page 46) are in the throws of refurbishing this pub on the green in the little village of Winchmore Hill. The interior is more colourful than that at The Greyhound, and rather more modern. The food though, under Dave Bennett, who also cooked at the Greyhound, is likely to be similar: that is classy, sophisticated but not overly complicated. It should be a winner.

the southeast

The southeast is easy to dismiss as crowded commuter-land. It *is* densely populated, but get off the main roads and you can lose yourself in the tight networks of green lanes in Sussex, walk by the beery hop fields and oast houses of Kent, or wander along the coast, enjoying its faded grandeur, ragged seaside cafés, amusement arcades, and the melancholia of salt-marshland and caravan sites. There are tarred net-drying sheds at Hastings; half-timbered, skew-roofed houses in Rye; ozone, pebbles and groynes in Whitstable.

Along with the fact that the Battle of Hastings was in 1066, the scrap of knowledge that is retained by every British schoolchild is that the Weald of Kent is the 'Garden of England', and it is like some kind of English Arcadia. The warm, rich soil is ideal for growing fruit and vegetables. There are orchards bursting with apples, pears, plums, cherries and nuts; gardens crammed with rhubarb and berries; hop fields and vineyards.

The region has benefited from the scores of traders and invaders who brought their own varieties of fruit with them. The great upsurge in fruit growing began in the 16th century, when many estates developed orchards, and soon the idea of market gardening, started mainly by immigrant French gardeners, was firmly established. Centuries later, the Weald was the first area in Britain to have farm

shops, and travelling here to pick-your-own was a summertime treat long before food writers started proselytising about fresh, seasonal produce.

The southeast has historic links with sheep-breeding, and the region's lamb is still famous for its superb flavour, whether it has been grazed on the turf of the chalk downs or the rich, salty marshes around Romney. Steve Harris, chef at the Sportsman in Seasalter, says that the local pork is unsurpassable, too — incredibly sweet, especially if it is from pigs which have grazed in the apple orchards, stuffing themselves with the windfalls. Then there are the fish and shellfish: oysters, sea-bass, turbot, brill, plaice and Dover sole.

You do see Mediterranean influences in the cooking of the southeast, as you do everywhere in Britain now, but the chefs in this chapter generally respect the area's position, beside a cold, grey sea that leads to France and continental northern Europe.

At the Stephan Langton Inn in Abinger Common, chef Jonathan Coomb has goulash soup and cured salmon with beetroot and horseradish on the menu. Steve Harris serves sea-bass with a tartare of cockles, cod with parsley sauce, and turbot with deep-fried oysters on a pea purée that is spiked with a little bit of malt vinegar so that the dish has a touch of chip-shop flavour. Tim Neal at The Chequers in Rowhook serves warm potatoes in a beer and mustard dressing alongside duck confit. And all over the place you'll find local asparagus served with hollandaise, locally smoked fish and poultry, and every berry ripened under the Kent sun.

Faversham Road
Seasalter
Whitstable
(01227 273370)
serves lunch and dinner tues to
sun lunch; bookings advised;
chidren welcome

the sportsman

Just before you get to the seaside town of Whitstable, take the slip road to Seasalter and you'll find yourself in a melancholy hinterland of pylons standing like sci-fi giants on flat marshland and beachhuts in shades as colourless as the sea. The Sportsman, a scruffy, butter-coloured pub by the road, looks like the kind of place where you might meet trouble. But the inside is awash with light. Happy families squeeze round the scrubbed, rickety tables; hunks in leather jackets knock back oysters and chorizo and even the odd celeb can be seen tucking into chef Steve Harris' sublime slow-roast chicken.

Here is a chef – self-taught, obsessive, enthralled by taste – who really thinks. He loves the flavours achieved by the culinary stars – it was a meal at Nico Ladenis' that made him give up his job as a newspaper sub and take to the stove – but he hates the ponciness of restaurants. 'I wanted to do haute cuisine stripped bare: Nico Ladenis food in a pub,' he says.

Lucky for diners that he made that choice, because here you get knock-out food at bargain prices, and Stephen's experiments with culinary science push his cooking ever further. His rhubarb sorbet, for example, is made by macerating the raw fruit in sugar for two days and then using the extracted juice. Paired with a little pot of burnt cream, this is a sensational taste experience, and it's only one of the many pleasures here. The Sportsman is a delight.

soda bread starters

Since you don't use yeast and there's no proving time, Irish soda bread is easy to make. Stephen hunted around for the best recipe before finally selecting one from Irish chef, Richard Corrigan, on which this is based. It is sweet and salty with a touch of treacly bitterness. These starters, all based on the bread, are simple and unfussy.

for the soda bread

makes 1 loaf

65g (2¹/2oz) white self-raising flour, plus extra for dusting

125g (4¹/2oz) wholemeal flour

65g (2¹/2oz) pinhead oatmeal

30g (1oz) bran

15g (¹/2oz) wheatgerm

5ml (1tsp) salt

5ml (1tsp) bicarbonate of soda

15ml (1tbsp) treacle

300ml (10¹/2fl oz) buttermilk

1 Preheat the oven to 220°C/425°F/gas mark 7. Dust a baking tray with flour.

2 Put all the dry ingredients into a mixer and mix thoroughly on a low setting for 2 minutes.

3 Warm the tin of treacle in a saucepan of hot water to make it easier to measure. Add the buttermilk and warm treacle to the dry ingredients and mix slowly for 1 minute to get a slightly sticky dough.

4 Shape the dough into an oval and put on the floured baking tray. With a sharp knife, cut 2 slashes in the top of the bread. Bake for 10 minutes in the very hot oven, then turn the oven down to 150°C/300°F/gas mark 2 and cook for a further 35 minutes, or until the bread sounds hollow when tapped on the base. Place on a wire rack to cool.

marinated salmon cured in vodka and lemon

serves 10

565g (1¹/4lb) side of salmon, filleted and pin-boned

300g (11oz) sea salt

150g (5oz) soft brown sugar

40ml (2¹/2tbsp) icing sugar

juice of 2 lemons

115ml (4fl oz) vodka

10 slices soda bread, about 1.5cm (¹/2 inch) thick

285g (10oz) cream cheese, such as Brillat-Savarin

black pepper

sorrel, shredded, or chives, chopped

1 Place the salmon flat on a large platter. Mix the salt and brown sugar together and spread over the surface of the salmon. Cover with cling-film and leave for 2 days in the refrigerator.

2 Wash all the salt and sugar mixture from the salmon with cold water and, using a sharp knife, slice the salmon horizontally, as thinly as possible (about 3mm/⅛ inch thick).

3 Stir the icing sugar into the lemon juice until it dissolves and then add the vodka. In a flat bowl, marinate the slices of salmon in the vodka dressing for 5–10 minutes.

4 Spread the slices of warm soda bread thickly with cream cheese and sprinkle with black pepper. Put the cured slices of salmon on the bread and pour over the vodka dressing. Garnish with shredded sorrel (in the summer) or chopped chives (in the winter).

smoked eel and horseradish

serves 4

225g (8oz) smoked eel fillets

4 slices soda bread, 1cm (3/8 thick)

115g (4oz) cream cheese

20ml (4tsp) horseradish sauce

4 sprigs watercress

olive oil and lemon juice

sea salt

1 Cut the room temperature smoked eel fillets into 7.5cm (3 inch) lengths.

2 Warm the soda bread. Spread the cream cheese thickly onto the slices of warm soda bread, then spoon on 5ml (1tsp) horseradish sauce.

3 Dress the watercress (or lamb's lettuce if you prefer) with a little olive oil, lemon juice and sea salt.

4 Put the smoked eel on the bread and top with a sprig of dressed watercress (or lamb's lettuce).

smoked mackerel and gooseberry jelly

serves 4

500g (1lb 2oz) gooseberries

250g (9oz) caster sugar

about 2 sheets gelatine

2 smoked mackerel fillets

4 slices soda bread, warm

115g (4oz) cream cheese

sorrel, shredded

1 Mash up the gooseberries and sugar in a bowl. Cover and leave in the fridge for a day or 2. Strain the gooseberries through a nylon sieve. Measure the thin purée, then soak 1 sheet of gelatine in cold water for every 200ml (7fl oz) of purée.

2 Gently heat the purée in a heavy-bottomed pan until it is hot, but do not boil. When the gelatine is soft (after about 5 minutes) squeeze out the excess water and add it to the purée. Stir thoroughly and leave to cool and set.

3 Halve the smoked mackerel fillets. Spread the soda bread thickly with cream cheese and gooseberry jelly. Put the mackerel on top and serve with shredded sorrel.

oysters and chorizo

This dish is based on the idea behind 'oysters *basquais*': ice-cold oysters and hot spicy sausages. It's one of the dishes that you can hear fellow diners raving about when you're eating at The Sportsman.

serves 4 as a starter

12 rock oysters (if necessary, ask your fishmonger for instructions on how to open them)

crushed ice

155g (5½oz) chorizo sausage, about 2.5cm (1 inch) diameter

1 Open the oysters straight from the refrigerator. Place them on a tray of crushed ice.

2 Slice the chorizo into £1 coin-sized pieces and grill or fry in a hot frying pan for 30 seconds.

3 Put a slice onto each oyster and serve while the chorizo is still hot.

asparagus soup with a soft-boiled egg

This is really luxurious and a fantastic dinner-party starter, as it is a treat but can easily be prepared in advance.

serves 4 as a starter

2 bunches dark green asparagus

unsalted butter

85ml (3fl oz) double cream

15ml (1tbsp) freshly grated Parmesan cheese

salt and pepper

4 medium eggs

to serve

4 slices soda bread, cut into soldiers (optional)

1 Cut each asparagus stalk into 3 pieces: the tip, middle and base.

2 Rinse the bases of the asparagus as they are likely to be gritty. Roughly chop, place in a saucepan and just cover with about 285ml (½ pint) water. Bring to the boil and simmer for 10 minutes. Strain and reserve the stock.

3 Preheat the oven to 200°C/400°F/gas mark 6.

4 In a large heavy-bottomed pan, fry the middles of the asparagus in 115g (4oz) of the butter until they start to soften but are still green. Add the reserved stock and simmer for 10 minutes.

5 Blitz the mix in a blender at high speed for 5 minutes, adding the double cream and Parmesan cheese. Strain the soup and adjust the seasoning.

6 Place the eggs in a saucepan of cold water. Bring to the boil and boil gently for 2¾ minutes.

7 While the eggs are cooking, roast the asparagus tips in on a baking sheet in the hot oven for 6 minutes, then dress with a knob of butter. Divide between 4 plates and serve immediately with a small bowl or little cup of the soup and a warm soft-boiled egg. Some soda bread soldiers (see soda bread recipe on page 59) are also good for dipping.

'this is based on a soup from a michelin-starred restaurant, but it's just as stunning when simplified.' stephen

charred maple-cured pork loin with grain mustard tartare

Smoked paprika gives the most wonderful intense Spanish flavour and heightens the sweetness of pork. This dish has such disparate components that you might be put off trying it – but it works very well.

serves 4

30ml (2tbsp) smoked paprika

60ml (4tbsp) maple syrup

30ml (2tbsp) groundnut oil, plus extra for frying

4 large pork loin chops

sea salt

to serve

about 225g (8oz) greens, finely shredded

knob of unsalted butter

lemon juice

black pepper

1 Mix the smoked paprika, maple syrup and groundnut oil together in a bowl and rub into the loin chops. Cover and refrigerate for at least 3 hours, or up to 3 days.

2 Preheat the oven to 140°C/275°F/gas mark 1.

3 Heat a frying pan and add a little groundnut oil. Fry each seasoned chop (don't wash off the marinade) until it starts to blacken, then transfer to a baking dish and bake in the preheated oven for 25 minutes, until tender.

4 Cook the shredded greens in boiling, salted water for 4 minutes. Drain and dress with butter, lemon juice and black pepper to taste.

5 Spoon the meat juices from the baking dish over the chops and season them with sea salt.

6 Serve with the greens and the grain mustard tartare sauce.

grain mustard tartare sauce

60ml (3tbsp) mayonnaise, either homemade or good quality commercial

1 small shallot, diced

55g (2oz) gherkins, diced

55g (2oz) chives, finely chopped

55g (2oz) capers

10ml (2tsp) moutarde de Meaux

1 Simply mix all the ingredients together.

bitter chocolate tart with blood orange ice-cream

This really is the most delicious, grown-up bitter chocolate tart I've ever tasted. The ice-cream is made in rather an unorthodox way: Steve has done a lot of experimenting to achieve the most intensely flavoured ice-creams and sorbets, and the results are stunning.

serves 12

for the pastry

255g (9oz) unsalted butter, softened

40g (1½oz) icing sugar

1 medium egg

500g (1lb 2oz) plain flour, sifted

for the chocolate filling

360ml (12fl oz) double cream

140ml (¼ pint) full-fat milk

400g (14oz) dark chocolate (at least 70% cocoa solids), broken into pieces

3 medium eggs, beaten

1 Preheat the oven to 180°C/350°F/gas mark 4. Place a baking sheet on the middle shelf in the oven.

2 Cream the butter and sugar in a food mixer, or in a bowl with a wooden spoon, until pale and fluffy, then add the egg.

3 Turn the food mixer to its lowest setting and add the plain flour. Mix until the pastry comes together. Wrap in cling-film and chill for at least 30 minutes.

4 Butter a 20cm (8 inch) tart ring or a loose-bottomed tart tin. Roll out the pastry into a circle 3mm (⅛ inch) thick and about 5cm (2 inches) bigger than the tart ring. Line the tart ring with the pastry, pressing it down gently and leaving a 2.5cm (1 inch) overhang.

5 Prick the base with a fork and blind bake (see page 19) in the preheated oven for 20 minutes, or until starting to brown. Remove and trim the overhanging pastry level with the top of the ring, using a sharp, heavy knife.

6 Turn the oven down to 130°C/250°F/gas mark ½ and make the filling. In a saucepan, heat the cream and milk until trembling, just under boiling point. Take off the heat.

7 Add the chocolate to the cream and milk and stir until fully blended, then add the eggs and mix again. Pour the chocolate mix into the tart case and bake in the preheated oven for about 1 hour. The tart is done when it is still a bit wobbly in the middle. Leave to set for at least 45 minutes before serving.

blood orange ice-cream

500g (1lb 2oz) blood oranges, preferably unwaxed

340g (12oz) caster sugar

6 medium egg yolks

200ml (7fl oz) double cream

400ml (14fl oz) full-fat milk

1 Grate the orange skins and quarter the fruits. Put the grated skins and quarters into a bowl and pour over 255g (9oz) caster sugar. Refrigerate for a day or 2.

2 Squeeze the juice from the mixture – start by using your hands and then press through a nylon sieve. Measure the juice.

3 Make the custard for the ice-cream by whisking the egg yolks and remaining sugar together until thick and pale (this should take 10 minutes in a food mixer).

4 Bring the cream and milk to the boil in a heavy-bottomed pan, then whisk the mixture into the eggs. Return this to the pan and cook gently, stirring constantly until the custard begins to thicken. You must not allow the mixture to boil or it will scramble. If you prefer, you can cook the custard in a bowl set over a pan of simmering water. Check whether it is thick enough by coating the back of a wooden spoon with the custard – if, when you slide your finger through it, it leaves a trail, it is ready. Remove from heat and cool.

5 Whisk the juice with one and a half times its volume of cooled custard, then churn in an ice-cream maker. Alternatively, pour the mixture into a freezerproof container and half freeze, then whisk again to remove the ice crystals. Return to the freezer.

pears poached in porter with lancashire cheese

You can add a good pinch of tobacco to the porter if you like. It adds a mysterious flavour – but do strain if off! This is one for people who miss the smell of a pub after a heavy Saturday night. Go and get yourself good Lancashire cheese, such as Mrs Kirkham's.

serves 4

1 litre (1¾ pints) porter, such as Shepherd Neame's

85g (3oz) caster sugar

good pinch of tobacco (optional)

4 large conference pears, peeled

225g (8oz) Lancashire cheese

1 Preheat the oven to 150°C/300°F/gas mark 2. Gently heat the porter in a saucepan with the sugar and tobacco, if using, stirring occasionally until the sugar has dissolved.

2 Bring the porter up to simmering point and poach the pears in it. When a sharp knife easily cuts into the pears, they are done. Remove the pears, cover and keep warm in the oven.

3 Strain the tobacco out of the porter. Bring the porter to the boil and boil rapidly until it has reduced by three-quarters and is syrupy.

4 Place each pear on a plate and pour over the syrup. Serve with a wedge of Lancashire cheese.

panettone 'perdu' with strawberries and cream

Butter-fried panettone, strawberries and thick cream – nothing could be simpler.

serves 4

225g (8oz) strawberries

120g (4¼oz) icing sugar

lemon juice

115g (4oz) unsalted butter

4 slices panettone, cut 2.5cm (1 inch) thick

to serve

untreated Jersey cream or the best thick cream that you can find

1 Preheat the oven to 150°C/300°F/gas mark 2. Place a baking sheet in the oven.

2 Hull and halve the strawberries, dust with 30g (1oz) of the icing sugar and a squeeze of lemon. Set aside.

3 In a heavy-bottomed frying pan, gently melt 30g (1oz) butter. Sprinkle 15g (1tbsp) icing sugar over the top of 1 slice of the panettone and, when the butter is foaming, place the panettone sugar side down in the pan. Fry until starting to brown and crisp. Sprinkle over another 15ml (1tbsp) icing sugar and turn the panettone over. Once the second side is brown and crisp transfer it to the baking sheet in the slow oven. Repeat with the next 3 slices.

4 Put each slice of panettone on a plate and scatter over the strawberries. Serve with thick cream.

'i love the cooking of marco pierre white and nico ladenis, where flavours are pushed to the limit. but i wanted to simplify it, strip it down to its essentials, and serve it in a pub.' stephen

the best of the rest

the dove

Plum Pudding Lane

Dargate

Kent

01227 751360

serves lunch tues to sun and

dinner weds to sat;

bookings advised;

children welcome; garden

The Dove, a red-brick Victorian pub surrounded by apple orchards, is an unhurried, old-fashioned place. There are green candles in wine bottles, scrubbed wooden tables, Liberty print curtains and windows of etched glass. It's far from high style – teddy bears dressed as chefs grace each end of the dining room – but big wine goblets on the tables indicate food and drink are taken seriously here.

Lighter dishes, such as sandwiches and croques, are listed on a blackboard by the bar. A printed menu's offerings include cep and Bayonne ham tart, sea-bass with crushed potatoes and tapenade, and fillet of beef with wild mushrooms and roasted salsify. The cooking is bold, if uneven, and there's good use of local produce. But a visit must be judged on the whole experience. The Dove is a proper pub with all the things that entails: good wines and beer, a warm fire, a bit of gossip and the odd dog, and is so cosy and welcoming that it's hard to drag yourself from the table.

the stephan langton inn

Friday Street

Abinger Common

Surrey

01306 730775

serves lunch and dinner

tues to sun lunch;

bookings advised;

children welcome; patio

Believe it or not, you can find odd patches of deeply hidden countryside in Surrey. The Stephan Langton Inn is in just such a place, down a single-track road beside a small lake. It's a rambling, old red-brick building, well-known in the area as a good pub, and now with a great dining room as well, overseen by chef Jonathan Coomb and his Brazilian wife, Cynthia. It's a big space, filled with dark pub furniture, but the Coombs have turned it into a gracious, understated dining room.

Jonathan worked at the Chiswick in London under Adam Robinson, a restaurateur famed for his savvy, bare-bones cooking, and the same restraint is evident here. The dishes are modern European; the menu is short and makes your mouth water: cod with clams, lentils and salsa verde; lamb with olives, capers and mint, and poached prunes with Armagnac ice-cream. It is straightforward, flavourful cooking, excellently done.

the horseguards inn

Tillington

near Petworth

West Sussex

01798 342332

serves lunch and dinner mon

to sun; bookings advised;

children welcome; garden

The white-washed Horseguards is a real find. It's like a French auberge – beams everywhere, wood-panelled walls, gleaming pieces of copper cookware, tables with linen napkins, sparkling glasses and bunches of flowers – that has a very English bar at its heart, with Badger Best Bitter and Wadworth 6X on tap. There's always a good smattering of drinkers as well as eaters; the owners are adamant that the Horseguards should be a real local as well as a dining pub.

The food ranges from the hearty – pies, braised faggots, sausages with onions and stout – to more refined dishes such as sea-bass with crushed new potatoes and fennel butter sauce. It's all skilfully cooked, with French classics and the old-fashioned British dishes, in particular, well done. There are plenty of family groups. The welcome is warm and the place is charming.

the jolly sportsman

Chapel Lane
East Chiltington
East Sussex
01273 890400
www.thejollysportsman.com
serves lunch and dinner tues to
sun lunch; bookings advised;
children welcome; garden

The Jolly Sportsman is not one of those pubs you 'ooh and aah' over. It's in the back of beyond and the cream-painted brick-and-clapperboard building isn't pretty. But inside it is buzzing with 30-somethings from Brighton and local families. You can eat in the hop-festooned bar or in the more contemporary dining room, with its wooden blinds and sage-green walls. The food is European mainstream: serrano ham with grilled radicchio, artichokes and white Spanish beans; sea-bass with lemon beurre blanc. You feel like ordering it all. The pud menu sports the usual suspects such as lemon tart and toffee pudding. The cooking is capable, the informality is refreshing and the range of whiskies and apéritifs will make you want to abandon the rest of the day to self-indulgence.

the chequers inn

Rowhook,
West Sussex
01403 790480
serves lunch and dinner mon to sun
lunch; bookings advised; children
welcome; garden

The Chequers, a white 15th-century cottage down a country lane near Horsham, is hard to find, but it's worth the search. They make no noise about the quality of food here, and there are plenty of customers who are just drinking, so you're not quite prepared for the high standard of cooking. Moist roast pheasant with juniper and root vegetables, their tips caramelized to sweetness; smoky pumpkin and smoked haddock risotto; rich duck-liver pâté, which comes to the table in a preserving jar, with cornichons and a beautifully dressed salad. It's all top notch.

the griffin inn

Fletching
East Sussex
01825 722890
serves lunch and dinner
mon to sun; bookings
advised (restaurant only);
children welcome; garden

Lunch at the Griffin, a 16th-century country pub in a village near Ashdown Forest, makes a great outing on a sunny day, when you can sit outside under big cream parasols or sprawl in the huge garden. There are often barbecues, sometimes with a jazz artist, and jugs of Pimms do the rounds.

Inside you'll find a classic country pub interior with wainscot walls, beams and open fires. The food is a mixture of country French, Mediterranean and old-fashioned British: pheasant with bacon, lentils and roast garlic; fish with hollandaise; game pie and cracking homely puds such as rhubarb and ginger crumble. The dishes are classic and unfussy, cooked well and served with warmth.

the lickfold inn

Lickfold
Near Lodsworth
West Sussex
01798 861285
serves lunch and dinner
mon to sun; bookings
advised; children welcome;
garden

The Lickfold, hidden in a dense network of Sussex lanes, is a charmer. A trail of smoke curls from its chimney and a pale blue and black sign, hand painted on its red brick herringbone wall, proclaims its name. You feel like you've stumbled across a story-book cottage that could disappear at any moment. The interior is warm and honey coloured, with old rugs on the floors and white candles twinkling in every available space. It's comfortable and stylish without trying too hard.

The cooking is simple – no stock reductions, no pretensions – and good: local asparagus with perfectly seasoned hollandaise; a salad of sweet queenie scallops with fried chorizo and rocket; Thai fishcakes with chilli and mango salsa. Corn-fed chicken with wild mushrooms and cream on sautéed new potatoes is the kind of dish you might find in a roadside bistro in France and proclaim that you could never find in England.

The Lickfold confers deep contentment. With a few culinary tweaks – vegetables are the standard carrots and mange-tout, and the pudding list could do with a few more fruity offerings – it would be a gem.

Gastropubs are now such an established feature of the London landscape that it's hard to remember a time when they didn't exist. But their ubiquity owes much to a pub that opened in 1991: the Eagle, in Farringdon Road. Its style was shabby chic; the food was gutsy southern Mediterranean; a blackboard listing the day's menu, with smudged clouds of chalk representing the dishes that had run out, made the place feel spontaneous and exciting, as did the open kitchen. You could see the raw materials that went into your food – big wire bowls of lemons, bottles of golden-green oil, bunches of sappy greenery – and smell them as they were cooked on the flames behind the bar.

The Eagle did feel British. It had big windows, a bar with pumps, and City types mingling with journos from nearby newspapers. But the colours, heat and speed of the place gave it an immediacy and rawness that transported you to a Madrid bar. It showed us that pubs could be full of light, energy and great food.

The influence of the Eagle, which is still going strong, has been astounding. It was an idea whose time had come. The high-spending expense-account dining of the 1980s had had its day; lavishing huge sums of money on food began to look obscene. Eating food that was overly complicated seemed outmoded and pretentious. Mediterranean peasant food, food that depended on good ingredients rather than complicated preparation, was popularized by restaurants such as the River Cafe and Alistair Little. Chefs began to talk about the importance of sourcing and 'simple' became a buzzword.

london

After Eagle-influenced refurbishments, there came the pub with a 'dining room': a place where you could eat in the bar but also dine from a more extensive menu in a room above or beside it. The Eagle's sister pub, the Fox, is one such place. Now we're seeing dining pubs that eschew rickety furniture and ad hoc decoration in favour of expensive, design-driven interiors. They may be serving dishes that sound similar to those at the Eagle, but a pub like The House in Islington goes one step further, styling itself as a dining pub 'with glamour'; hence the bespoke furniture, smoked mirrors and ex-Marco Pierre White chef.

London is not a region in the way that the rest of the areas in this book are. It doesn't have its own produce or regional specialities, but it does influence the rest of the country. The capital is the great laboratory, the culinary catwalk, and the success of its dining pubs has had an effect on the whole country. While most rural chefs are not, thank God, imitating any-and-every London fashion, London gastropubs have opened the eyes of cooks, entrepreneurs and breweries to the potential of pubs everywhere.

137 Westbourne Park Road
London W2
020 7221 3395
serves lunch and dinner
mon din to sun;
children welcome at lunch;
terrace

Most gastropubs in London function as neighbourhood restaurants: you eat in them if you live or work nearby, or if you are visiting the area. But the Oak, a converted corner pub in Notting Hill, has diners coming from as far away as Kew and Hoxton. The chef, Mark Broadbent, who set the style here, worked at The Brackenbury – a groundbreaking, simple neighbourhood restaurant in West London, in its glory days – and you can see its influence in the directness of his food.

In a big, high-ceilinged room with dark slatted blinds and chocolate-brown walls, you can get first-rate pizzas from the wood-fired oven, and modern European dishes that are way ahead of the usual offerings both in terms of authenticity and execution. There's a bit of the Mediterranean – caponata with goat's cheese and zarzuela of fish with saffron, for example – but it is the hearty French and British dishes, such as a knock-out confit of pork with Jerusalem artichokes and black pudding and a chocolatey daube of venison with Agen prunes and wild boar sausage, that are the real hitters.

the oak

The place is always packed with a huge cross-section of Londoners: mummies with kids in tow, serious elderly diners and hip media types. It's the sort of sprawling, inclusive, feel-good eatery that every city should have. The Oak is definitely worth crossing London for.

lamb shanks with mint and harissa sauce on pea couscous

Serve this with a bowl of Greek yoghurt – and a little extra harissa mixed with olive oil for those who like their food spicy.

serves 4

4 lamb shanks

salt and pepper

vegetable oil, for frying

795g (1¾lb) tinned tomatoes

5ml (1tsp) rose harissa

½ bunch coriander, stems and leaves roughly chopped

½ bunch mint, stems and leaves roughly chopped

5ml (1tsp) cumin seeds, toasted and crushed

5ml (1tsp) paprika

5ml (1tsp) ground allspice

565ml (1 pint) chicken stock

1 Preheat the oven to 180°C/350°F/gas mark 4. Season the lamb shanks. In a large heavy-bottomed pan, heat a little vegetable oil and then seal the meat until brown all over. Add the tinned tomatoes, rose harissa, coriander, mint, cumin, paprika, allspice and chicken stock.

2 Bring to the boil, then lower the heat, cover and braise for 2 hours in the oven until the lamb is soft and tender.

3 Remove the shanks to a plate, cover with foil and rest.

4 Bring the cooking liquor to the boil and reduce until it's the consistency of full-bodied gravy. Strain through a sieve.

5 Divide the couscous between 4 warmed plates, place the lamb shanks on top and spoon over the sauce.

couscous

340g (12oz) couscous

zest of 1 unwaxed lemon

85g (3oz) peas, freshly blanched

medium bunch of mint, leaves finely shredded

small bunch of coriander, shredded

handful of pine nuts, toasted

1 medium cucumber, peeled, seeds removed, and cut into 1cm (3/8 inch) dice

salt and pepper

extra virgin olive oil

1 Mix the couscous with 285ml (½ pint) boiling water in a bowl. Add lemon zest to taste, freshly blanched peas, shredded mint and coriander, toasted pine nuts and diced cucumber, salt, pepper and a good slug of olive oil.

2 Mix thoroughly with a fork.

herb-crusted scallops with roasted tinkerbell chilli

If you can't find tinkerbell chillies, use poblano chillies, or any other large, mild chilli you can find

serves 1

55g (2oz) fresh breadcrumbs

15g (1/2 oz) piquillo pepper, diced

pinch of lemon zest

1 clove garlic, finely chopped

handful of flat-leaf parsley, shredded

30g (1oz) nibbed almonds

extra virgin olive oil

5 queen scallops in shell, cleaned and seasoned

to serve

lemon wedges

salad leaves

extra virgin olive oil

lemon juice

1 Preheat the oven to 180°C/350°F/gas mark 4. In a small bowl, mix the breadcrumbs, piquillo pepper, lemon zest, chopped garlic, parsley and nibbed almonds. Moisten with olive oil. Cover the scallops in their shells with the mixture.

2 Place the filled scallop shells on a baking tray and bake in the preheated oven for 10 minutes, then finish under a hot grill until golden brown.

3 Serve the warm scallops with the roasted tinkerbell chilli (at room temperature), lemon wedges and some salad leaves dressed with olive oil and lemon juice.

roasted tinkerbell chilli

1 tinkerbell chilli, cut in half through the stalk and deseeded

2 cherry vine tomatoes

1 clove garlic, halved

1 small leaf basil, torn in half

olive oil, for drizzling

1 Preheat the oven to 180°C/350°F/gas mark 4.

2 Fill the tinkerbell chilli halves with tomatoes, garlic halves and basil. Drizzle with olive oil. Place in a roasting tin and roast for 1 hour in the preheated oven.

free-range chicken with smashed neeps, ceps and madeira

Use other wild mushrooms, or a mixture of wild and cultivated mushrooms if you prefer. This is good served with buttered spinach.

serves 4

olive oil, for roasting

2 cloves garlic, crushed

salt and pepper

2 sprigs thyme, leaves only

4 x 225g (8oz) free-range chicken breasts, skin on

unsalted butter

12 ceps, cleaned

for the smashed neeps

55-85g (2-3oz) unsalted butter

3 large carrots, peeled and diced

1 small swede, peeled and diced

for the Madeira sauce

2 shallots, finely chopped

1 small carrot, peeled and finely chopped

1½ celery sticks, finely chopped

1 medium leek, white only, finely chopped

2 cloves garlic, finely chopped

125ml (4½fl oz) Madeira

125ml (4½fl oz) red wine

285ml (½ pint) chicken or veal stock

90ml (3½fl oz) double cream

1 Preheat the oven to 220°C/425°F/gas mark 7. Put a little olive oil in a roasting tin and heat in the oven. Meanwhile, sprinkle the garlic, seasoning and thyme leaves over the chicken breasts and lightly press onto the skin.

2 Transfer the roasting tin from the oven to the hob and add a knob of butter. Put the chicken breasts, skin side down, in the oil and butter to seal quickly. Transfer the tin to the oven and cook for 15–20 minutes. Place the chicken on a plate to rest.

3 Heat a knob of unsalted butter in a pan and quickly cook the ceps. Season.

4 Divide the smashed neeps between 4 warmed plates, place the chicken on top with the ceps and spoon around a little Madeira sauce.

smashed neeps

1 In a heavy-bottomed pan, heat 55g (2oz) butter. Add the vegetables (you need an equal amount of carrots and swede) and a splash of water, cover and sweat until soft – this will take about 15 minutes. You may need to add a little splash of water from time to time.

2 Break up with a fork, adding seasoning and butter if required. Don't overmash.

madeira sauce

1 Put the shallots, carrot, celery and leek into a heavy-bottomed saucepan. Add the garlic, Madeira and red wine.

2 Bring to the boil and reduce by half to a syrup. Add the stock and reduce by half again. Stir in the double cream, heat through but do not boil, then strain through a fine sieve.

cod with brown shrimp butter
and parsley mash

A lovely, very English dish. Don't stint on the parsley, and serve with some buttered carrots.

serves 4

4 x 170–200g (6–7oz) cod fillets, skin on

sea salt and pepper

zest of ½ unwaxed lemon

1 sprig fresh thyme, leaves only

4 large Desirée (red skin) potatoes, peeled and cut into equal pieces

400g (14oz) unsalted butter, chilled

a splash of double cream

5ml (1tsp) Dijon mustard

30g (1oz) flat-leaf parsley, finely shredded

½ bottle dry white wine

4 shallots, finely chopped

lemon juice

30ml (2tbsp) cooked brown shrimp, shelled and chopped

1 small bunch chives, snipped

1 small bunch dill, lightly chopped

olive oil, for frying

1 Lightly salt the cod fillets and sprinkle over the lemon zest and thyme leaves. Cover and refrigerate for a couple of hours.

2 Preheat the oven to 220°C/425°F/gas mark 7.

3 Bring a large pan of water to the boil and cook the potatoes until tender. Drain and mash with 55g (2oz) of the butter, the cream, mustard, parsley and some salt. Keep warm.

4 In a small heavy-bottomed saucepan, bring the wine to the boil. Add the chopped shallots and boil until the liquid has reduced by three-quarters and is a light syrup. Gradually whisk in the remaining cold, diced butter, season with lemon juice, salt and pepper, then stir in the chopped brown shrimp, chives and dill.

5 Meanwhile, heat a little olive oil in a frying pan over a moderate heat and very quickly crisp the cod fillets, then place in a roasting tin, skin side down, and roast in the oven for 6–7 minutes.

6 Serve the cod on warmed plates with the brown shrimp butter and the parsley mash.

'i am very influenced by simon hopkinson and alastair little. i like their blend of home food and fantastic technique.' mark

bramley apple crumble

Pre-cooking the apples and the crumble may be unorthodox, but it does make a particularly rich dish.

serves 4–6

6 large Bramley apples, peeled and diced

225g (8oz) unsalted butter

light soft brown sugar to taste

1 cinnamon stick

2 star anise

115g (4oz) plain flour

zest of 1/4 unwaxed lemon

zest of 1/4 unwaxed orange

55g (2oz) nibbed almonds

30g (1oz) ground almonds

55g (2oz) muscovado sugar

to serve

1 Bramley apple

140g (5oz) granulated sugar

double cream or custard

1 Preheat the oven to 190°C/375°F/gas mark 5. In a heavy-bottomed pan, sauté the apples in half the butter. Add the light soft brown sugar, cinnamon stick and star anise and cook for 10–15 minutes, until the apples are caramelized and soft.

2 Make the crumble by putting the flour and remaining butter in a food processor and whizzing until the mixture resembles breadcrumbs. Alternatively, sift the flour into a large bowl and lightly rub in the remaining butter with your fingertips. Stir in the lemon and orange zest, nibbed and ground almonds and muscovado sugar.

3 Spead the crumble on a baking tray and cook in the oven for 10 minutes. Move it around with a fork. Put the sautéed apples in an ovenproof dish and cover with the crumble. Cook for 15 minutes in the preheated oven.

4 If you want to serve the crumble with caramelized apple slices, cut 8-12 very thin slices from the centre of the apple. Make a sugar syrup by heating the sugar with 285ml (½ pint) water, until it has dissolved. Boil to a syrupy consistency. Dip each apple slice in the syrup, then set them on a wire rack somewhere warm to dry out a little. Put the slices under a medium grill and caramelize on each side. Serve each portion of crumble with a couple of apple slices and cream or custard.

'i love working on simple dishes like crumble, finding ways to make them taste sensational.' mark

63-69 Canonbury Road,
London N1
020 7704 7410
serves lunch and dinner mon
dinner to sun; bookings advised;
children welcome; terrace

the house

The House's owner, a well-bred, fresh-faced young man called Barnaby Meredith, doesn't look old enough to be drinking here, let alone running the show. In fact, he has been around the block a few times, working mostly as a restaurant manager for Marco Pierre White. The informality and 'no rules' ethos of gastropubs always appealed to him, but he thinks that the original shabby chic look isn't for everyone and that the food is often sub-standard. So he decided to bring glamour and Michelin-standard cooking – though not Michelin-style dishes – into a pub environment.

The talented Jeremy Hollingsworth, who trained under Marco Pierre White and gained a Michelin star at Quo Vadis, is in the kitchen. This man can cook. He turns out a redoubtable jambon persillé with a salad of warm potatoes and grain mustard dressing, revitalizes shepherd's pie by making it with sweet chunks of braised lamb shank, delivers a mean eggs Benedict and a damned fine roast chicken. The food is largely traditional French, with a few American and British classics thrown in, and is neither fussy nor fashionable.

The House has moved the gastropub along, but not so far away from the original idea that it loses its *raison d'être*. Meredith is right when he says that now that gastropubs are no longer a novelty in London, each one will stand or fall by its cooking. This one will stand.

seared beef, red onion and roquefort salad

The vinaigrette makes a larger quantity than you need for this recipe, but keep the rest in the fridge and use to dress other salads. You can make a very English salad by using Stilton instead of Roquefort and watercress instead of rocket.

serves 4

275g (10oz) top-quality strip steak

salt and pepper

150ml (5½fl oz) soured cream

200g (7oz) Roquefort cheese, crumbled

handful of rocket, wild if possible

1 medium red onion, very finely sliced

1 clove garlic, crushed

aged balsamic vinegar

for the croûtons

½ French ficelle loaf, cut in paper-thin slices

olive oil, for frying

1 Sprinkle the beef with salt and roll in freshly ground black pepper. Place on a hot chargrill and cook on each side for 5–6 minutes, until medium rare. Leave to rest for 5 minutes.

2 To make the croûtons, deep-fry the ficelle slices in olive oil until golden. Drain on kitchen paper.

3 For the Roquefort dressing, blend the soured cream with 150g (5½oz) of the Roquefort, until smooth.

4 Place the rocket, croûtons, onion, garlic and the rest of the Roquefort in a bowl. Season and dress the salad with some of the vinaigrette.

5 Divide the salad between 4 plates, then slice the beef thinly and lay it on top. Drizzle with the Roquefort dressing and a little aged balsamic and serve.

vinaigrette

makes about 500ml (18fl oz)

225ml (8fl oz) olive oil

115ml (4fl oz) groundnut oil

155ml (5½fl oz) white wine vinegar

2–3 sprigs tarragon, chopped

¼ bulb garlic, chopped

salt and pepper

1 Mix the oils and vinegar together and add the tarragon, garlic and seasoning to taste.

2 Leave for an hour to infuse, then strain to remove the garlic and tarragon. Store in the refrigerator.

shepherd's pie

Good, creamy mash and chunks of sweet lamb shank take the House shepherd's pie into another league. Comfort food of the highest order.

serves 4

4 lamb shanks

salt and pepper

vegetable oil, for frying

2 large onions

2 large carrots, peeled, topped and tailed

2 celery sticks

4 cloves garlic, chopped

1 bay leaf

2 thyme sprigs

chicken stock, to cover

small bunch of flat-leaf parsley, finely chopped

for the mash topping

3 large red potatoes, peeled

150ml (5¹/₂fl oz) double cream

100g (3³/₄oz) unsalted butter

1 Preheat the oven to 180°C/350°F/gas mark 4.

2 Season the lamb shanks well. Heat a little vegetable oil in a hot frying pan, then brown the lamb all over.

3 Put the shanks in a large casserole with the whole vegetables, garlic, bay leaf and thyme, and cover with chicken stock.

4 Place a round of greaseproof paper on top of the meat and vegetables and put in the oven to braise for 2½–3 hours, until the meat is falling off the bones.

5 Remove the meat and vegetables from the stock and pick out the sprigs of thyme. Bring the stock to the boil and reduce by about two-thirds.

6 Pick the meat off the bones and flake. Cut the vegetables into small pieces and put both meat and vegetables in a bowl with the reduced stock and chopped parsley. Check the seasoning, then transfer to a shallow ovenproof dish.

7 Cook the potatoes until tender, drain and let them rest for 3–4 minutes. In a small saucepan, slowly bring the cream and butter to the boil. Remove from the heat. Mash the potatoes, adding the hot cream and butter mixture, and season. Pipe or spread the mash on top of the meat, then cook in the preheated oven for 25 minutes, until the mash is golden brown. Serve.

'i really felt that in the best restaurants people were paying for the frills and not the cooking. i wanted to offer great cooking but cut down on the frills.' barnaby

roast chicken with vinaigrette, new potatoes, leeks and chillied hazelnuts

Sometimes you wonder how a chef makes a simple dish such as roast chicken taste so good, then you examine how he does it and you find it isn't quite so simple after all. Making the *jus gras* takes a bit of effort, but it's gorgeous. If you're short of time, use a well-flavoured chicken stock and reduce it to a light syrupy consistency.

serves 4

2 x 680g (1½lb) corn-fed poussins

½ bulb garlic, halved

2 sprigs thyme

salt and pepper

vegetable oil, for frying

12 new potatoes

4 finger leeks, trimmed and thoroughly washed

500ml (18fl oz) jus gras

vinaigrette (see page 81)

4 shallots, finely chopped

small bunch of chives, chopped

to serve

20 whole shelled hazelnuts

sweet Thai chilli sauce

medium bunch of chervil

for the *jus gras*

makes about 1.5 litres (2½ pints)

1 boiling fowl, from a good butchers

chicken stock, to cover

¼ bottle Madeira

1 Preheat the oven to 200°C/400°F/gas mark 6. Prepare the poussins by removing the wing tips with a sharp knife. Place the garlic and thyme inside. Season well.

2 Heat some vegetable oil in a hot frying pan. Brown the birds all over before putting them in a roasting tin, and roasting for about 45 minutes. Remove to a plate, cover loosely with foil and leave to rest.

3 Cook the new potatoes and leeks separately in boiling salted water. Remove and allow to cool. Put the *jus gras* in a large saucepan, add a good splash of vinaigrette and the shallots, new potatoes and leeks, and bring up to a simmer. Remove the breasts and legs of the poussin, place in the hot *jus*, season and add the chives.

4 Meanwhile, for the chillied hazelnuts, dry-fry the hazelnuts in a heavy-bottomed pan. Coat with sweet Thai chilli sauce, to taste.

5 To serve, place a leg and breast in each of 4 warmed deep bowls, spoon over the new potatoes, then the leeks and finally the sauce. Sprinkle chillied hazelnuts over the chicken and garnish with chervil.

jus gras

1 Preheat the oven to 180°C/350°F/gas mark 4. Place the fowl in a roasting tin and roast for 2–2 ½ hours, until cooked and dark brown. Put the bird in a large heavy-bottomed pan and cover with the stock. Place the roasting tin over a medium heat, pour in the Madeira and stir, boiling until the liquid has reduced by half. Add to the chicken pot and simmer on a very low heat for 2½ hours. Take off the heat.

2 Remove the bird and place in a colander with a bowl underneath to catch the juices. Cover in clingfilm and place a heavy weight on top. Leave overnight to press out all the juice. Add this juice to the rest of the sauce, bring to the boil and reduce until there is about 1.5 litres (2½ pints) left, then skim to remove any fat.

chargrilled rib of buccleuch beef with a shallot crust and gratin dauphinoise

Jeremy Hollingsworth, the chef at The House, serves this with *jus gras* (see opposite) finished with a few knobs of unsalted butter whisked into it and, rather unorthodoxly, a drop of HP sauce. You could serve the beef with some well-flavoured reduced veal or beef stock instead, or with no sauce at all.

serves 2

5ml (1tsp) Dijon mustard

5ml (1tsp) Pommery mustard

1 Buccleuch rib-eye steak

5 large shallots, finely chopped

200ml (7fl oz) port

200ml (7fl oz) Madeira

salt and pepper

130ml (4½fl oz) jus gras (see opposite)

knob of unsalted butter

dash of HP sauce

to serve

watercress

green beans, steamed

1 Mix the mustards together. Let the beef come to room temperature.

2 Place the shallots in a small saucepan with the port and Madeira, bring to the boil, and boil rapidly until the liquid has gone.

3 Season the beef, then place on a hot cast-iron grill-pan. Cook on each side for 15 minutes, until medium rare.

4 Remove from the griddle and smother one side of the meat with the mustard and then the shallots. Leave to rest for 10 minutes.

5 Heat the *jus gras*, if using, in a small saucepan. Whisk in a knob of unsalted butter and a dash of HP sauce.

6 Thinly slice the rib-eye steak and put on 2 warmed plates with the gratin, some watercress and green beans. Spoon some *jus gras* round the beef.

gratin dauphinoise

butter, for greasing

500ml (18fl oz) double cream

salt and pepper

3 cloves garlic, crushed

5ml (1tsp) grated nutmeg

3 large red potatoes, peeled and finely sliced

1 Preheat the oven to 190°C/375°F/gas mark 5. Butter a small ovenproof dish.

2 Heat the cream in a heavy-bottomed pan with salt and pepper, garlic and grated nutmeg. Bring to the boil, then add the sliced potatoes and stir to thoroughly coat them.

3 Pour into the ovenproof dish and bake in the oven for 40 minutes, until the top is golden and the potatoes are tender.

Chocolate, Peach + Blackcurrent

pear tarte tatin

People get nervous about making tarte tatin and think it's best left to restaurants. In fact, it's pretty simple - you don't even have to make any pastry. Just make sure that the butter and sugar are properly caramelized, but not burnt, and leave the tart for about 5 minutes to cool slightly before turning it out, though don't leave it for longer or it will start to stick.

serves 2

3-4 large, firm William pears, peeled

80g (2¾oz) unsalted butter

100g (3¾oz) caster sugar

1 sheet ready-made puff pastry

to serve

whipped cream or crème fraîche

1 Preheat the oven to 180°C/350°F/gas mark 4. Halve the pears lengthways and remove the cores. Place the butter and sugar in a 18cm (7 inch) pan that can go on the stove-top and in the oven. Lay the pears on top, outer surface down.

2 Put the pan on a medium heat to melt the butter and sugar, then cook until the sugar caramelizes – but do not burn! Remove from the heat and allow to cool.

3 Roll out the pastry to 6mm (¼ inch) thick. Cut out a 20cm (8 inch) circle and cover the pears, tucking the pastry under at the sides. Bake for about 25 minutes.

4 Remove from the oven and allow to cool slightly. Turn out onto a plate and serve with whipped cream or crème fraîche.

the best of the rest

the duke of cambridge

30 St Peter's Street
London N1
020 7359 3066
serves lunch and dinner
mon to sun;
bookings advised;
children welcome;
outside seating

The Duke was the first gastropub to be certified by the Soil Assocation. As well as the food, 80 per cent of the wines – and even the cigarettes – are organic. There's a good choice of beers, including the light, spritzy Eco Warrier, the Freedom Brewery's organic Pilsner and a deep, rich beer called Singboulton, which is specially brewed for the Duke by the Pitfield Brewery and named after the pub's owners.

Game and fish are either wild or from sustainable sources and the pub's broader ethos, such as responsibility to the community and the use of salvaged materials in the building, is written up on a blackboard near the loos (loos which, incidentally, are candle-lit, presumably an aesthetic rather than an ethical decision, and a good one).

Does all this translate into good eating? Well, yes, mostly. Dishes, such as belly pork with baked pear, roast cod with chorizo and scallops with soba noodles and Chinese greens, are mostly fresh, hearty and robust. There's good bread and olive oil – which comes in a brown beer bottle – to chew on while you wait for your order to arrive, and you can eat in the pretty, candle-lit extension if you're not the gregarious type. All in all, the Duke is a cheerful, genuine neighbourhood pub, much loved by the laid-back, black-clad Islingtonians who frequent it.

Owners Esther Boulton and Geetie Singh are also responsible for the Crown (223 Grove Road, London E3), a lovely pub in a Grade II listed building with a bar downstairs and smart dining rooms with balconies upstairs. It's a gracious, relaxing place – great for family outings and big get-togethers – and the kitchen knows what it's doing.

the draper's arms

44 Barnsbury Street
London N1
020 7619 0348
serves lunch and dinner mon
to sun lunch;
bookings advised;
children welcome; garden

A classy place, this. A big, double-fronted Georgian building, off the beaten track in smart residential Islington, it has been revamped with panache and a fair amount of money.

Downstairs there's a large bar, polished wooden floor and leather sofas, all glowing in the light that pours in through the big windows. Upstairs it's sparse but glam, with bare boards, upholstered chairs, brass chandeliers, soothing pale blue walls and a few large canvases.

The food is modern, straightforward brasserie stuff: chorizo, squid and artichoke salad, linguini with crab, goat's cheese tart, seared tuna with peppers and caper berries and, the Ivy classic, frozen berries with warm white chocolate sauce. It's mostly well done, but can be hit and miss. Regulars, though loyal, whinge about its lack of consistency but still love the place.

Since this is trendy Islington you might get to do a bit of celebrity spotting if you come here: purveyors of Britart, comediennes and rock chicks have all been sighted dining at the Draper's Arms.

the highgate

Highgate Studios
53-79 Highgate Road
London NW5
020 7485 8442
serves lunch and dinner
mon to sun; bookings
advised (restaurant only);
children welcome
(lunchtime only);
outside seating

Very hip, the Highgate, but completely unaffected. Decoratively, it feels like an Italian airport lounge circa 1974: big open space, huge windows and a clean-lined wood-veneered bar with a vast array of colourful liquors behind it. As the girders that support the ceiling suggest, it's actually a converted warehouse. The styling is blunt and urban – plain sturdy tables and chairs, a few banquettes and the odd leather sofa. There are a couple of pop art canvases and an old Italian advertising poster on the walls. Piles of help-yourself paper napkins and bottles of malt vinegar and HP sauce indicate that the kitchen has no pretensions, and indeed it does turn out solid, robust grub. Dishes are Mediterranean or heartily English: stickily melting steak and kidney pie, properly fishy fishcakes, well-wrought risottos and pastas. A blackboard by the bar lists 'the big five' – daily lunch specials such as grav lax with cucumber salad or a gargantuan sausage sandwich – at a knock-down price.

The punters are young and savvy – media types, Camden girls, wide-boys – and loads of office workers from the area use it as their unofficial canteen. There's no pressure to eat, even during the busiest times, and staff are so languid it's amazing they bother to take your money. A downstairs restaurant offers more complicated modern European fare in an equally laid back atmosphere.

The team behind the Highgate also own The Gunmakers, (13 Eyre Street Hill, London EC1), a great pub in Clerkenwell that has been simply madeover, and serves the sort of old-fashioned food you *should* be able to find in a British pub: a pint of prawns with bread and butter, sausages and mash, and the sort of puds – jam roly poly, rice pudding – that make central heating redundant.

the salusbury pub and dining room

50-52 Salusbury Road
London NW6
020 7328 3286
serves lunch and dinner
mon eve to sun;
bookings advised; children
welcome (lunchtime only);
outside seating

With old LP covers and blown-up, black-and-white cityscapes on the walls, tables so bashed that some have completely lost their veneer and John Coltrane on the sound system, this place is hip, urban and much loved by local twenty- and thirty-somethings.

You can eat either in the bar with its ox-blood walls and Victorian fireplace, or the dining room, which is full of dark junk-shop tables, already laid. The menu is the same throughout and offers food that is no-frills Italian - poussin with white wine and rosemary, roast cod with basil and chilli, fontina ravioli with butter and sage - and is genuine and delicious. There are some great Italian wines and plenty of punters come in just to drink.

the ladbroke arms

The Ladbroke Arms
54 Ladbroke Road
London W11
020 7727 6648
serves lunch and dinner
mon to sun;
bookings accepted;
children welcome; terrace

Situated in Notting Hill, an area where restaurants seem to come and go and standards are inconsistent, The Ladbroke Arms is a safe bet for a really good meal. The place is elegant but unfussy, with an old-fashioned bar dominated by a magnificent mirror bearing the pub's name. The cooking is deft and the waiting times for certain dishes (indicated on the menu – and you'll think it's worth it for the chocolate fondant) signal that this is a serious kitchen.

The food, which changes daily, is European mainstream – pea and mint risotto, linguini with tomato and basil, duck confit, fishcakes with aioli. They do excellent hearty braises, very good tarts, such as Jerusalem artichoke, pumpkin and taleggio, with perfect, crisp pastry, and the odd more unusual dish such as tuna with a soft boiled egg and bottarga. Sorbets and ice-creams are ace and the clientele is young, cool and solvent.

st john's

91 Junction Road

London N19

020 7272 1587

serves lunch and dinner

mon dinner to sun;

bookings advised;

children welcome; patio

The dining room at St John's is an astonishing, theatrical space: there are big, high, gold-painted ceilings, deep-red velvet banquettes, battered chesterfields, old chandeliers and pea-green walls covered in large pictures. The place feels louche and bohemian; reminiscent of Paris or Berlin in the 1930s. There's a mixed crowd of contented locals – middle-aged professionals, svelte pierced young girls, Nick Hornby-reading guys, elderly couples and acutely trendy types. Everyone fits in.

The menu is on a massive blackboard and sports hearty, homely fare. There might be *borscht*, potted shrimps, pork with roast apples and mustard sauce, and rice pudding with baked plums. The cooking isn't always consistent – they're catering for big numbers here – but when it's good, it's great. Mussel chowder is rich and spicy, the velvety broth stuffed with fish; duck confit with plums is sweet and succulent. Portions are huge and service is swift and intelligent. You can eat the same food in the large bar at the front, another stunning space but very different in character; sparse with a big handsome bar, natural colours on the walls and semi-industrial lighting.

the eagle

159 Farringdon Road

London EC1

020 7837 1353

serves lunch mon to sun,

dinner mon to sat;

no bookings;

children welcome;

outside seating

This is the grand-daddy of them all, the place where the London gastropub revolution started. Opened in 1991 by two friends, Mike Belben and David Eyre, its blend of raw energy, attitude and theatre – the result of a truly open kitchen – changed the face of London dining for ever. Many have tried to imitate its style, a chic-shabbiness, achieved by mixing junk-shop furniture with mismatched china and bits of modern art, but few have done it with such ease and panache.

David Eyre has long since left the stoves, but the food is still gutsy Mediterranean stuff with a bias towards Portugal and Spain. It can be inconsistent but, when it's good, it brings a blast of Iberian colour and warmth to the tastebuds. Think of Portuguese *caldo verde*, salt cod tortilla, Asturian pork and butter bean stew. The menu changes as dishes run out and is chalked up on blackboards, and there's usually a marinated steak sandwich, a Spanish or Italian cheese, and those delectable Portuguese tarts, *pasteis de nata*. The coffee, which you get in your own Bialetti, is ace.

Mike Belben believes that many of the 'gastropubs' opening now are so far removed from the original Eagle idea – too much like restaurants and not enough like pubs – that he doesn't even like the term 'gastropub' to be applied to The Eagle.

the well

180 St John St

London EC1

020 7251 9363

serves lunch and dinner

mon to sun;

bookings accepted;

children welcome;

outside seating

The Well, which has the same owners as Islington's The House (see page 80), is not cosy. There's the usual mix of battered tables and chairs, but the surroundings are modern: full-length windows, semi-industrial lighting and exposed brick. A young crowd, mostly of workers from surrounding offices, use it for supper or a drink on the way home. It's confident, lively and very London.

The food is robust, no-nonsense stuff, and well executed. There might be artichoke and pancetta tart, cottage pie, fish and chips and old-fashioned puddings such as apple crumble and custard. The belly of pork with artichokes, wild mushrooms and leeks (unctuous, earthy and richly autumnal) was one of the best dishes I ate while researching this book.

The bar seems to stock every drink under the sun: there are 6 teas on offer, plus, hoorah, excellent Irish coffee. The staff are smart and efficient. The Well is definitely a cut above the rest.

the fox

28 Paul Street
London EC2
020 7729 5708
serves lunch and dinner
mon to fri;
bookings accepted;
children welcome; terrace

The Fox is always humming. City workers and journalists drink round the big central bar, or perch on chairs which are rapidly losing their stuffing, tucking into plates of rillettes and salt-beef on rye.

Upstairs the dining room is all junk-shop chic – mismatched china, jugs full of flowers, a whole wall of mirrors you could have stolen from your gran's, and candelabras, lit even at lunch time, on every table. It's pretty and, unusually for a pub, very feminine.

The food is from the no-mucking-about school of cookery: exemplary rustic terrines, well-flavoured soups such as rocket and potato, home-style braises such as rabbit with flageolet beans and new season's garlic, and a couple of pasta dishes. It's country cooking from France, Italy and Britain – real food, very well done.

the cow

89 Westbourne Park Road
London W2
020 7221 5400
serves lunch and dinner
mon to sun;
bookings advised
(dining room only);
children welcome
(lunchtime only); outside
seating

Owner Tom Conran has pulled off quite a difficult feat here: he has managed to sell us Irishness, in as stylish a way as his father Terence sold us France, by creating a pub that does indeed feel Irish – noisy, smoky and filled with alcohol-fuelled energy – but isn't the least bit faux or themed. Come for a drink when there's a rugby international showing on the telly above the bar and you'll think you've been transported to Dublin.

This downstairs Irish bar has its own menu: duck confit, moules marinière, shepherd's pie and oysters, which are shucked before your eyes. There's nothing particularly Irish about the dining room upstairs, except the Guinness poster above the fireplace, but the decor is fittingly plain: burgundy-coloured banquettes, bentwood café chairs, tables covered in paper cloths. The food, from chef Jamie Rix, is a mix of classic French, Italian and British dishes, and is seriously good: intense fish soup with a warm and spicy rouille, silky potato and cep ravioli with truffle butter, a hefty, perfectly cooked *côte de boeuf* with sauce bordelaise. Puds are the weakest link. The bill is on the scary side – an evening at the Cow can cost substantially more than the average gastropub – but the quality is high. Eat downstairs if you're watching the purse strings; that's where the fun is.

the pilot

56 Wellesley Road
London W4
020 8994 0828
serves lunch and dinner
mon to sun;
bookings advised;
children welcome; garden

An evening at the Pilot, a handsome pub surrounded by gracious houses in Chiswick, shows you just what a vital part of a neighbourhood a good dining pub can be. Even on a Monday night the place is like 'Cheers' – everybody does seem to know everybody elses' name – but with better food. You won't feel left out, though, if you don't live nearby. The decor is plain but smart: aubergine-coloured tongue and groove and modern black and white photos on cream walls.

The style and standard of the cooking was set by Mark Robinson, who used to work at the sterling Havelock Tavern and is now behind the stoves at its sister pub, The Earl of Spencer. It's robust, big-flavoured stuff, very well executed. You might find thick, spicy split pea soup with yoghurt and coriander, melting steak with horseradish cream, salsify and mash, and butternut squash and spinach risotto with goat's cheese. There's a good wine list, a decent range of beers and a short cocktail menu. An exemplary neighbourhood eatery.

the anglesea arms

35 Wingate Road
London W6
020 8749 1291
serves lunch and dinner
mon to sun;
no bookings;
children welcome;
outside seating

The Anglesea Arms divides people. Its detractors complain of varying standards, long waits between courses and the no-bookings policy. All of this is justified; but I adore the place. Why? Because of the flashes of fire you see in the open kitchen, the sound of chopping, sizzling and banging, the stark, gutsy simplicity of much of the food, and the noise and enthusiasm of the diners. All these give the Anglesea an excitement and a rawness more common in the bars of Madrid and Barcelona than a neighbourhood pub in Britain. There isn't a flamenco dancer or a Portuguese fado singer trailing sultriness and passion round the place, but you half expect it.

The blackboard menu always has a good selection of Iberian dishes and all the food is earthy, peasanty and vibrant. Hake with slow-roast tomatoes and patatas bravas, roast Pyrenean milk-fed lamb, salad of broad beans, chickpeas, tomatoes, cumin and mint, a charcuterie plate with chorizo, serrano ham, a rough-textured terrine and roast vegetables: there are days when you think the kitchen has taken pots of saffron-yellow and paprika-red and painted instead of cooked.

The cooking isn't always consistent but it does have soul. It is rare that a dish will taste the same twice, but why should it? This is food born of passion and spontaneity, honest and genuine.

The Anglesea, and the style of its creator, Dan Evans, has had a big influence on other chefs' cooking in pubs, firing them with an enthusiasm to do similarly 'real' food. Evans is no longer at the helm here, but he's left a terrific legacy. It's worth getting to The Anglesea early and waiting for that table.

the havelock tavern

57 Masbro Road
London W14
020 7603 5374
serves lunch and dinner
mon to sun; no bookings;
children welcome; terrace

Smoky, noisy and, especially in the evenings, bursting at the seams, the Havelock is very much a pub. There's been no expensive make-over. A lick of paint, assorted furniture and big vases of flowers haven't so much transformed as revamped the place. It's in a predominantly residential area of west London and serves locals and the tv people who work in the nearby production companies.

The menu is written up at the last minute – the chef is often still making up his mind at ten to seven – which creates a feeling of excited anticipation and guarantees that the food is fresh and considered. The cooking is no-nonsense and very, very good. A mix of Mediterreanean, old-fashioned French and British dishes all cohere well together. Terrines are first-rate, as is the accompanying bread; soups, such as spinach and lentil with crème fraîche and pancetta, are perfectly judged, and fish – monkfish in Parma ham with asparagus and lemon butter sauce being as fancy as it gets – is deftly cooked.

There's a quietish room at the back of the pub, but the majority of diners and drinkers spread out round the huge central bar. It's a bit of a pain that you can't run a tab or pay by credit card – you pay as you order, by cash or cheque – but this is in keeping with the style and ethos of the place.

The owners of the Havelock also run The Earl Spencer (260 Merton Road, London SW18), an equally unpretentious local with a similar style of food: first-class home-made pasta, Middle Eastern classics and sturdy English puddings. This team know how to run a great local dining pub.

ealing park tavern

222 South Ealing Road
London W5
020 8758 1879
serves lunch and dinner
mon dinner to sun;
bookings advised;
children welcome; garden

This red-brick Victorian corner pub with huge windows has the same owners as the estimable St John's in north London (see page 90), but the food here is several notches higher.

In the bar-room, a cavernous, gorgeously plain space – dark ancient bar, junk-shop furniture, no extraneous adornment – they serve tapas that really are good rather than pale wine-bar imitations.

A full menu operates in the dining room. As at St John's, this a bold, high-ceilinged room, though the decor is restrained: wood-panelled walls, industrial lighting and moody charcoal sketches. The open kitchen turns out satisfying, unpretentious stuff. There's usually a terrine and a savoury tart, plus a few of the usual suspects – calves' liver and bacon, sausages and mash – and fish – perhaps mussels with beer and bacon or hake with boulangère potatoes and pastis cream. It's superior cooking. Desserts, such as rhubarb crème brûlée and rice pudding with Armagnac-soaked prunes, are superb, and service, under the management of an ex-Ivy staffer, is slick but warm.

the salisbury tavern

21 Sherbrooke Road
London SW6
020 7381 4005
serves lunch and dinner
mon to sun;
bookings advised
(restaurant only);
children welcome
(restaurant only)

The Salisbury Tavern is very Fulham – full of ex-public school boys in chinos and Johnny Boden shirts eating steak sandwiches, and well-bred girls with expensive highlights tucking into salads. Nothing on the outside indicates the classiness of the clientele, nor the standard of the food.

The sight of three big TV screens above the bar, all transmitting Sky, may make your heart sink and don't be under any illusions – the place is often noisy, smoky and very busy – but it's far from being an old boozer. The walls are partly wood-panelled and the sofas, in leather or chintz, pristine.

In the bar they serve good versions of pub standards – fish or cottage pie, fish and chips and pork and leek sausages – while the restaurant offers more complex, but not too fussy, dishes, including a cup-winning chicken liver and foie gras parfait with pear and saffron chutney, gnocchi with roast vegetables and rocket pesto and smoked haddock with creamed leeks and mussels. The Salisburys' owners have a similar place, the Admiral Codrington (17 Mossop Street, London SW3), a solid, smart pub in Chelsea with equally good food and a more subdued atmosphere.

the victoria

10 West Temple
Sheen
London SW14
020 8876 4238
www.thevictoria.net
serves lunch and dinner
mon to sun;
bookings advised;
children welcome; garden

The Victoria is a bit off the beaten track but it's worth making a trip here as the food is outstanding. Ask to eat in the bar: it's light and bright, with a white-washed wooden floor and lilac walls.

The cooking, from chef and co-owner Darren Archer, is first-rate French and Mediterranean fare: beautiful velvety soups, such as Jerusalem artichoke with truffle oil, pastas, such as spaghetti with sweet mussels, chorizo and gremolata, and several old-fashioned French classics such as bourride with garlic mayonnaise and a hefty cassoulet. Puds are first-rate too, particularly the tarts, and sorbets are mouth-puckeringly intense. The place opens for breakfast and the sofas are usually taken up by mums and toddlers by mid-morning. They're brilliant with children: toys and drawing materials are provided and there's a smart little playground with wooden play equipment outside.

At the Victoria you get restaurant quality food, served in elegant, laid back surroundings, at bargain prices. Darren's business partner, Mark Chester, was a head honcho in the Conran empire for years, opening and running many of its gastro palaces; the Victoria is his best production yet.

If the identity of a region could be summed up in a colour, then the heart of England would be burnished gold. This isn't just because the manor houses, cottages and churches are built of warm, honey-coloured Cotswold stone; it is also because gold signifies richness, and the Heart of England is the region in which I found the greatest sense of abundance in the food.

Travelling around, you see signs for local cider, chance upon farmers' markets where local apples, pears and squash are piled up in mountains, and drive by fields of red and white Herefords – the cattle prized for their marbled meat. In Herefordshire there are apples, pears, plums and hops; in the Vale of Evesham in Worcestershire, asparagus, gooseberries and strawberries; in Leicestershire you'll find potted meats and pork pies, and around every corner there seems to be superb beef, lamb, pork and cheeses. The sense of plenty is overwhelming.

As well as the riches that are indigenous to the region, there has been an explosion of artisan producers and specialized farmers. Chefs here can even be specific about the breed of animal from which they want their meat.

The area has a greater density of good dining pubs than any other part of Britain. This is partly due to the relative affluence of areas like the Cotswolds, but excellence and local ingredients are part of the culinary culture. Good cooks want to open establishments in places where they can buy good produce, but once quality becomes valued, producers respond, and even increase in number.

This is why there's a strong 'food network'. Information on sourcing is

heart of england

passed between chefs, and some put up notices asking their neighbours for windfalls and surplus garden vegetables. You can sit in a pub, as I did at the old red-brick Three Crowns in Ullingswick in Herefordshire, and enjoy local cheeses accompanied by a single ripe fig from the tree outside the window, and a slice of quince cheese made from fruit picked in a neighbouring garden.

Something special happened when I was eating at the Stagg Inn in Titley in Herefordshire. This was the first pub in the country to win a Michelin star, and is an admirably unpretentious place which serves simple, excellently sourced food, brilliantly cooked. The people at the table next to me decided to have a cheese course. I watched the co-owner, Nicola Holland, wheel a groaning trolley of cheeses towards her customers and talk them through each one. Every cheese had come from within a 40-mile radius. The diners, a happy band dressed in fleeces and jeans, were not interested in food fashion, but they did discuss which beer or cider they should order to accompany the cheese. This, I thought, is a picture of how food and taste could develop in Britain. And I saw it in a pub.

Titley
near Kington
Herefordshire
01544 230221
www.thestagg.co.uk
serves lunch and dinner tues
to sun lunch;
bookings advised;
children welcome; garden

the stagg inn

Trelough duck with elderflower; lamb with fennel and garlic purée; roasted pineapple with vanilla ice-cream: it's difficult to believe, as you read chef Steve Reynolds' menu, that he used to be 'a doner kebab and six pints of lager man'; that, apart from a short stint at the Roux brothers' Le Gavroche restaurant, he is entirely self-taught; and that he's never been to France. Difficult because his pub, the Stagg Inn (the first pub in Britain to get a Michelin star) is the kind of unpretentious country eatery you find in provincial France: it serves delicious but restrained cooking, it's doggedly regional and it's full of locals.

Steve was an architectural photographer when he got fed up with London and moved back to his native Herefordshire. He started to cook in a pub owned by friends and his style developed as he cooked and read Raymond Blanc and Prue Leith. Perhaps it's because he hasn't experienced sustained exposure to restaurants that his cooking is so unshowy. He admits to cooking in 'a kind of bubble'. He never knows what is fashionable; he just sources top-quality produce and doesn't do anything too complicated with it.

Nearly all the food he serves is right on his doorstep, not because he has a romantic notion about 'localness', but because the produce here is very good, and because he and his partner Nicola want to support and feed the community. In this, as in so much else, the Stagg Inn is a beacon.

seared scallops with pea purée, crispy bacon and mint oil

This combination has now become a bit of a classic, but Steve has put his signature on it with the mint oil. You must use the oil on the same day it's made or the mint will discolour.

serves 6

for the pea purée

225g (8oz) English garden peas, shelled weight

4 leaves of mint

salt and pepper

55g (2oz) unsalted butter

for the scallops

6 slices good-quality streaky bacon, rind removed and cut into thirds

18 large king scallops (preferably Cornish), with muscle and roe removed

Maldon sea salt

mild olive oil, for frying

for the mint oil

100ml (3¹/₂fl oz) mild olive oil

3 large sprigs mint, stems removed

1.25ml (¹/₄tsp) caster sugar

for the honey vinaigrette

100ml (3¹/₂fl oz) light olive oil

15ml (1tbsp) white wine vinegar

2.5ml (¹/₂tsp) Dijon mustard

5ml (1tsp) runny honey

to serve

salad leaves such as frisée or lamb's lettuce

1 To make the mint oil, put all the ingredients in a blender and whizz. Chill for 2 hours to let the flavour develop, then strain.

2 Cook the peas with the mint in salted, boiling water until just tender but not soft. Drain and refresh in very cold water.

3 Purée the peas in a blender until very smooth, or push through a sieve.

4 Grill the bacon, put it on kitchen paper and keep warm.

5 Heat 2 large frying pans until very hot but not smoking. Season the scallops on both sides with sea salt. Add 15ml (1tbsp) mild olive oil to each pan and then put in the scallops. They should sizzle. Cook each scallop for 45 seconds on each side, then remove from the pan and keep somewhere warm.

6 Whisk all the honey vinaigrette ingredients together.

7 Divide the pea purée between 6 warmed plates and place 3 pieces of bacon across each portion. Arrange 3 scallops around the purée and drizzle with the mint oil. Put some salad leaves dressed with honey vinaigrette on top.

gressingham duck breast with rhubarb sauce

You can use good, strong chicken stock for this recipe instead of homemade
duck stock – it won't be as rich, but it's better than not cooking the dish at all as it
is heavenly!

serves 4

2 Gressingham ducks

salt and pepper

mild olive oil, for frying

for the rhubarb sauce

285ml (1/2 pint) red wine

*6 sticks forced rhubarb, cut
into 1.5cm (1/2 inch) chunks*

55g (2oz) caster sugar

*1 vanilla pod, cut in half
lengthways and seeds
scraped out*

4 star anise

1 cinnamon stick

*140ml (1/4 pint) reduced duck
stock*

**for the reduced duck
stock**

mild olive oil, for frying

*4 large carrots, roughly cut
into 2.5cm (1 inch) dice*

*2 celery sticks, roughly cut
into 2.5cm (1 inch) dice*

*2 large Spanish onions,
roughly cut into 2.5cm
(1 inch) dice*

3 cloves garlic, chopped

4 litres (8 pints) water

1 Preheat the oven to 180°C/350°F/gas mark 4. With a sharp knife, cut the breasts
and legs from the ducks. Keep the legs for another dish (see page 42).

2 Put the carcasses in a roasting tin and cook in the oven for 1–1½hours, until
brown. Remove the browned carcasses.

3 Put the roasting tin containing the meat juices over a medium heat and stir in
the red wine for the rhubarb sauce. Bring to the boil and reduce until the liquid
is syrupy.

4 To make the duck stock, heat a little olive oil in a heavy-bottomed pan and fry
the carrots and celery until light brown. Add the onions and garlic and cook,
stirring, until golden brown, then add the duck carcasses and cover with water.
Bring to the boil and simmer for 4 hours, skimming off any scum that rises to
the surface.

5 Strain the stock into a clean saucepan. Bring to the boil and reduce until it is
thick enough to coat the back of a spoon.

6 Preheat the oven to 200°C/400°F/gas mark 6. Season the duck breasts. Heat a little
olive oil in a very hot frying pan and quickly sear the breasts until golden on both
sides, then roast in the hot oven for approximately 10 minutes. Rest the meat for
5 minutes.

7 Meanwhile, to make the rhubarb sauce, poach the rhubarb in 565ml (1 pint)
water with the sugar, vanilla seeds, star anise and cinnamon until the rhubarb is
tender but still chunky. Remove the whole spices and gently stir in 140ml (¼ pint)
reduced duck stock and the red wine reduction.

8 Thinly slice the duck breasts and spoon around the rhubarb sauce.

pedro ximénez sherry cheesecake

Nicola, Steve's wife, likes this dessert more than any of his others, mostly because you have to eat it with yet more Pedro Ximénez sherry. If you don't want to splash out on the real McCoy, use another good, sweet dark sherry.

serves 8–10

for the base

170g (6oz) digestive biscuit crumbs

40g (1½oz) skinned, roasted and crushed hazelnuts

40g (1½oz) unsalted butter, softened

grated zest of ½ lemon

for the filling

1.5kg (3½lb) cream cheese

225g (8oz) icing sugar, sieved

3 medium eggs

2 vanilla pods, cut in half and the seeds scraped out

10ml (2tsp) vanilla extract (not vanilla essence)

100ml (3½fl oz) Pedro Ximénez sherry

finely grated zest of 2 lemons

to serve

shelled and skinned whole hazelnuts, toasted and roughly chopped

1   To make the base, combine all the ingredients. Press the mixture into a 22.5 x 6.25cm (9 x 2½ inch) springform tin that has been lined with greased parchment paper. Chill.

2   Preheat the oven to 175°C/335°F/gas mark 3½.

3   To make the filling, put the cream cheese in a blender and blend until smooth. Add all the other ingredients except the lemon zest and blend well. Then add the lemon zest – do not be tempted to add it earlier or the mixture will split.

4   Pour the filling on to the chilled base and bake for 45 minutes. Only the outside 2.5cm (1 inch) of the cake will appear to be cooked; the middle should be wobbly. Cool completely and then chill for 2 hours, or until set.

5   Serve at room temperature. Place a slice on a plate and scatter on the toasted hazelnuts. Serve with large glasses of chilled Pedro Ximénez sherry.

'we made a conscious decision to be part of the local community, a neighbourhood eatery.' steve

baked figs with honey and whiskey ice-cream

It's hard to believe that a Michelin-starred establishment would serve a dessert that's this simple, but good cooking is about knowing when to leave well alone. Steve prefers Irish whiskey for the ice-cream, but you can use Scotch.

serves 6

100ml (3½fl oz) whiskey

140ml (¼ pint) full-fat milk

285ml (½ pint) double cream

6 medium egg yolks

55g (2oz) clear honey

1 Heat a heavy-bottomed saucepan. Add 75ml (2¾fl oz) of the whiskey and flame to burn off the alcohol. Once the flames have died down, stir in the milk and cream. While this is coming to the boil, whisk the egg yolks and honey together in a food mixer until they have doubled in size and become fluffy.

2 Take the milk and cream off the heat and pour half onto the egg yolks. Whisk until combined, then put to one side.

3 Put the remainder of the milk and cream back onto the heat and, when it is boiling, add the egg mixture, turn down the heat and whisk constantly for approximately 1 minute.

4 Pour into a large bowl to lower the mixture's temperature and stir in the last 25ml (¾fl oz) whiskey. Cover and chill.

5 Once thoroughly cool, churn in an ice-cream machine. Alternatively, pour into a freezerproof container, put in the freezer and beat every 20 minutes until set.

6 Place the warm figs in 6 shallow bowls or on 6 plates, pour over some syrup and put a scoop of honey and whiskey ice-cream in the centre.

baked figs

15 fresh figs, halved

425g (15oz) Demerara sugar

750ml (26fl oz) port

1 Preheat the oven to 170°C/325°F/gas mark 3.

2 Halve each fig lengthways through the stalk. Place the figs in a baking dish and sprinkle evenly with the sugar and port. Bake for about 40 minutes, or until the figs are soft with a good thick syrup.

Market Square
Stow-on-the-Wold
Gloucestershire
01451 830364
www.kingsarmsstowonthewold.co.uk
serves lunch and dinner
mon to sun lunch;
bookings accepted
(dining room only);
children welcome

the king's arms

Peter Robinson, the chef-owner here, has a pretty stellar cv. He worked at Bibendum and Stephen Bull in London, then the eminently classy seaside hotel, The Tresanton in Cornwall, before winding up in this refurbished pub in Gloucestershire.

Peter's culinary hero is Alice Waters, the mother of modern Californian cooking. When he feels down, he goes back to the introduction to Waters' first book, *The Chez Panisse Menu Cookbook*, to remind himself that it's the flavour of good ingredients and the basic cooking skills employed to bring that out which are important.

The word 'simple' crops up a lot in *The Gastropub Cookbook*, but Peter's cooking style is simpler than simple; it is so pared down that it could almost be described as elemental. He does practically nothing with ingredients except cook them. You will get eight fat, sweet langoustines with a dollop of basil mayonnaise and half a lemon; cured salmon with a soft boiled egg and a caper salad; warm, pink duck breast with a green olive relish and a handful of dressed rocket.

With dishes like these, there are no tricks to hide behind. It is the kind of cooking that helps you to understand what the word 'taste' really means. And if the food alone isn't enough to entice you, it is served in two rustic but elegant rooms. Peter Robinson is an exceptional chef cooking in a lovely space. This place is worth queueing in the rain for.

squid piri piri

In Portugal they have entire restaurants devoted to piri piri dishes, served with nothing more than salad and bread or sauté potatoes. It's fantastic on chicken (leave the skin on) as well as on fish.

serves 6

3 red peppers

2 dried chillies, crumbled

6 medium red chillies (or more), halved and deseeded

4 cloves garlic, roughly chopped

5ml (1tsp) ground coriander

extra virgin olive oil

6 good sized fresh squid, roughly 2kg (4¹⁄₂lb) in total, cleaned and beaks removed from tentacles (ask your fishmonger to do this)

15ml (1tbsp) red wine vinegar

juice of 1 lemon

to serve

lemon wedges

salad leaves

extra virgin olive oil

lemon juice

1 Heat the grill to high and grill the peppers on all sides until the skin is blackened and blistered. Place in a plastic bag and leave to cool. Peel away the skin, halve, deseed and roughly chop.

2 To make the piri piri marinade, put the peppers, dried and fresh chillies, garlic and coriander into a food processor. Blitz, adding enough olive oil to make a loose paste. Alternatively, finely chop the peppers, mix with the chillies, garlic and coriander and push through a sieve or a mouli before adding oil.

3 Using a sharp knife, cut the squid in half lengthways, and score each half in a criss-cross pattern – but don't cut it all the way through.

4 Spread half the piri piri over the squid and marinate for at least 4 hours. Mix the remaining paste with 15ml (1tbsp) olive oil and the red wine vinegar to make a dressing.

5 Heat a griddle pan until smoking, then cook the squid for 1 minute on each side. Squeeze some lemon over the squid and serve immediately with a little piri piri dressing, lemon wedges and salad leaves lightly dressed with olive oil and lemon juice.

gypsy eggs

You have to get chorizo that needs to be cooked for this recipe, not the cured type. Don't assume that baked eggs – which is basically what this dish is – are boring. This is fantastically rich, spicy and warming. Peter shamelessly stole the idea from The Eagle, the seminal London gastropub, where Spanish and Portuguese dishes dominate the menu.

serves 4

115g (4oz) Serrano ham, finely sliced and roughly chopped

115g (4oz) cooking chorizo, roughly chopped

olive oil, for frying

1 medium onion, finely chopped

2 cloves garlic, finely sliced

5ml (1tsp) smoked paprika

115g (4oz) peas, fresh or frozen

2 x 400g (14oz) tins tomatoes in thick juice

285ml (1/2 pint) chicken stock

8 medium eggs

extra virgin olive oil

black pepper

to serve

good coarse country bread

1 Preheat the oven to 200°C/400°F/gas mark 6.

2 In a frying pan, slowly cook the ham and chorizo in a good slug of olive oil for about 5 minutes. Remove the meat, then sweat the onion and garlic in the oil until soft.

3 Add the smoked paprika, peas, tomatoes, reserved ham and chorizo and the chicken stock and cook for about 10 minutes, until the mixture is sloppy rather than very liquid.

4 Divide between 4 x 10cm (4 inch) ovenproof dishes, crack 2 eggs on each, grind over some black pepper and bake for 5–10 minutes, depending on how you like your eggs.

5 Serve with thick slices of good country bread.

lemon, oregano and black pepper chicken with warm bean and olive salad

This dish is pure summertime. Use chicken breasts that haven't been boned if you prefer, but you'll need to increase the cooking time.

serves 4

4 x 200g (7oz) chicken suprêmes or breasts, skin on

handful of oregano, roughly chopped

1 dried chilli, flaked, seeds removed

juice and finely grated rind of 1 unwaxed lemon

15g (1tbsp) black peppercorns, cracked

extra virgin olive oil

for the salad

2 handfuls French beans

450g (1lb) new potatoes, preferably organic or, when in season, Jersey Royals

2 shallots, cut into thin rings

handful of flat-leaf parsley, roughly chopped

100g (3¹/₂oz) Kalamata olives, pitted

5ml (1tsp) rosemary or thyme vinegar

extra virgin olive oil

salt and pepper

to serve

lemon wedges

1 With a sharp knife, make 3 cuts all the way through the chicken from the wing bone to the fillet end.

2 In a bowl, mix the oregano, chilli, lemon juice, lemon zest and black pepper with a good slug of olive oil. Rub into the chicken pieces, cover and leave to marinate for 2 hours.

3 Tail the beans and boil for 3 minutes, until tender. Drain.

4 Boil the potatoes until tender. Drain and, while still warm, cut them in half and mix with the beans, shallots, parsley, olives, vinegar and a slug of olive oil. Season.

5 Cook the chicken on a hot griddle pan, or under the grill, for 6–7 minutes on each side. Squeeze some more lemon juice over the chicken and serve it on top of the salad, with extra wedges of lemon.

'better to cook simple food well than complicated food badly. there's nothing worse than finding a yawning gap between the description on the menu and what ends up on your plate.' peter

torta della nonna

An easy, homely, but elegant tart. Serve in thin slices with Italian dessert wine or cups of strong espresso.

serves 8

for the pastry case

250g (9oz) plain flour, sifted

115g (4oz) unsalted butter, softened

2 medium eggs

140g (5oz) icing sugar, sifted

5ml (1tsp) vanilla extract

for the filling

340g (12oz) fresh ricotta cheese

140g (5oz) pine nuts, toasted

170g (6oz) caster sugar

juice and finely grated rind of 2 unwaxed lemons

10 medium eggs, beaten

1 First make the pastry case. Butter a 25cm (10 inch) loose-bottomed tart tin. Preheat the oven to 190°C/375°F/gas mark 5. Place a baking sheet on the middle shelf.

2 Tip the flour onto a board. Make a well in the centre and add the butter, then the eggs, sugar and vanilla.

3 Gently mix the butter, eggs, sugar and vanilla together to form a paste with the fingertips of one hand. Then quickly mix in the flour, lightly kneading until it's a smooth dough – but don't overknead. Wrap in clingfilm and chill for an hour.

4 On a lightly floured board, roll out the dough into a 33–35cm (13–14 inch) circle, 3mm (⅛ inch) thick. Carefully line the tart tin, leaving a 4cm (1½ inch) overhang.

5 Line the pastry case with greaseproof paper and fill with dried beans or rice to weigh the pastry down. Put the tin straight onto the preheated baking sheet and bake for 8 minutes. Remove the paper with the beans and bake the pastry case for a further 5 minutes, so the pastry no longer looks glassy. Remove from the oven and, using a sharp knife, trim the excess pastry level with the top of the ring.

6 Turn the oven down to 180°C/350°F/gas mark 4.

7 Mix all the filling ingredients together well and pour into the partially baked pastry case. Bake for 20–25 minutes, until firm to the touch.

Bleak Acre
Ullingswick
Herefordshire
01432 820279
www.threecrownsinn.com
serves lunch and dinner
tues to sun;
bookings advised; children
welcome; garden

three crowns inn

'I've got my own little Provence here,' says Brent Castle, chef-owner of the red-brick, lopsided Three Crowns, as he stands in front of his pub surveying the Herefordshire countryside. 85 per cent of the fruit and veg Brent uses come from an organic market gardener who lives just up the road, or from the pub garden. Brent also has an ever-growing network of home gardeners who supply him with gooseberries, rhubarb, quinces and even the walnuts that he pickles and serves with his goat's cheese and onion tart. Few eating places source so carefully or so locally, and this seems to affect the atmosphere as well as the food.

A feeling of ease and plenty suffuses the Three Crowns. It's a proper pub. There's a small bar with grapes carved into it, traditional wooden wall lights with little cream shades, curtains that look like they're made from old pyjamas and plenty of drinkers.

Diners tuck into country dishes – rustic in origin, refined in execution – such as confit shoulder of Marches lamb, cassoulet and steamed treacle pudding, smiling at one another as if they're all in on a well-kept secret. Chris, the barman, will seduce you with local ciders, or slip the list of 'special wines' onto your table if he thinks you'd be interested. I wish there was a pub like this hiding behind every hedgerow in Britain.

twice-baked swede and farmhouse cheddar soufflé

If you would rather not bake the soufflés twice, just serve them as soon as they come out of the oven the first time, but reheating them at the last minute makes this a very easy starter.

serves 6

butter and finely grated Parmesan cheese, for preparing the ramekins

225ml (8fl oz) full-fat milk

1 shallot, halved

55g (2oz) swede, finely grated

1 bay leaf

salt and pepper

freshly grated nutmeg

40g (1½oz) unsalted butter

40g (1½oz) plain flour

100g (3¾oz) mature farmhouse Cheddar cheese

4 medium eggs, separated

to serve

285ml (½ pint) double cream

115g (4oz) Parmesan cheese, finely grated

finely chopped parsley

1 Prepare 6 ramekins by brushing them with melted butter. Make sure that all surfaces, including the rims, are totally covered. Dust the insides of the moulds with grated Parmesan cheese, again coating all the surfaces, including the rim. Put the ramekins in the refrigerator to chill.

2 In a small saucepan, bring the milk to simmering point with the shallot, swede, bay leaf, salt, pepper and nutmeg. Take off the heat and leave to infuse for 3 minutes. Remove the shallot and the bay leaf.

3 Preheat the oven to 150°C/300°F/gas mark 2. Make a roux by melting the butter in a saucepan, stirring in the flour and cooking this for 2 minutes over a medium heat.

4 Take the roux off the heat and gradually add the milk mixture in stages, incorporating the liquid before adding more. Put the sauce back on the heat and bring to the boil, stirring. Turn the heat down and cook gently for 4–5 minutes, stirring often.

5 Add the grated Cheddar and take the pan off the heat. Lightly whisk the egg yolks and mix well into the sauce. Season to taste with salt, pepper and nutmeg.

6 Whisk the egg whites to soft peaks and stir 2 tbsp into the sauce to loosen it. Fold a third of the whites into the sauce. When this is incorporated, fold in the rest.

7 Fill each ramekin to the top and place in a bain-marie (a roasting tin is fine). Pour boiling water into the tin to a depth of 6mm (¼ inch) and bake for 30–45 minutes, or until the soufflés have risen and the tops are pale and firm to the touch. Cool the soufflés in the bain-marie. When cool, remove them from the ramekins and put them in the refrigerator. They'll keep well overnight.

8 To serve, preheat the oven to 200°C/400°F/gas mark 6. Bake the soufflés a second time, top side down, on a silicon paper-lined baking tray, for about 15 minutes, until golden brown and crusty.

9 While the soufflés are baking, bring the cream to the boil in a saucepan and reduce by about a third. Place the soufflés, top side up, onto warmed plates. Pour the cream around them, sprinkle with Parmesan and parsley and serve immediately.

grilled mackerel with marinated cucumber and mustard crème fraîche

This is a lovely, simple summery starter. Adjust the amount of mustard that you put into the crème fraîche to suit your taste, or leave it out of the dish altogether if you prefer.

serves 4

4 plump mackerel fillets

salt and pepper

lemon juice

olive oil

for the marinated cucumber

115ml (4fl oz) white wine vinegar

1 bay leaf

1 small red chilli, deseeded and finely chopped

55g (2oz) caster sugar

1 medium cucumber

55ml (2fl oz) olive oil

2 shallots, finely sliced

15ml (1tbsp) chopped chives

for the mustard crème fraîche

15ml (1tbsp) chopped dill

15ml (1tbsp) Dijon mustard or grain mustard, or more to taste

170g (6oz) crème fraîche

1 For the marinated cucumber, mix the vinegar, bay leaf, chilli and sugar together in a small saucepan. Bring to the boil. Strain and allow to cool.

2 Peel the cucumber, split in half lengthways, and deseed. Sprinkle with salt and allow to stand in a sieve or colander for 15–30 minutes.

3 Wash off the salt, dry the cucumber and cut into segments approximately 6mm (¼ inch) thick.

4 Combine the vinegar mixture with the olive oil, shallots, cucumber and chives. Mix carefully so as not to break up the cucumber slices. This can be made up to 3 days ahead and kept in the refrigerator.

5 For the mustard crème fraîche, stir the dill and mustard into the crème fraîche, then season with a little salt.

6 Season the mackerel with salt, pepper and lemon juice. Brush with a little olive oil, then grill them, skin side up, for 2–3 minutes, until the skin is bubbled and crisp.

7 Serve with the marinated cucumber and the mustard crème fraîche.

'working with rick stein had a big influence on me. he knows when to leave a dish alone.' brent

grilled pork chop with braised pork belly and cassoulet of chorizo sausage

This recipe does take a bit of effort, but it's well worth it. To cut down on the hassle, you can prepare it in easy chunks over a few days.

serves 6

700g (1lb 9oz) pork belly, skin scored with a sharp knife

7g (¼oz) coarse sea salt

250g (9oz) dried haricot beans

1 bouquet garni (thyme, rosemary and sage)

1 large onion, sliced

1 medium carrot, halved

1 small chorizo sausage, or 170g (6oz) piece

olive oil, for frying

1 medium onion, diced

2 celery sticks, finely sliced

1 bulb garlic, cloves separated and peeled

100g (3¾oz) tomato passata

a good pinch of paprika

salt and pepper

6 pork chops, approximately 170g (6oz) each

1 The day before you plan to eat the dish, rub salt onto the skin side of the pork belly, wrap it well in clingfilm and refrigerate. Soak the haricot beans in cold water overnight.

2 The next day, preheat the oven to 150°C/300°F/gas mark 2. Wash the salt off the pork and place in a deep roasting tray with the bouquet garni, sliced onion and halved carrot. Cover with water, place on the cooker and heat to simmering point.

3 Cover with foil and put in the oven. Braise for about 1½–2 hours, or until the pork is soft and tender. Remove the pork carefully, put it into a roasting tin or on a large plate, cool and refrigerate as soon as possible. Reserve the cooking liquor in a large, covered container and refrigerate that as well.

4 Drain the soaked beans and place in a saucepan with plenty of fresh, cold water. Boil vigorously for about 15 minutes, then drain.

5 Cut the chorizo into fairly chunky pieces. In a heavy-bottomed pan, heat a little olive oil and quickly fry the chorizo. Add the diced onion, celery, garlic, the part-cooked beans, tomato passata and paprika.

6 Remove the fat that has risen to the top of the reserved braising liquor (and solidified). Add 15–30ml (1–2tbsp) of the fat to the bean and chorizo mixture at this point – it helps to make them soft and unctuous.

7 Next add enough of the braising liquor to cover the beans and chorizo. Cover the pan and cook very gently either on the hob or in a slow oven (150°C/300°F/gas mark 2), stirring from time to time and adding more liquor or water as necessary. It will take about 1½ hours for the beans to soften. Once they are quite soft, season. (Adding salt to beans before they have softened makes them hard.)

8 Turn the oven up to 200°C/400°F/gas mark 6. Cut the pork belly into 5cm (2 inch) squares and place on a baking sheet in the oven for 20 minutes to finish and crisp the skin. Cook the pork chops in a hot frying pan, with a little olive oil, until well browned on each side and just cooked.

9 To serve, spoon a ladleful of cassoulet beans into 6 large warmed bowls and put some pork belly and a chop on top of each one.

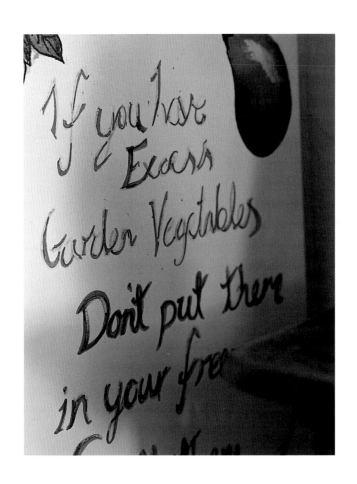

geranium-scented panna cotta with red gooseberries

Brent uses red Lancashire Lad gooseberries for this, grown for him by a friend who lives near the pub. You can use ordinary green gooseberries, or just serve the panna cotta with uncooked summer berries.

serves 6

155ml (5¹/₂fl oz) milk

600ml (22fl oz) double cream

6 rose-scented geranium leaves or about 15ml (1tbsp) rosewater

3 gelatine leaves

150g (5¹/₂oz) caster sugar

1 In a large saucepan, heat the milk and cream with the geranium leaves until the liquid just begins to simmer. Take the pan off the heat and let the leaves infuse for about 30 minutes. (If you are using rosewater, see below.) Remove the leaves.

2 Put the pan back on the heat and carefully simmer to reduce the liquid by a third – this normally takes about 5 minutes. Meanwhile, soak the gelatine leaves in a little cold water until they go soft and floppy.

3 Once the cream has reduced, add the sugar and stir to dissolve thoroughly, and then add the rosewater, if using. Gently squeeze the water out of the gelatine and add it to the cream. Carry on stirring until the gelatine has dissolved. Strain and leave to cool.

4 When the panna cotta mixture is quite cool, pour it into 6 moulds or small teacups and put them in the refrigerator to set for at least 3 hours.

5 To unmould the panna cottas, dip the moulds or teacups in a little lukewarm water, upend each one onto a plate and give it a good shake – it should slide out easily. (A little splash of water on the plate beforehand helps to reposition the panna cotta, should it plop out in the wrong place). Spoon some of the gooseberries and their syrup around each panna cotta and serve.

red gooseberries

340g (12oz) red gooseberries

285g (10oz) caster sugar

1 Preheat the oven to 170°C/325°F/gas mark 3.

2 Mix the gooseberries with the sugar and a drizzle of water in an ovenproof dish. Cover with foil and bake in the moderately slow oven for 20 minutes, or until the gooseberries are soft and the juices are syrupy. Leave to cool.

the best
of the
rest

lough pool inn

Sellack

Herefordshire

01989 730236

serves lunch and dinner

mon to sun;

bookings advised

(dining room only);

children welcome; garden

Stephen Bull, the owner and co-chef at the Lough Pool Inn, has had several lives. He worked first as an advertising executive and then as the chef-proprietor of several top-notch London restaurants, before moving to Herefordshire to run this country pub.

Perhaps because he has got the restaurant business out of his system, Bull has had the confidence to leave the place as he found it. A black-and-white, half-timbered building with a crooked roof, the Lough Pool is a proper pub. There are red, fringed lampshades on the wall lights and a Sooty charity box on the bar. A printed menu in a folder with Bull's signature scrawled over it is the only concession to restauranty-ness. Alongside the bar is a bright yellow, cottagey dining room, but the same food is offered in both.

And the fancy monogrammed menu? It's a pleasure to read: no obeisance to fashion, no flashiness, no fireworks. You might find hare terrine with prunes, fish soup, paupiettes of pork with anchovy cream, damson Bakewell tart. Bull just cooks what he wants to cook – what he is interested in – and he does it damned well. The food has integrity and the prices make it a real bargain.

The whole place is low-key, even when busy; service is efficient and – as befits a pub – not over-fussy.

the olive branch

Main Street

Clipsham

Rutland

01780 410355

www.theolivebranchpub.com

serves lunch and dinner

mon to sun lunch;

bookings accepted;

children welcome; garden

Even from the outside, The Olive Branch fills you with a warm glow of anticipation. It's a spick-and-span old stone farmhouse with a gravelled arbour, huge aged terracotta planters and an antique wooden wheelbarrow by the door. Odd collections of garden implements, walls covered in lids from wooden wine crates, and eclectic furniture – choir pews, old rockers, Heidi-style carved chairs – give it a real quirkiness.

The clientele runs from babes in arms to crotchety old ladies, but the place overall exudes a youthful feel, probably because it is owned and run by three 30-somethings. They all met when they were working at the nearby country-house hotel, Hambleton Hall, so there was a danger that they'd try to replicate the country-house style of cooking in their pub, but they haven't. The menu is a roll-call of modern classics – tomato tart, cassoulet, chargrilled rib-eye with béarnaise sauce, fish pie – with the odd wild card thrown in, such as tandoori-style monkfish with raita. It's well done, though perhaps not as polished as it might be.

The great thing about this place is that all the distinctive touches – the little blackboard on each reserved table with the customer's name, the cigar menu, the wedge of steaming bread that comes to your table with a decent knife and a pot of black olive butter – come together to produce a pub that is truly individual. You'll leave feeling happy, well-fed and cosseted.

new inn

Coln St. Aldwyns

Gloucestershire

01285 750651

www.new-inn.co.uk

serves lunch and dinner

mon to sun;

bookings accepted

(dining room only);

children welcome; terrace

This is a little bit of heaven in the Cotswolds. An old, creeper-covered 16th-century hostelry in a small village among some of the gentlest (and emptiest) Gloucestershire countryside, the New Inn is pretty, superbly run and serves great food.

The Courtyard Bar is cosy but elegant, with bits of copper, scrubbed tables, dried hops, richly coloured fabrics and mellow-yellow walls. The food is up-to-the-minute without being over-wrought. Chef Sarah Payton seems to get the tone just right, mixing contemporary dishes such as tomato, courgette and sweet onion tart with modern pub classics such as calves' liver with mustard mash and smoked bacon or fishcakes with aïoli. And boy, can she cook! Sure technique, precision, generosity: when you apply this level of skill to dishes this simple, you get dream pub food.

There's a separate, small, dining room with a tartan carpet, country pine furniture and cream napery. In style, it's very like an English version of a French *auberge,* and there's a set-price menu here if you want something slightly more formal.

The New Inn is a quiet, civilised place, full of smart middle-aged couples treating themselves, posh ladies-who-lunch with equally posh daughters, and a smattering of keen walkers. The staff wear bottle-green waistcoats, but it makes them look smart rather than corporate, and they're a lovely, warm, helpful bunch. Prices are keen. This is quite simply one of the best pubs in Gloucestershire. Go.

the hundred house hotel

Bridgnorth Road

Norton

Shropshire

01952 730353

www.hundredhouse.co.uk

serves lunch and dinner

mon to sun;

no bookings for bar;

children welcome; garden

The Hundred House, a red-brick roadside inn, is a one-off. Enter through the old swing doors, complete with stained-glass panels and the words 'Temperance Hall', and you don't know where to focus. There's a network of small pubby areas with colour everywhere: patchwork leather cushions, paintings and old advertising posters. The importance of the garden, established and tended by one of the owners, Sylvia Phillips, can be felt everywhere. Its produce is used to decorate the pub, there's a pot of herbs on every table and packets of seeds are on sale.

The Hundred House, owned by the Phillips family, is very much a family affair. Mother, father and one son run the place, while the other son, Stuart, is the chef. He cooks both brasserie and more sophisticated restaurant-style food and the menu roams all over the place. You might find a great, gutsy Italian soup of beans, tomato and sausage, beautifully cooked local lamb chump with rosemary *jus*, or scallops with rice cakes and a carrot, ginger and tamarind sauce. Portions are on the hefty side and side dishes of vegetables pile up around you, but the food is tasty and consistent and the ingredients well-sourced. The simpler the dish, though, the better the cooking. Both the lasagne and the sausages with mash and onion gravy are top-notch.

There's a huge garden with an orchard, herbs, topiary, and weird and wacky artefacts (there's even a teddy bear's picnic area), which you can explore, maps supplied. The Hundred House is original, eccentric and has real warmth. It's had a great reputation for years, but if you don't know about it and happen to be in Shropshire, it's worth a special trip.

the falcon inn

Fotheringhay
Northamptonshire
01832 226254
www.huntsbridge.com
serves lunch and dinner
mon to sun;
bookings accepted;
children welcome; garden

This place is a breath of fresh air. Chef and co-owner Ray Smikle likes big sunny flavours and he does a good bit of culinary globe-trotting in pursuit of bold, unusual dishes. You'll find Jamaican jerk chicken with sweet potato and avocado and tuna carpaccio with lime and wasabi cream alongside excellent versions of pub classics such as beer-battered fish with tartare sauce.

The Falcon is part of the Huntsbridge Group (chaired by Master of Wine John Hoskins), which owns the Pheasant in Keyston and the Three Horseshoes in Madingley (see East Anglia), and it is run with the same high degree of professionalism while remaining distinctive. Like the other pubs in the group, it has one menu and different eating areas with varying degrees of informality, so there's a bar, dining room and conservatory, all full of flowers, soft colours and polished tables.

Smikle's food explodes into all this good taste, which is perhaps why it attracts quite a young crowd, as well as smart middle-aged diners. The drinks include Adnams, a couple of guest ales and an inspiring wine list put together by Hoskins.

the bull's head

Craswall
Herefordshire
01981 510616
serves lunch and dinner
mon to sun;
bookings accepted
(dining room only);
children welcome; garden

If you're looking for elegance and grace, don't go to The Bull's Head. The ancient wallpaper is peeling, the huge fireplace is surrounded by old kettles, the books and bottles are overlaid with several years worth of dust, and the bar is a hole in the wall with makeshift shelves. A Belfast sink is home to a motley collection of plants. It's almost as if some old geezer just decided to open a pub in his living room. But The Bull's Head has real charm and offers good country cooking.

The menu is mostly British: lamb from the farm up the road, braised in cider and mint, or Craswall pie, a hearty offering of beef, gammon and beer in shortcrust pastry. There are also usually a couple of more Mediterranean dishes on offer, such as seared tuna with red chard, olives and tomatoes. Chips are home-made and there's malt vinegar on every table.

The two dining areas are swish compared to the bar, with stone walls, ironwork sconces and wobbly lamps. The Bull's Head is tucked away on the Welsh border – in fact, you despair of ever finding it – but if you like down-to-earth pubbiness and no-nonsense food, it's worth seeking out.

the howard arms

Lower Green
Ilmington
Warwickshire
01608 682226
www.howardarms.com
serves lunch and dinner
mon to sun;
bookings accepted;
children welcome; garden

Turn up here at twilight, when the lamps inside have just been turned on, and you'll be instantly seduced. Spare, uncluttered and elegant, The Howard Arms is a glowing Cotswold stone pub dating from the 17th-century, sitting in the shade of a chestnut tree overlooking the village green.

Inside, the place has been opened up. The more pubby area, with its low ceilings, polished flagstones and fires, leads onto a graceful dining room. You can eat anywhere; the menu is the same throughout. Tall arched windows with checked cloth shutters, oil paintings, antique furniture and ceramic lamps make the dining room feel grand, but the tables aren't laid and you order from a blackboard menu. The robust dishes, such as beef, ale and mustard pie and Cumberland sausages with white beans and tomatoes, are better than the more refined ones. Puds, such as orange panna cotta with poached plums, or sticky pear and ginger pudding, are the business.

It's very much a local, with plenty of regular drinkers at the bar, but outsiders get a warm welcome too. The clientele is pretty county – loafers and wellies abound.

the red lion inn

Red Lion Street

Stathern

Leicestershire

01949 860868

www.theredlioninn.co.uk

serves lunch and dinner

mon to sun lunch;

no bookings; children

welcome; garden

Very mellow, this one. In fact, it's so comfy that most of the punters look like they're in their own living rooms. Teenagers lounge on battered chesterfields, children clamber over the settles, lovers eat with hands entwined and old-timers sit at the bar. People seem to settle in for hours at a time. The walls are a warm sandy colour and sport collections of old kitchen paraphernalia, and you can hear the low hum of jazz on the sound system. It has the same kind of easy-going, cared-for feel as the Olive Branch at Clipsham, and is owned by the same group of friends.

The food is pretty similar to that at the Olive Branch: modern brasserie fare that nods to all corners of the globe – duck confit, Thai-style mussels, chicken kebab with Bombay potatoes – alongside a few British pub stalwarts, such as a very pukka pork pie from nearby Melton Mowbray, served with home-pickled shallots and piccalilli. The food has a generous, homely quality. There's good walking country round about, and they even provide a wooden chest for storing muddy boots.

the fox

Lower Oddington

Gloucestershire

01451 870555

www.foxinn.net

serves lunch and dinner

mon to sun;

bookings accepted;

children welcome; garden

The Fox is comfy, relaxed, elegant and full of personal touches. The daily papers and a copy of *Hello* are on the table by the door and there are piles of old Penguin paperbacks and country flowers everywhere. Pitch up on a cold evening, when the candles flicker in the windows and the fire in the inglenook fireplace is lit and you'll think you're in heaven.

The food is country cooking, largely French and English – lovely tarts, good terrines, braises, steak and kidney pie and fishcakes – and suits the place perfectly. The dishes feel as though they've been made by a good home cook rather than a team of chefs. Puddings, such as plum crumble or steamed pear and ginger pudding with thick cream, are scrumptious.

The clientele is mostly 45-plus, and there are plenty of cravats and tweed jackets in evidence. Service is delightful. It wouldn't be worth coming here for the food alone, but the whole package is quintessentially English and utterly charming.

the sun inn

Marton

Shropshire

01938 561211

serves lunch and dinner

tues eve to sun lunch;

bookings accepted;

children welcome; garden

The young chef at The Sun Inn, Steve McCallum, retained a Michelin star for the Airds Hotel in Port Appin, where he cooked before he bought this ivy-covered stone inn near the Welsh border with his parents and brother.

McCallum is not aiming for a Michelin star here, but he turns out sophisticated dishes nonetheless. Starters and fish dishes are terrific. There's a lusciously rich risotto of smoked salmon with poached egg and chive cream, and precisely-cooked turbot with herbed mashed potatoes, braised fennel and mustard sauce. Puds, such as whinberry crème brûlée with elderflower sorbet, are also strong, but meat dishes can be disappointing in comparison with the rest of the food.

The Sun Inn is very much a pub. There's a darts board, a pool table, standard issue pub furniture and hops hanging over the bar: definitely no gastropub makeover here. Perhaps it isn't worth driving hundreds of miles for, but it's a good find if you live in Shropshire or are visiting the area. And that risotto is definitely worth going out of your way for.

the churchill arms

Paxford

Gloucestershire

01386 594000

www.thechurchillarms.com

serves lunch and dinner

mon to sun;

no bookings;

children welcome; garden

Paxford is a small Cotswold village of honey-coloured stone, with just a handful of houses, an old church and the Churchill Arms. Bentwood café chairs, duck-egg blue and cream paintwork, and the open-plan layout make it unusually bright for an old country pub, and the place is unaffected.

The menu is chalked up on a collection of blackboards around a pillar in the middle of the room, ensuring an almost constant traffic jam. It offers a good mixture of robust and light, traditional and contemporary dishes. There's good solid lamb shank with dauphinoise potatoes, bacon chop with bubble and squeak, and halibut with aubergines and spring onions served with a pineapple relish. Chefs Sonya Brooke-Little and Ivan Reid pull off the more daring flavour combinations and the cooking is very sure and ungimmicky. Arkells 3B and Hook Norton are on draught and there's a good, interesting wine list, with nine wines offered by the glass.

The Churchill has long been a popular dining destination and gets crowded with locals, plus plenty of others who feel it's worth a drive, so get there early.

the king's head

Aston Cantlow

Warwickshire

01789 488242

serves lunch and dinner

mon to sun;

bookings accepted;

children welcome; garden

This really is a modern local. The customers range from 18 to 80, and include spivs out on dates, suited business people, builders and glam Brummie ladies, and there are as many drinkers as diners. The bar and waiting staff – Aussies, Kiwis and South Africans – could give classes in how to do this job properly. They seem to know everyone and imbue the place with breezy good humour.

The 16th-century building is timber-framed and creeper-clad and, supposedly, where Shakespeare's parents got hitched. Inside it feels pubby but smart, with the usual oak beams, flagstone floors and plenty of different areas to sit in, but vibrant colours, big cushions and modern cartoons on the walls give it a touch of modernity without sacrificing its oldness.

A few traditional pubby dishes, such as calves' liver with mash, make an appearance, but the food is mostly modern and spans the globe: pasta with pumpkin and Gorgonzola, squid with chilli aioli, salmon and coriander fishcakes. The cooking is good, if inconsistent: bad seasoning, flaccid batter and a slightly over-cooked pasta have all marred otherwise fine meals.

the trouble house

Cirencester Road

Tetbury

Gloucestershire

01666 502206

www.troublehouse.co.uk

serves lunch and dinner

tues to sun lunch;

bookings accepted;

children welcome

(dining rooms only); garden

The Trouble House is a big, white-washed stone pub sitting right on the busy A433 near Cirencester, and the traffic does thunder past, though when the place is busy you barely notice.

Chef and owner Michael Bedford turns out robust stuff: ox cheeks braised in red wine with mushrooms, roast pigeon with black pudding and walnut salad, smoked haddock risotto. Bold and confident, with great depth of flavour, it's predominantly French, though the odd ingredient like chorizo or couscous does turn up, subsumed into the French style. You'd be pleased if you were served food this good in a Paris bistro (most French bistros aren't actually up to this standard). To find it in a roadside pub in England is amazing. Bedford knows how to cook.

The place has been given the usual gastropub makeover – sisal carpet, scrubbed pine tables and colourful prints of the French countryside – and it slightly lacks character and the confident feel of somewhere established. It needs to grow into itself a bit more, but when it develops that 'been-here-for-years' cosiness, it will be an absolute corker.

the village inn

Barnsley

Gloucestershire

01285 740421

www.thevillagepub.co.uk

serves lunch and dinner

mon to sun;

bookings advised;

children welcome

(in dining areas only);

terrace

Barnsley, just four miles outside Cirencester, is a small but perfectly formed village. Even the sign outside The Village Inn is the embodiment of taste and restraint – a burgundy-painted square with plain gold lettering – and sets the tone for the pub itself.

The style is uncluttered country, with bare brick and honey-coloured walls, pale-wood floors and rugs. And the furnishings are more antique than junk shop. There is no separate dining room here; you can eat or drink in any of the rambling areas. Parts of the pub, like the bar itself, are plain but pretty; other areas show more boldness and a sense of humour. One area has stunning striped wallpaper and an *art naif* mural of farmyard animals.

Tweedie middle-aged types and young Porsche drivers happily rub shoulders together. The Village Inn is a very up-market venue, but don't make the mistake of thinking it's grand. The staff are young and warm and the atmosphere is laidback.

The food, from chef Graham Grafton, who has cooked at The Ivy, Le Caprice and Bibendum in London, is classy without being fussy, and the menu is a comfortable blend of modern European, classical French and old-fashioned British dishes: white onion risotto, veal blanquette and Bramley apple crumble all make appearances. There's a marked absence of swirls and drizzles; this is genuine food cooked very well. Desserts, such as elderflower and wine jelly with poached peach, or apricot and almond tart, are luscious and show impeccable taste and technique.

Barnsley's a good place for a stroll and, if you're horticulturally inclined, you can visit the garden of Rosemary Verey, just across the road from the pub, though you need to make an appointment in advance.

the crabmill

Preston Bagot

Claverdon

Warwickshire

01926 843342

www.thecrabmill.co.uk

serves lunch and dinner

mon to sun lunch;

bookings accepted;

children welcome; garden

Urban gastro-chic meets smart country pub at the Crabmill. The outside is spare – cream-painted and anonymous, if rather handsome – but nothing about it quite prepares you for the inside.

Open the door and you can smell the money. The bar is a huge, bright space with exposed oak joists, gorgeously chunky flagstones and a touch of the baroque in the imposing white-and-brushed-gold mirror and the ironwork chandelier. There's a meandering network of smaller dining areas in rich colours, each one individual (a bit of Scandinavia here, a bit of the Raj there) and the hand of the designer is felt everywhere. There are selected pieces of rural pub style – church pews and a huge fireplace – but they have been mixed with contemporary leather sofas, a handsome zinc bar and various *objets*: bowls of fruit as art, plaster busts and framed modern cartoons. It may be a bit brash for some, but it seems to work and the place is always busy.

The clientele is a real mixture. Everyone, from elderly couples who greet the bar staff by waving their walking sticks to trendy young Brummies, seems to feel at home here. You're welcome to just lounge around and drink, but the food – modern, brasserie-style French and Italian stuff, such as mussels with apples, leeks and cider and spring onion and taleggio tart – generally avoids the usual gastropub clichés and is very well done. The staff, black t-shirted Kiwis and Aussies, are keen, friendly and understand the menu.

If you fancy a pint in the country but are tired of horse brasses and uncomfortable settles, you'll find the Crabmill a tonic.

East Anglia is the place that time forgot, its bulbous curve as self-contained as a cat curled in on itself. People talk about travelling to the Norfolk coast as 'going to the edge', and with its wide skies and frayed coastline, where marshes, creeks and sea run into one another, you do feel like you could fall off the edge of the world. East Anglian scenery is quiet but unmanicured. The rickety tarred fishermens' huts in seaside Walberswick, the lanes, elms and watermills of Constable country, the colour-washed, lime-timbered houses in the ancient market town of Lavenham: they're all picturesque, but real.

As far as food goes, fish and game are the things. Foraging is both a job and a pastime here. Oysters, shrimps and Cromer crabs are often advertised on makeshift boards outside flint cottages, along with an occasional notice announcing the availability of samphire, that green tentacular vegetable that is eaten, like asparagus, with melted butter. Most chefs have a 'mussel man' who delivers sacks of inky shells. Boats bring in skate, plaice, sole and sea-bass, and smokeries lend the scent of wood to local herring, eel and prawns.

When it comes to game, you can see why many chefs are happier to work in a dining pub than a restaurant. If the man up the road turns up with 15 partridges he has just shot – and most chefs have this kind of relationship with local shooters – the pub kitchen, which often has half a dozen specials every day, can put it on the menu immediately. Chefs in pubs are not hide-bound by an *à la carte* menu; they don't have to have 30 or 40 portions of everything.

east anglia

The best cooking here resonates with a sense of the local. At the Hoste Arms in Burnham Market you'll be served grilled lemon sole with a lemon and cockle dressing. At the Wildebeast Arms, just outside Norwich, you'll get lightly curried Norfolk mussel soup, while at the Three Horse Shoes in Madingley, near Cambridge, you can order a pizza of local asparagus with ricotta and mint.

A Mediterranean influence is much in evidence, but East Anglia is distinctive for the preponderance of Asian ingredients, perhaps because they marry so well with fish, or perhaps because there's a good sprinkling of Kiwi and Aussie chefs working here, plus English chefs who've travelled and cooked 'down under'. Chef Richard Stokes at the Three Horse Shoes, for example, serves English partridge on an Asian cabbage salad he discovered in California. The clean sweet-sour flavours, he says, go better with partridge than any British accompaniment he can think of. It's a culinary leaning that British cooks have displayed since they embraced the spices brought back by the Crusaders. Now they're borrowing from Sydney and Singapore as well.

High Street
Madingley
Cambridgeshire
01954 210221
www.huntsbridge.com
serves lunch and dinner
mon to sun lunch;
bookings accepted;
children welcome; garden

three horse shoes

The quietly spoken Richard Stokes, the chef and co-owner of the Three Horse Shoes, has worked at the River Café and numerous restaurants in San Francisco. But he likes cooking in this gracious thatched English pub better than anywhere. 'I'm not hide-bound by an unchanging *à la carte* menu. If a local shooter brings me 20 mallards I can serve them until they run out. I can do a slow roast every day if I want to. I can serve puddings as simple as ripe figs with mascarpone and a honey that I discovered in Tuscany. I can tinker around with ideas,' he says.

The Three Horseshoe's daily-changing menus are full of modern Asian and Italian touches that Richard picked up in San Francisco. You might find green papaya and crab salad with chilli, lime and soy, or a pizzetta with ricotta, pumpkin and rosemary. It is gloriously sunny food, modish without being overwrought.

In the kitchen, Richard has demi-johns full of raspberries in Campari or vodka, so he can make boozy sorbets in June before the fruit comes into season, and there are jars of fig, grape and apple chutney. Side dishes, such as fontina potato cake and braised leeks with ham and cream, are divine, and there's always something interesting behind the bar, such as home-made lemonade or prosecco with freshly squeezed blood orange juice. Here is a chef who goes the extra mile.

sardine 'sandwiches'

This is a slight variation on a dish that Richard learnt at the River Café in London. It's not unlike the Sicilian dish *sarde a beccafico*, but the good thing here is that you don't have to fiddle about rolling up the stuffed fish.

serves 4

85g (3oz) coarse white breadcrumbs

zest of 1 unwaxed lemon, and the juice of 1/2 lemon

115g (4oz) pine nuts

2 dried bird's eye chillies, crumbled

small bunch of flat-leaf parsley, finely chopped

3 sprigs mint, stems removed and leaves torn

1/2 large bulb fennel, very finely shredded

salt and pepper

olive oil

12 fresh plump sardines, filleted and each fillet cut in 2

1 Preheat the oven to 200°C/400°F/gas mark 6.

2 In a bowl, mix together the breadcrumbs, lemon zest, lemon juice, pine nuts, chillies, parsley, mint, fennel, seasoning and enough olive oil to make a paste.

3 Brush a small baking dish with 40ml (2½tbsp) olive oil. Lay half the sardine fillets in the dish, skin side down, and then sprinkle evenly with half the breadcrumb mixture.

4 Repeat with another layer of sardines and then sprinkle on the rest of the breadcrumb mixture.

5 Drizzle with olive oil and cook in the hot oven for 5–6 minutes, until the dish is golden brown.

asparagus and dandelion salad with gulls' eggs, anchovies and pecorino

Gulls' eggs are only available for 3 weeks in the year, and are collected specially for Richard, but hens' eggs are just as good. There are infinite variations on this salad – add black olives or halved, just-cooked new potatoes to make it more substantial, or use cured ham instead of the anchovies if you prefer. You can use other greens as well if you can't get dandelion leaves. A mixture of frisée and watercress or rocket would be good.

serves 4

8 gulls' eggs

150g (5¹/₂oz) tender asparagus, trimmed

olive oil, for cooking

16 anchovy fillets in brine or olive oil, drained

extra virgin olive oil

lemon juice

black pepper

celery salt

2 celery sticks, finely shredded

small bunch of flat-leaf parsley, finely chopped

2 heads dandelion leaves, separated

170g (6oz) Pecorino cheese, shaved

1 Bring a saucepan of water to the boil and boil the gulls' eggs in their shells for 4 minutes, then refresh them in cold water.

2 Brush the asparagus with a little olive oil and cook on a hot, ridged griddle pan until they are tender but still have bite. This will take about 4 minutes, depending on how thick the asparagus is.

3 Rinse the anchovies in cold water and dry on kitchen paper. Cut in half.

4 Mix 60ml (4tbsp) extra virgin olive oil with a squeeze of lemon juice and season with pepper and celery salt.

5 To assemble the salad, mix the celery, parsley and dandelion leaves together. Coat evenly with the dressing and divide between 4 plates. Quickly peel and halve the eggs and put 4 halves on top of each pile of salad with 8 anchovy halves, the asparagus and some shaved Pecorino. Drizzle each plate with a little more extra virgin olive oil and serve.

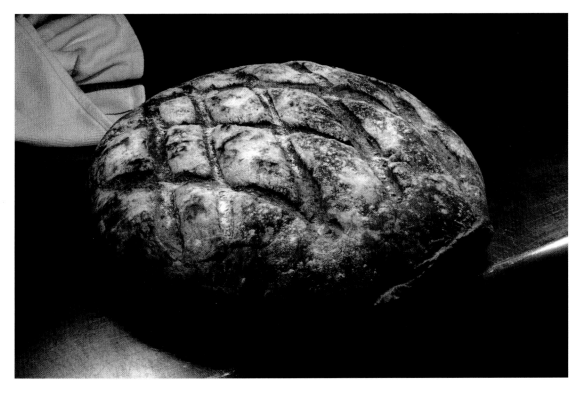

roast partridge with vietnamese cabbage salad

Rau ram is a herb that tastes like slightly minty basil. It's hard to get hold of, except in specialist Asian stores, but you can use a mixture of basil and mint instead. The pecans might seem a bit of a hassle, but this is the authentic Vietnamese way to candy nuts.

serves 4

4 partridge

groundnut or sunflower oil

for the marinade

1 bird's eye chilli, seeds removed and finely chopped

1 clove garlic, finely chopped

small handful coriander stems, finely chopped

salt and pepper

120ml (4¼fl oz) groundnut oil

for the caramel fish sauce

115g (4oz) demerara sugar

55ml (2fl oz) water

115ml (4fl oz) fish sauce

for the salad dressing

2 cloves garlic, crushed

2 bird's eye chillies, deseeded and minced

55ml (2fl oz) rice vinegar

150ml (5½fl oz) light soy sauce

55g (2oz) caster sugar

juice of ½ lime

for the cabbage salad

400g (14oz) red cabbage, very finely shredded

100g (3¾oz) jicama or mouli, very finely shredded

1 pink grapefruit, segmented

small bunch of coriander, finely chopped

small bunch of rau ram, finely chopped

1 Place the partridge in a large dish. Mix the marinade ingredients together in a small bowl and spoon over the partridge. Cover and leave to marinate for 24 hours in the refrigerator, turning the birds over every so often.

2 To cook the partridge, preheat the oven to 200°C/400°F/gas mark 6. Heat a little oil in a large heavy-bottomed pan and add the partridge. Brown them on all sides, over a high heat, but don't cook through. Put the birds into a roasting tin and roast them for 15 minutes. Rest for 5 minutes.

3 Meanwhile, mix all the ingredients together for the caramel fish sauce. Mix the ingredients for the salad dressing with 55ml (2fl oz) water.

4 Mix the salad ingredients together and dress. Divide the salad between 4 plates, add the pecans and put the partridge on top. Drizzle over the caramel fish sauce.

candied pecans

225g (8oz) pecans, shelled

3 medium egg whites

85g (3oz) caster sugar

a pinch of salt

1 Preheat the oven to 150°C/300°F/gas mark 2. Toast the pecans for 2 minutes on a baking sheet to warm through but not to colour them.

2 Cover a separate baking sheet with Bakewell paper.

3 Whisk the egg whites with the sugar and salt until they are stiff. Stir in the pecans, then spread the mixture onto the baking sheet and cook in the slow oven for about 25 minutes, until the egg whites are golden brown and have collapsed around the nuts.

4 Stir the mixture with a spoon to break it up, then put the nuts back into the oven for a further 15 minutes, until they're nicely toasted.

grilled peaches with zinfandel granita

This is the kind of simple, elegant dessert that Richard is great at. The granita also goes well with raspberries, and the peaches are good on their own served with whipped cream that has a little Amaretto liqueur stirred into it.

serves 4

1 bottle red Zinfandel wine

285g (10oz) caster sugar

juice of 2 lemons

1 Mix the Zinfandel with the sugar and lemon juice in a saucepan. Heat slowly until the sugar has dissolved. Turn the heat up, bring to the boil and reduce the liquid to 565ml (1 pint).

2 Pour the liquid into a shallow freezerproof tray and freeze for 30–40 minutes, then break up the ice crystals with a fork.

3 Repeat this process every half an hour, until the mixture is set into lovely dry crystals. This will take about 2 hours.

grilled peaches

4 peaches, halved, stone removed

1 vanilla pod

40ml (2½tbsp) caster sugar

to serve

crème fraîche

1 Preheat the oven to 170°C/325°F/gas mark 3 and set the grill to high. Place the peaches, cut side up, in a baking dish.

2 Split the vanilla pod in half lengthways and scrape out the seeds. Mix the seeds with the sugar. Using a pestle and mortar, pound them together to a powder and sprinkle over the peaches.

3 Grill on a high heat until the tops are charred and caramelized, then finish cooking in the moderately slow oven until the peaches are soft. Serve the peaches warm or cold.

4 Put 2 peach halves on a plate, add a blob of crème fraîche and a good scoopful of the granita. Alternatively, put the granita into a little glass beside the peach.

'my food is a mixture of english, italian and southeast asian. i get a lot of ideas on trips to california, and working at the river cafe had a big influence on me.' richard

raspberry lemonade

This is so refreshing and easy to make. You can mix it with freshly squeezed
orange juice if you want to stretch it a bit.

serves 4

450g (1lb) raspberries

*55g (2oz) caster sugar, plus
extra to taste*

*finely grated rind and juice of
4 unwaxed lemons*

1 litre (1³/4 pints) soda water

1 Purée the raspberries with the caster sugar in a food processor and then push
through a nylon sieve.

2 Mix the sieved purée with the lemon zest and juice and the soda water. Add
extra sugar to taste and chill.

'i love raspberries. i make raspberry
lemonade once they're in season,
but i also preserve them in alcohol so that
i can make raspberry and
campari or raspberry and vodka
sorbet from June onwards.' richard

the best of the rest

the swan

Monks Eligh,
Suffolk
01449 741391
serves lunch and dinner
weds to sun lunch;
bookings advised;
children welcome; garden

Although he originally hails from the north of England, Nigel Ramsbottom, the Swan's chef and owner, is in love with all things East Anglian. Here you'll find Suffolk asparagus with melted butter, smoked prawns from Orford with lemon mayonnaise, and an 'all-day-breakfast' salad of local bacon, black pudding, fried potatoes and poached egg with a warm vinaigrette.

Summer menus offer a pick-and-mix of modern European cooking, such as seared tuna with couscous and stewed peppers, while winter fare has more British leanings: dollops of home-made picallili accompany a gutsy pork terrine; beef from the butcher in nearby Long Melford is braised till melting and topped with dumplings; rabbit is made into a soothing stew with bacon, cream and English mustard. This is seriously comforting stuff.

Nigel used to be head chef at Franco Taruschio's legendary Walnut Tree Inn in Abergavenney (a forerunner of the contemporary gastropub), and you can tell: his sourcing is brilliant and every ingredient sings with flavour.

The varnished pine furniture, bamboo chairs, check curtains and carnations on every table make you feel like you're in a café-cum-tea-shop rather than a dining pub. No-one has done a gastropub makeover on The Swan and, although Nigel carries out improvements when he can afford to, it will always be homely and unpretentious. It's food, not decor, that matters here.

the white horse

Brancaster Staithe
Norfolk
01485 210262
www.whitehorse
brancaster.co.uk
serves lunch and dinner
mon to sun;
bookings advised;
children welcome; terrace

You might not bother with the White Horse if you were passing. It looks like a modern suburban home and, beside the flint cottages along this part of the Norfolk coast, it doesn't quite make the grade in the charm stakes. But you'd be missing a treat. Firstly, because the view from the large, modern conservatory is one of the best in England: flat tidal marshes and reed beds fraying into the sea and a broad, curved, empty sky; secondly, because the food is fresh, zippy and modern.

As much as 70 percent of the menu here is fish and the young local chef, Ben Handley, makes the most of what's on his doorstep. You may even catch sight of his mussel man as he pulls his haul up from the sea's edge through the pub car park. When they're in season, Ben uses more mussels than anything else, usually for *moules marinière*. There's also crab from just along the coast at Cromer, dressed in the English way, or served in a salad spiked with chilli and soy, or made into a sauce for spaghetti with parsley and garlic.

Ben learnt to cook at his parents' pub nearby, but he has spent a lot of time cooking 'down under', and there's plenty of Pacific Rim influence in dishes such as grilled bream with Vietnamese pickled coleslaw, though it's incorporated in a way that respects the locale rather than paying homage to fashion. There are also great sandwiches, such as honey roast ham with mustard and tomato chutney (at lunch only) if you don't want a full meal.

the hoste arms

Burnham Market

Norfolk

01328 738777

www.hostearms.co.uk

serves lunch and dinner

mon to sun;

bookings advised;

children welcome; garden

Paul Whittome, who owns the Hoste Arms, is one of the most passionate enthusiasts you could meet and his conversation is peppered with the pubs, restaurants and hotels he loves. He bought the Hoste Arms in 1989 with the not inconsiderable aim of turning it into 'the best inn in Britain'. He has made a pretty good job of it – the Hoste is overwhelmingly popular – and he has always maintained the innate pubby casualness of the bar and dining rooms, influenced by Denis Watkins' Angel Inn at Hetton in Yorkshire, one of the first gastropubs in the country.

The bar has been restored and is a beautiful space: deep red walls, settles, an exposed brick fireplace and handsome aged tables, all overlooked by a huge landscape of the Norfolk coast in all its flat, marshy glory by the photographer Harry Cory-Wright.

Of the several dining rooms, the one by the bar, with its chunky pine furniture and wooden floor, is the most casual. Tea-lights glowing behind silver shades and expensive fabrics indicate that the Hoste is a bit posher than your average gastropub, but the atmosphere is laidback, even ebullient, there are no cloths on the tables and you can order something as simple as a beefburger.

The menu encompasses brasserie dishes, such as bang bang chicken, modern pub classics such as steak with crispy onions, and restaurant cooking, such as black pudding risotto with foie gras. There's a Pacific Rim influence, not surprisingly since the chef is Australian, and a wealth of local fish such as Brancaster oysters with shallot vinaigrette and dressed Cromer crab. The simpler dishes work best and some robust offerings, such as honey glazed ham hock, are bang on.

Burnham is a model of seaside chicness: luxury food shops, a terrific milliners and stylish boutiques – no wonder half of Kensington decamp here at weekends. Bring your credit card.

the bell

High Road

Horndon-on-the-Hill

Essex

01600 750235

www.bellinn.co.uk; serves

lunch and dinner

mon to sun;

bookings accepted;

children welcome; terrace

You don't feel hopeful, travelling out through the flatlands of East London, down the A13, past Thurrock Lakeside shopping centre. But take the turning for Hordon-on-the-Hill and you'll find a little bit of half-timbered England and a cracking place to eat.

The Bell, a pale primrose, flower-bedecked building, has been owned and run as a dining pub by John and Sally Vereker for 30 years. There is a small dining room with printed menus and tables you can book, but go for the more casual, characterful option and eat in the old oak bar, with its chunky flagstones, dark beams, settles and newspapers on poles. The room is dominated by a huge blackboard that lists the dining-room menu plus a few more pubby offerings such as beer-battered fish with chunky chips.

The 'smart dining' dishes can be pretty fancy: there are usually a few aerated sauces, variously called 'froths' or 'cappuccinos', and the odd dish has taken adventurousness too far, such as raspberry pavlova with watercress ice-cream. But when chef Finlay Logan's talents are reined in, he cooks some lovely stuff: smoked cheese risotto with caramelised cauliflower; terrine of bacon knuckle with a deep-fried egg; pot-roast chicken with salsify, mussels and mustard. And the veg? Just the business. Creamy cauliflower purée you could happily sup on its own and crisp, 'fat chips' which should really be described as 'obese'. Meat comes from the butcher next door, the herbs from the back garden.

The Verekers know what they're doing.

the pheasant

Keyston
Cambridgeshire
01832 710241
www.huntsbridge.com
serves lunch and dinner
mon to sun;
bookings accepted;
children welcome; terrace

The Pheasant, a white, thatch-roofed cottage right beside the green, is the most dominant feature of the little village of Keyston. The pub looks as English as cricket and cream teas, but walk through the low front door and you'll swear you're in provincial France.

A basket of cheese sits on a bar made of wavy rafts of timber, with a hefty wooden platter covered with bottles of glowing amber – whiskies, Cognacs, brandies and liqueurs – alongside it. Large vases of flowers, highly polished old country furniture, smart table lamps, big, elegant fireplaces, walls the colour of damson fool: all is calm and tasteful, and makes you feel utterly cosseted. Only a couple of stuffed pheasants, a handful of hunting scenes and well-kept Adnams bitter give away the fact that you are in England. The Pheasant combines a quintessential Englishness with the polish and informality of a French *auberge*.

You can eat either in the dining room, where the tables are already laid, or in the bar area, with its comfy leather chairs, baskets of toys for children and bowls of top-notch nuts. The food, as you might expect from a dining pub that is partly owned by John Hoskins (its sister pubs are the Three Horse Shoes in Madingley and the Falcon at Fotheringhay), is even better than you'd find in a reputable French *auberge*. Ox tongue on rocket, shaved fennel and Italian lentils with horseradish dressing; pork terrine with apple chutney and poached foie gras; brioche *pain perdu* with port-poached figs and gingerbread ice-cream. This is seriously refined cooking, and it's very well executed, even if it can, at times, be a bit too complex.

Despite the ambitiousness of the food, there is no pressure to go for the full monty. The menu explicitly encourages you to opt for one course, two starters, or even just a pudding, and drinkers are every bit as welcome as diners. The Pheasant does want to be an English pub, after all.

the crown

High Street
Southwold
Suffolk
01502 727200
www.adnams.co.uk
serves lunch and dinner
mon to sun;
children welcome; terrace

The Crown, in the story-book seaside town of Southwold – with its ice-cream hued beach huts and handsome 19th-century houses – reflects the elegance and civility of its surroundings. Here are tall windows, walls in warm gold and sage green, battered antique tables and settles with leather cushions. There's no frippery, just an imposing grandfather clock, a few old Adnams posters (this is Suffok brewer's Adnams flagship pub), and a portrait in oils above the fireplace.

The clientele is classy: well-groomed families with well-behaved children, genteel elderly couples sharing the *Daily Telegraph*, groups of artistic locals and moneyed metropolitans up from London. And it's a jolly place, so much so that you're willing to forgive some inconsistencies in the food.

Chef Chris Coubrough, a New Zealander, is inclined to go for unsuccessful swims in the Pacific Rim – Thai fish and watermelon curry isn't great in the imagination and it's worse on the palate – but more classic dishes are well executed. Ragoût of chicken and wild mushrooms in a Dijon mustard sauce is hearty and delicious, as is lamb's liver with black pudding and bubble and squeak. Puddings, such as chocolate fondant or apple-crumble parfait, elicit 'oohs' and 'aahs' as they're carried from the kitchen, and the wine list and the ales are superb.

There's a charming small bar where you can play shove ha'penny, dominoes or cribbage, but it's for drinking only. A separate restaurant serves more complex food in an atmosphere that is less enjoyable, so stick to the main bar.

the george

Cavendish

Suffolk

01787 280248

www.georgecavendish.co.uk;

lunch and dinner served

sun to mon;

bookings advised;

children welcome; garden

The George's chef-owner, Jonathan Nicholson, as well as doing stints for Marco Pierre White, worked for the Conran empire (his last job was head chef at Bluebird in London's King's Road) and the menu at this 600-year-old pub is full of Conranesque brasserie dishes: tiger prawns with Thai green curry, entrecôte with béarnaise and chunky chips, Moroccan spiced lamb with roast sweet potato and stuffed pimento. There are also proper lunchtime dishes such as fish and chips and eggs Benedict. The food is accomplished: meat and fish perfectly cooked, soups splendid and seasoning spot-on.

Jonathan and his wife Charlotte, who does front of house, have made a great job of refurbishing the place too. There's a careful mixture of original features – chunky oak beams and joists, exposed brickwork, a big fireplace – and modern touches, such as thick hessian blinds, cream ceramic wall lights, sisal carpeting and contemporary photographs. The staff are young and smiling, the punters span all ages, and the place is full of cheer. There's beer from the local brewery, Nethergate, and an interesting wine list with (praise be) a good selection of half bottles. This is one to watch.

the crown

Snape

Suffolk

01728 688324

www.snapevillage.org.uk

serves lunch and dinner

mon to sun;

bookings accepted;

no children under 14;

garden

The Crown is an ancient, butter-coloured pub a stone's throw from Snape Maltings, the home of the Aldeburgh Music Festival and the Pears Britten Music School. The food is simple and genuine, like that of a really good home cook: plump sweet scallops with chunks of bacon on well dressed, springy leaves; fishy salmon and cod cakes with tartare sauce; homemade brown bread ice-cream.

Diane Maylott, who's been cooking here for more than 10 years, doesn't have any truck with fancy restaurant cooking. She shops well, then lets the ingredients speak for themselves. Her three dining rooms are country-cottage comfy: beamed ceilings, herring-bone brick floors and farmhouse chairs. Tea-lights sit in little hand-painted pots and there are preserves on the shelves. If you get there early, you should be able to bag a table in the 'codgers" bar, a small area created by the curving of two magnificent high settles round the big inglenook fireplace.

The clientele covers blue-stockings who've been to a concert up the road, bikers and groups of over-60s fighting over shared puddings. The puds – slices of tart, deep-dish lemon pie and big wedges of summer pudding – are a highlight. If only more places did things this simply and so well.

the wildebeest arms

Stoke Holy Cross

Norfolk

01508 492497

serves lunch and dinner

mon to sun; bookings

advised; children welcome;

garden

You might expect to find exotic foods such as bison and ostrich in a place called the Wildebeast, but the menu here is modern European, with a bias towards the French. The decor, though, is 'safari lodge chic': ethnic tapestries, African artefacts, and tables made from slices of tree trunk.

The words 'nage' and 'jus' crop up on the menu, signalling grand ambitions, but most dishes are less complicated than they sound. Best end of lamb with cocotte potatoes, green beans and niçois jus is perfectly pink meat accompanied by cooking juices flavoured with black olives, for example. The food is at its best when it's not trying too hard, so go for straightforward dishes, such as lightly curried Norfolk mussel soup or smoked salmon risotto with dill cream and poached eggs.

Great bread and big chunky chips are made on the premises and the desserts are a real highlight: homemade ice-creams, big creamy clouds of meringue with poached peaches and mascarpone, and passion fruit tart with sorbet. Waiting staff are young, keen and smart.

wales

Wales is a country set apart, full of landscapes where it's still possible to feel far away from it all. The writer Wynford Vaughan Thomas described the Gower Peninsula, that coastline of sheer cliffs, prehistoric dolmens, tiny flowers and broom, as 'a secret which people hug to themselves'. In north Wales, the alien-looking slate heaps near Blaenau Ffestiniog – their edges dark and wavy like stacks of half-burnt newspapers – are just some of the dramatically isolated elements of Snowdonia, with its sheer mountain passes and the strong, clear, pyramid-shaped peak of Snowdon itself.

Of course, the Welsh language also sets the country apart. You can appreciate the musical cadences in its flow, even if you don't speak Welsh. There seem to be no breaks between words, and you will smile at the poetic meanings of town names such as Llanrhaeadr-y-Mochnant: 'the holy place on the waterfall of the pig-stream'.

This difference, and Wales' history of non-conformism, have always made the place attractive to people who want to follow their own path. Potters, painters, sculptors, hippies, ecologists, writers and cheesemakers – all have loved Wales for the fact that they could be themselves there, and do something distinctive.

In the area of food, it was an Italian who came to Wales to do something distinctive. When Franco Taruschio and his English wife Anne took over The Walnut Tree in Abergavenny in 1963, they created ripples that are still having an effect on British cooking and eating today. They cooked good Mediterranean food in a country in which Italian cuisine meant only plates of spaghetti and outsize pepper mills; they mixed this Mediterranean food with Welsh dishes; and they cared about their ingredients, sourcing the best Welsh produce. They created the first gastropub, in effect, even though the term hadn't yet been coined. It was the mix of good food and informality that made the Walnut Tree great: a place that felt like a pub, but with better food than you would find in most restaurants.

Travelling around Britain, I lost count of the number of chefs with their own dining pubs who told me that they just wanted to do 'what Franco did'. There is now a string of superb dining pubs in the Brecon Beacons, all individual, and all influenced by him. They source the best produce they can — Welsh cheeses, lamb and venison, beef from the Welsh Marches or Herefordshire, coracle fished sea-trout, laverbread — with its iodine, rock-pool flavour — and cockles. And of course they also serve the Welsh bitter that was so loved by Dylan Thomas for 'its live, white lather, its brass-bright depths... the salt on the tongue, the foam at the corners.'

What is special about the pubs in this chapter is that they are all individual — more varied than I have found in any other area. Franco Taruschio may have influenced the trend, but nobody has slavishly copied him. They have instead done what Wales allows people to do: be distinctive.

Nant-y-Derry
Monmouthshire
01873 881101
www.thefoxhunter.com
serves lunch and dinner
tues to sat;
bookings advised;
children welcome; terrace

The menu at The Foxhunter reads prosaically: artichoke soup, herb risotto with mascarpone, smoked haddock fishcakes with wild garlic mayonnaise. There are no fancy phrases, or even much detail about cooking methods, so the impact – when the food is delivered – is all the greater. There aren't many meals that make you wonder what tricks the chef has pulled off to make the food taste this good. Chef-owner Matt Tebbutt, who trained in London with Alistair Little, is a bold, confident, gifted cook. His risottos are among the best you will eat, here or in Italy. His sorbets are so intense they stop you in your tracks. There just isn't a duff dish on the menu. If Tebbutt's food were fancier, he'd be in line for a Michelin star, but thankfully that's not his aim. He just cooks modern classics, from the Med to Thailand, with skill and polish.

The place itself is contemporary-country: flagstones and woodblock floors, slick beech furniture, big church candles burning in uncurtained windows, and wooden bowls of pears and gourds on the shelves. There's a log fire, open to the bar and the dining room, and watercolours and pastels by local artists.

Tebbutt comes out to chat to people, often with his baby in his arms. The Foxhunter is a calming, civilized place – worth a trip even if you have to drive for miles.

the foxhunter

home-cured duck with wasabi, soy and melon

Matt has adapted this from a recipe in Rick Stein's book, *Food Heroes*. It's very simple and a great dish to prepare in advance. Slices of mango are just as good as melon.

serves 4

2 large duck breasts

for the cure

2.5ml (1/2tsp) coriander seeds

2.5ml (1/2tsp) black peppercorns

5ml (1tsp) thyme leaves

2 bay leaves

55g (2oz) caster sugar

40g (1 1/2oz) salt

to serve

8 thin slices melon, the ripest available

wasabi

dark soy sauce

1 Blitz the cure ingredients to a fine powder in a food processor; alternatively, grind them to a powder in a pestle and mortar. Spread half the cure on the bottom of a dish. Put the duck breasts, skin side down, in the cure and sprinkle the rest of it over and around the breasts. Cover and chill for 12 hours, or overnight.

2 Preheat the oven to 170°C/325°F/gas mark 3. Wash the cure off the duck breasts and place them in a roasting tin or shallow pan. Add 250ml (9fl oz) water, or just enough to come about halfway up the side of the duck breasts. Cook in the oven for 20–25 minutes.

3 Remove the duck breasts from the oven, take them out of the tin and leave to cool on a plate until firm enough to slice. Serve half a duck breast, sliced, per person, with 2 neat slices of melon, a dab of wasabi, and a little dipping bowl of soy sauce on the plate beside the duck.

deep-fried whitebait with paprika mayonnaise

Elevated pub-grub; delicious with a glass of ale.

serves 4

vegetable oil, for deep-frying

handful of flat-leaf parsley, perfect leaves only

4 large handfuls whitebait

seasoned flour

to serve

paprika mayonnaise

lemon wedges

1 Heat the oil in a deep-fat fryer, or a heavy-bottomed pan. Take a handful of perfect parsley leaves. Make sure they are dry, then throw them into the hot oil; they will splutter furiously. As soon as they have stopped spitting, scoop them out with a slotted spoon onto kitchen paper and salt them sparingly.

2 Shake the whitebait in a bag with the seasoned flour. Sieve off any excess flour and split the whitebait into 2 batches. Deep-fry the fish in simmering oil for a few minutes, until crisp and golden. Lift out, drain on kitchen paper and salt lightly.

3 Pile the whitebait into a big bowl, scatter with the deep-fried parsley and serve immediately with the paprika mayonnaise and lemon wedges.

paprika mayonnaise

2 medium egg yolks

7.5ml (1/2tbsp) Dijon mustard

1 clove garlic, crushed

pinch of sea salt

250ml (9fl oz) sunflower oil

250ml (9fl oz) olive oil

white wine vinegar

paprika

1 Whisk the egg yolks, mustard, crushed garlic and salt together in a bowl.

2 Very slowly, add the oils, a dribble at a time, whisking vigorously, and thoroughly incorporating each drop of oil before adding any more.

3 Once the mayonnaise has thickened and all the oil has been whisked in, add a splash of white wine vinegar. Season carefully with paprika until the mayo's as spicy as you want. Cover and refrigerate.

rack of lamb with umbrian lentils and salsa verde

The lentils and salsa verde here are also good with roasted or seared fish, such as cod, bass or tuna.

serves 4

250g (9oz) Umbrian or Puy lentils

½ medium Spanish onion, halved again

3½ celery sticks and finely chopped leaves

1 large carrot, halved

½ bulb garlic, halved again

½ dried chilli

1 bouquet garni (thyme, rosemary, parsley, bay leaf)

4 racks of lamb

salt and pepper

olive oil, for frying

30g (2tbsp) roughly chopped flat-leaf parsley

extra virgin olive oil

lemon wedges

1 Preheat the oven to 220C/425°F/gas mark 7. Check through the lentils for grit, then put them in a heavy-bottomed pan with the onion, celery sticks (but not the celery leaves), carrot, garlic, dried chilli and bouquet garni. Cover generously with cold water and bring to the boil. Skim off any scum that rises to the surface, then turn the heat down and simmer until the lentils are just tender (start testing them after 10 minutes).

2 Drain through a sieve and pick out the vegetables and bouquet garni from the cooked lentils. Reserve the cooking liquor.

3 To cook the lamb, season it all over. Heat a little olive oil in a heavy-bottomed pan, add the lamb and quickly brown it all over, but do not cook through. Put the lamb into a roasting tin and roast for 12 minutes for rare, 15 for medium. Transfer the racks to a plate, cover with foil and let them rest for 10 minutes.

4 Put the cooked lentils in a bowl and throw in the chopped celery leaves and parsley. Season and moisten with some extra virgin olive oil and a little of the lentil cooking liquor.

5 Divide the lentils between 4 warmed plates. Slice each rack of lamb into 4 and place on top of the lentils, spooning some of the lamb cooking juices around it. Drizzle with a little extra virgin oil and add a good dollop of salsa verde. Serve with wedges of lemon.

salsa verde

4 anchovy fillets, in oil

1 clove garlic, crushed

5ml (1tsp) Dijon mustard

10ml (2tsp) red wine vinegar

handful each of basil and mint

2 handfuls flat-leaf parsley

250ml (9fl oz) extra virgin olive oil

1 Put the anchovies, garlic, mustard and vinegar in a blender and blend to a paste. Add the herbs and blend, then add enough olive oil to make a loose sauce.

2 Alternatively, pound the first 4 ingredients into a smooth paste with a pestle and mortar. Finely chop the herbs and mix thoroughly into the paste, then add enough olive oil as above.

rosé wine jelly with mulberries

Mulberries are not essential here, Matt just has a ready source from a neighbour.
You can use raspberries, tayberries or loganberries instead, or even a mixture.

serves 4

4¹/₂ gelatine leaves

300ml (10¹/₂fl oz) stock syrup, made from 150g (5¹/₂oz) caster sugar and 150ml (5¹/₂fl oz) water, heated to dissolve the sugar

¹/₂ bottle rosé wine, the best you can muster

Grenadine (optional)

170g (6oz) mulberries

to serve

Jersey double cream

1 Soak the gelatine in cold water for about 5 minutes, until it is completely soft.

2 Gently heat the stock syrup and pour into a large jug with the rosé wine. To enhance the colour, add a few drops of Grenadine.

3 Lift the gelatine out of the water and squeeze out the excess liquid. Add to the warm sugar syrup and let it dissolve for 30 seconds before stirring. Let this cool.

4 Pour a little jelly into 4 x 200ml (7fl oz) jelly moulds – about a third of the way up – then refrigerate for at least 45 minutes, until set.

5 Put a few mulberries onto the set layer of jelly and add just enough jelly liquid to cover the fruit. Allow this layer to set for 20 minutes before adding the rest of the jelly liquid. (If the jelly liquid starts to set before you have added it to the moulds, melt it again by warming it over a very low heat, but do not allow it to boil as this would destroy the gelatine and the jelly won't set.) Chill the jellies for 45 minutes, until firmly set.

6 Unmould the jellies by briefly dipping the moulds into hot water to loosen the set, then upend each one onto a plate and give it a good shake – it should slide out easily. Scatter some more mulberries around the jellies and serve with cold, thick Jersey cream.

'i really moved to the Brecon Beacons because of the walnut tree. i wanted to do what franco taruschio had done.' matt

seville orange marmalade bread and butter pudding

If you don't want to make the 'quick' marmalade you can use a bought one, but you won't have slices of orange covering the top.

serves 8

for the 'quick' marmalade

2 Seville oranges

300ml (10¹/₂fl oz) water

300g (10¹/₂oz) caster sugar

juice of 2 Seville oranges

for the pudding

300ml (10¹/₂fl oz) full-fat milk

300ml (10¹/₂fl oz) double cream

salt

2 vanilla pods, split in half

5 medium eggs

45g (1³/₄oz) caster sugar

handful of mixed dried fruit

handful of mixed candied peel

1 large brioche loaf

250g (9oz) unsalted butter, melted

to serve

clotted or Jersey double cream

1 First make the 'quick' marmalade. Slice 2 oranges into semi-circles 6mm (¼ inch) thick. In a heavy-bottomed pan, bring the water and sugar to the boil. Add the orange juice and slices. Cook over a low heat for about 2 hours, stirring occasionally, until the orange skin has softened and the liquid is jammy and thick. Set aside.

2 Preheat the oven to 140°C/275°F/gas mark 1. Brush the inside of a baking dish with the remaining melted butter.

3 In a heavy-bottomed pan, heat the milk with the cream, a pinch of salt and the vanilla pods until almost boiling. Take off the heat, pour into a bowl and leave to infuse for at least 10 minutes.

4 Whisk the eggs and sugar together in a large bowl. Sieve the warm cream mixture and then add it to the eggs and mix thoroughly.

5 Cover the base of the baking dish, 5–7.5cm (2–3 inches) deep, with the mixed fruit and peel. Slice the brioche and brush liberally with most of the butter. Cut each slice into 2 triangles and arrange in the dish in overlapping layers. Pour the cream mixture over and push the bread down to help absorb the liquid. Leave for half an hour.

6 Place the baking dish in a roasting tin. Fill the tin with boiling water to come one-third of the way up the sides of the baking dish. Put in the oven and cook for 30 minutes, until the pudding is slightly souffléd and wobbly, with just a little 'give' in the middle. Leave to cool.

7 Gently heat the marmalade. Interleave the orange segments from the jam over the top of the brioche and brush the liquid over the pudding's surface. Glaze under a hot grill, or in a hot oven (200°C/400°F/gas mark 6), for 10 minutes. Serve with thick cream.

Felin Fach

Powys

01874 620111

www.eatdrinksleep.ltd.uk

serves lunch and dinner

tues to sun;

bookings advised;

children welcome; garden

the felin fach griffin

Owner Charles Inkin wanted the Felin Fach Griffin to feel as relaxing as someone's home, and indeed this is one of the most laid-back, comfortable and characterful pubs in the country.

Charles, who cooks as well as running the place, trained at Ballymaloe Cookery School in Ireland and as soon as you sit down to eat you know this. The menu has rural seasonality written all over it: creamy parsnip soup with chives, Tregoyd pheasant with wild mushrooms and mash, Welsh venison with braised red cabbage. Garnet wine-poached pears with thick streams of Welsh cream running down their sides was one of the most beautiful desserts I have ever seen. It's lovely, unfussy country cooking: each ingredient tastes of itself and the seasoning – which can often let down food that's this simple – is spot-on.

The Griffin was a tumbledown stone farmhouse when Charles bought it, and it still feels domestic. In the bar, there's a coffee table with piles of newspapers and squashy leather sofas round the fire. The curtains are made from thickly woven Welsh blankets and everything – the scrubbed pine, the big wooden bowls of lemons and gourds and the locally made furniture – is chunky and genuine. Charles Inkin is a charmer who welcomes you as if you're coming to his own home, and there are simple but luxurious bedrooms upstairs if you want to make a weekend of it. Book one, or you'll regret it.

salmon and leek tartlets

You can use bought puff pastry for this if you prefer. Prick the circles of pastry with a fork, brush with beaten egg and cook at 220°C/425°F/gas mark 7 until golden, about 15 minutes, then proceed as in the recipe.

serves 4

good knob of butter

4 x 85g (3oz) salmon fillets, each cut into 3

dry white wine

240ml (8½fl oz) double cream

2 medium leeks, green part only, cut lengthwise into 7.5cm (3 inch) slivers

salt and pepper

a squeeze of lemon

30g (2tbsp) finely chopped chives

for the shortcrust pastry

140g (5oz) plain flour

pinch of salt

85g (3oz) chilled butter, cut into large dice

40g (1½oz) clarified butter

to serve

salad leaves

lemon juice

extra virgin olive oil

sea salt

1 To make the pastry, put the flour, salt and chilled butter into a food processor and whizz for a couple of seconds, until the mixture resembles fine breadcrumbs. Alternatively, sift the flour and salt into a medium-sized bowl, add the butter and rub lightly together with the fingertips until the mixture resembles fine breadcrumbs.

2 Add 30-40ml (2-2½tbsp) cold water gradually, mixing lightly with a fork until the pastry just holds together. Cover with clingfilm and refrigerate for at least 30 minutes.

3 Preheat the oven to 200°C/400°F/gas mark 6. Grease a baking sheet.

4 Roll out the pastry to a square 3mm (⅛ inch) thick. Using a 10cm (4 inch) round cup as a guide, cut out 4 circles from the pastry. Put the circles on the baking sheet, brush with clarified butter and bake for about 15 minutes, until lightly browned.

5 For the filling, in a heavy-bottomed pan, melt the knob of butter, then add the salmon chunks and a generous slug of white wine and cook gently for 30 seconds until the fish is sealed but not coloured. Using a slotted spoon, transfer the salmon to a plate and cover.

6 Add the cream to the pan and, without stirring, allow to reduce slowly. Watch that the cream does not catch and burn.

7 Add the leeks and salmon to the cream sauce. The leeks will cook very quickly – roughly 30 seconds – you want them to be slightly crunchy (*al dente*). Season well, then add a squeeze of lemon and the finely chopped chives.

8 Put the warm tart bases onto individual plates and gently place some of the salmon and leek mixture on top of each one. Serve with salad leaves simply dressed with olive oil, lemon juice and a pinch of sea salt.

conwy mussels with coconut milk and coriander

You can use any mussels for this, and add a little chopped fresh chilli to the shallots if you prefer a spicier version.

serves 1

knob of butter

1 shallot, finely sliced

450g (1lb) Conwy mussels, in the shell, cleaned

125ml (4½fl oz) coconut milk

salt and pepper

big bunch coriander, roughly chopped

wedges of lime or lemon

1 Melt the butter in a wide heavy-based pan over a high heat, but ensure the butter does not burn. Add the finely sliced shallot, sweat for about 1 minute, then add the mussels in 1 layer – cook in batches if your pan is too small – with about 60ml (4tbsp) water. Cover immediately with a tight-fitting lid.

2 Cook for 30 seconds, then check to see if any mussels are open. Remove these to a bowl. Replace the lid and cook for another 15 seconds, then check again for opened mussels. Repeat once more, then discard any mussels that remain closed.

3 Pour the coconut milk into the mussel pan, stir and gently warm through just to simmering point. Check the seasoning.

4 Return the mussels to the pan, stir and serve immediately in a large bowl, sprinkled with chopped coriander and wedges of lime or lemon on the side.

'i always wanted the griffin to feel like somebody's home.' charles

tregoyd pheasant with celery leaf and thyme barley and honeyed parsnips

This barley dish is a fantastic earthy alternative to risotto. You can use other wild mushrooms instead of girolles, or a mixture of wild and cultivated mushrooms. It isn't essential to make stock with the pheasant bones, though it's a pity to waste them. Well-flavoured chicken stock is a fine alternative.

serves 2

1 cock pheasant, oven ready

1 large carrot, halved

1 celery stick

1/2 medium Spanish onion

125ml (41/2fl oz) red wine

125ml (41/2fl oz) white wine

1 bay leaf

vegetable oil

5ml (1tsp) crab apple jelly

unsalted butter

handful of fresh girolles

salt and pepper

for the barley risotto

850ml (11/2 pints) vegetable or chicken stock

1/2 medium Spanish onion

vegetable oil

unsalted butter

225g (8oz) pearl barley

5ml (1tsp) thyme leaves

15g (1tbsp) chopped celery leaves

1 Ask your butcher to bone the pheasant, keeping the skin on the breasts and legs.

2 Preheat the oven to 200°C/400°F/gas mark 6. To make a quick stock, roughly chop the carcass and place it in a roasting tin with the carrot, celery and onion. Roast for about 20 minutes, until brown.

3 Put the roasting tin over a medium heat and pour in the red and white wines. Bring to the boil, stirring, and reduce for a few minutes to evaporate the alcohol. Add 565ml (1 pint) water and the bay leaf. Bring back to the boil and cook for 1½ hours, strain, then boil to reduce the stock to 255ml (9fl oz).

4 Heat a little vegetable oil in a heavy-bottomed frying pan. When the pan is smoking, put in the pheasant breasts and legs, skin side down, and seal for 1 minute. Turn the meat over and seal on the other side for just less than 1 minute. Place the meat, skin side down, in a roasting tin and roast in the preheated oven for 10–15 minutes, until cooked through. Put the pheasant on a plate and rest for 5–10 minutes.

5 To finish the sauce, strain the reduced stock through a very fine sieve, warm through and whisk in the crab apple jelly and a small knob of butter.

6 Drop the fresh girolles in a hot pan with a knob of butter. Toss together for 30 seconds and season.

7 Divide the pearl barley risotto between 4 warmed plates. Pour the sauce around the barley and place the parsnips, girolles and a pheasant breast and leg on top.

pearl barley risotto

1 Pour the stock into a small saucepan. Bring to the boil, then turn the heat down to simmer.

2 Dice the onion half. Heat a wide heavy-bottomed pan with a little vegetable oil and butter and sweat the onion for 1 minute. Add the pearl barley and stir for a few minutes.

3 Add a ladle of hot stock and stir until it has been absorbed. Gradually add the rest of the stock in the same way, ladleful by ladleful, stirring constantly for about 20–30 minutes, until the barley is cooked.

4 Stir in the thyme and celery leaves. Season well, then stir in a small knob of butter just to add a slight glaze to the pearl barley. Serve immediately.

honeyed parsnips

2 medium parsnips, peeled

vegetable oil

butter

15ml (1tbsp) runny honey

1 Halve, then quarter the parsnips lengthways and cut into 5cm (2 inch) batons.

2 Heat a little vegetable oil and butter in a small saucepan and cook the parsnips until tender. Stir in the honey and heat through, until lightly caramelized.

gemma's raspberry crème brûlée

Gemma Jenkins makes all the puddings at The Griffin – this is her recipe. It's a good idea to start the brûlée the day before you want to eat it.

serves 4

1 vanilla pod

565ml (1 pint) double cream

3 medium egg yolks

50g (1³/4oz) caster sugar

115g (4oz) raspberries

40ml (2¹/2tbsp) demerara sugar

1 Cut the vanilla pod in half lengthways and scrape out the seeds. Mix both with the double cream in a small saucepan. Heat gently until just before the cream boils, then remove from the heat.

2 Preheat the oven to 180°C/350°F/gas mark 4.

3 In a large bowl, whisk the egg yolks with the sugar until they are light and fluffy. Strain the cream and add to the egg yolks. Whisk quickly for 1 minute, then leave to stand for 3 minutes. Skim all the bubbles off the surface.

4 Divide the raspberries between 4 x 140ml (5fl oz) ramekins. Pour the egg mixture into each ramekin. Place in a roasting tin and pour just-boiled water into the tin to come three-quarters up the ramekins' sides. Cover the tin with a tea-towel and a piece of foil and place in the oven for 20–30 minutes until just set. Leave to cool.

5 When the 'custard' is cold, sprinkle 10ml (2tsp) sugar over each ramekin and shake gently to distribute the sugar evenly. Preheat the grill to its highest setting, or use a cook's blowtorch. Heat the sugar until it is blistering, melted and deep golden brown. Let the crème brûlées cool before serving.

the best of the rest

the bell at skenfrith

Skenfrith

Monmouthshire

01600 750235

www.skenfrith.com

serves lunch and dinner

mon to sun;

bookings advised;

children welcome; garden

The Bell, a white-washed, slate-roofed, 17th-century inn, is bit of a gem. After 18 months of refurbishment, when the whole place was decked out in warm oak, natural floors and old country furniture, it opened its doors in 2001 and has been busy ever since. There are two bars – one a fully functioning games room with snooker table and darts board, the other a simple, laid-back country dining room (no tablecloths anywhere) – and a host of bedrooms that are straight out of *Country Living*. Owners William and Janet Hutchings have created a rarity: a place that is both simple and luxurious.

The cooking ranges from hearty country to ambitious restaurant fare. Alongside the likes of Gloucester Old Spot pork with home-made chutney and mash, you'll find dishes like Trelough duck breast with celeriac mash, Puy lentils, figs and raspberry and pistachio oil. The food is cooked with real skill, but is most successful when the chef isn't putting too many flavours onto one plate. Roast cod and mussels on a risotto cake, for example, is divine.

Raw materials are carefully sourced. A blackboard in the bar lists suppliers: Minola for smoked goats' cheese, English Natural Foods in Herefordshire for Trelough duck, cream from Bower Farm just up the road. It makes you want to order before you've even read the menu. Main courses are pretty heavy on the purse, but they are copious and top-quality ingredients don't come cheap.

The punters are classy: well-heeled locals, genteel elderly folk, city-dwellers recharging their batteries and young famillies. Staff manage to be friendly and super-professional, and you have ruined castles, the River Monnow and glorious walking in the Golden Valley on your doorstep.

the penhelig arms hotel

Aberdovey

Gwynedd

01654 767215

www.penheligarms.com

serves lunch and dinner

mon to sun;

bookings advised;

children welcome; garden

Few activities bestow a feeling of well-being in the way that eating fish by the sea can, so hurray for the Penhelig Arms! It's a big, white-washed, old-fashioned hotel on the seafront in Aberdovey, a small, unspoilt little town on the Dovey estuary, opposite a beach strewn with shells and seaweed.

The Fisherman's Bar, a self-contained pub with slate walls, wood panelling, bits of maritime paraphernalia and a few salty old seadogs with pints, serves much the same food as the hotel's restaurant. The cooking is unfussy, and simple dishes such as beer-battered haddock with homemade tartare sauce and deep-fried whitebait are tip-top. Chef Jane Howkins likes Mediterranean touches and the odd salsa, so you might find roast cod with rouille, a spicy mayonnaise from the south of France, or chargrilled swordfish with roast tomatoes and Mexican salsa.

The starters could do with some attention but puds, such as raspberry and frangipane tart or bread-and-butter pudding spiked with marmalade, are well done. So enjoy watching the seaside light sparkle on the melted herb butter drenching your fried plaice – and walk off the meal afterwards on the beach.

the seland newydd

Pwllgloyw

Powys

01874 690282

serves lunch and dinner

tues din to sun lunch;

bookings advised;

children welcome; garden

Young chef Paul Thomasson, together with his mother and her partner, bought the Seland Newydd (Welsh for New Zealand) from the Kiwi owners who put it on the map, and he's maintaining its solid reputation.

Paul has worked in Michelin-starred establishments, and skill and care are evident in his cooking. Sensibly, he has resisted the temptation to turn out dishes that are too complicated for their setting. French finesse is applied to traditional British and local Welsh ingredients, resulting in highly flavoured dishes such as barley and haggis risotto with duck (a real triumph) and guinea fowl with mustard lentils and honey-roast parsnips. He's fond of terrines and parfaits served with various chutneys, and his more snacky dishes, such as Welsh rarebit with smoked bacon, or a baguette of hot Welsh beef with horseradish, are scrumptious.

Vegetables are specific to each dish, something other pubs might think about, and the flavoured breads, such as Parmesan bread, are exceptional and arrive at your table warm.

If you're booking for the dining room, ask for the small one, with its little fireplace, ticking mantel clock and cupboard full of china; it's much more characterful than the other one. The bar itself, though, is the loveliest part of the pub: vibrant salmon-pink in colour with glossy green windowsills dotted with plants, and striking furniture such as Singer sewing-machine tables.

Paul claims he loves diners to come and talk to him in the kitchen and is happiest when they say, 'I don't need to see the menu; just cook me the most wonderful dish you can.' Tempting.

the clytha arms

Clytha

Monmouthshire

01873 840206

www.clytha-arms.com

serves lunch and dinner

tues to sun lunch;

bookings advised;

children welcome; garden

The Clytha Arms, a pale pink, former dower house in the middle of nowhere, is the real McCoy. It pays no heed to fashion or style: with its table-skittles, darts board, and collection of old kitsch teapots, it feels part pub, part Granny's living room. You can have a cup of tea here as well as a pint of real ale or cider, and the sale of home-pickled eggs, Chuppa Chop lollies and jelly beans is further evidence that the chef-owner, Andrew Canning, does things his way.

The cooking, by Canning and his daughter Sarah, runs from gutsy dishes such as wild boar sausages with potato pancakes, to more refined offerings such as halibut with crayfish sauce. It can be a bit hit-and-miss, but the food is so good when everything comes together – genuine, simple, with the mark of a single cook rather than a brigade on it – that it's worth risking it occasionally missing the mark.

The menu takes in both French and Spanish influences, but is well rooted in local flavours. There are plenty of regional and solidly old-fashioned dishes on offer, such as cockles with laverbread and bacon, smoked haddock with Y-Fenni cheese and faggots with beer and onion gravy. Canning has a surer hand with fish than meat, and puddings, such as Sauternes cream with spiced prunes or raspberry and Chianti sorbet, are real humdingers.

The pub has four friendly dogs, comfily-attired regulars are all but soldered to their bar stools, old ladies totter in on sticks and babies sit in their car seats beside trendy parents. Everybody seems to come here, which means the place is full of surprises. You might expect two dishevelled old geezers playing draughts to be talking about changing traffic regulations or government subsidies, but here they could just as well be discussing the latest Coldplay CD.

the walnut tree inn

Llanddewi Skirrid
Monmouthshire
01873 852797
www.thewalnuttreeinn.com
serves lunch and dinner
tues to sun lunch;
bookings advised;
children welcome; garden

In 2001, the Taruschios sold their legendary pub (see Wales introduction) to Francesco Mattioli, a former manager of Antonio Carluccio's Neal Street Restaurant. The balance has tipped towards it being, in truth, more of a restaurant than a dining pub. The little pub tables have been topped with squares of dark, polished wood (and you can now book them); there are new, comfortable (and matching) chairs; and the service is slick rather than chatty. It is less crowded, less chaotic and less 'pubby' than it was, and it has consequently lost some of its charm and *joie de vivre*.

But the food is still wonderful. Some of the Taruschios' classic dishes, such as *vincigrassi*, a pasta dish of béchamel, Parma ham and wild mushrooms, and Llady Llanover's salted duck, are still on the menu, and new classics have been added. Breadcrumbed belly of pork with fennel, lemon and capers is an astonishing mixture of fatty and fresh flavours; lamb with potato torta is deeply savoury and satisfying; panna cotta with strawberries in basil syrup is a beautifully scented, summery dish.

In the Taruschios' day, no one, in the end, went to the Walnut Tree just to drink – you came to drink and eat. Yet it retained the informality of a pub, kept its little bar and gave you the freedom to order nothing more than a plate of pasta. The Walnut Tree no longer feels like a pub, though you can still come in and have a beer or a glass of wine by the fire along with a plate of warming gnocchi.

I'm including the present reincarnation of the Walnut Tree in this directory, even though it only just squeezes into the definition of being a gastropub, because this book would not be complete without a recommendation for such a seminal place: it was the Walnut Tree that first allowed the idea of the pub as a casual, lively, enjoyable place for good drink *and* good food, to take root.

the white swan

Llanfrynach
Powys
01874 665276
www.the-white-swan.com
serves lunch and dinner
weds to sun;
bookings advised;
children welcome; garden

A pukka refurbishment has been carried out on this country pub, which is tucked away in a calm and gracious village in the Brecon Beacons. The bar has oak beams, flagstones, squashy leather sofas and full-length windows looking out onto the garden. A separate dining room is a bit more swish, with exposed brickwork, ceramic lamps, upholstered chairs and driftwood on the walls.

The menu visits all corners of the globe. There's a good choice of pubby dishes and more high-flown ones: local sausages with bacon and chive mash and onion gravy, chilli polenta with chargrilled chicken and an aubergine and pepper relish, pheasant terrine with foie gras and caramelized apples. They also do a good ploughman's with home-made chutney and pickles and an ace steak sandwich (something I wish was on more pub menus), here with caramelized onions and flat mushrooms.

Some dishes, such as a salad of roasted Mediterranean vegetables with goat's cheese, are really well done and good value for money; others seem to fall at the last hurdle. A beautifully cooked bit of cod on a bed of pea purée came without its advertised slow-roast tomatoes, but instead had a drizzle of chilli sauce which tasted as if it had come from a bottle. So, good materials, well cooked, but sometimes a slight lack of attention to detail.

A lot of money has been spent to make this a smart, modern country pub. It's so pristine that it lacks character, but given time and fine tuning in the kitchen, it will rank alongside the area's best.

the nantyffin cider mill

Brecon Road
Crickhowell
Powys
01873 810775
www.cidermill.co.uk
serves lunch and dinner
mon to sun between June
and Sept; weds to mon
Oct to May;
bookings advised;
children welcome; garden

The Nantyffin Cider Mill plays a trick on you. It's a pink, pretty-as-a-picture, roadside pub, the kind of place where you'd expect to get a good bowl of soup and a decent piece of pie. Inside, two pubby rooms, painted a startling orange-pink, are kitted out with unremarkable furniture and a collection of books on apples. Then you venture through to what they humbly refer to as the 'dining room' and your jaw drops. In a huge, beamed barn of a place – once the old apple mill – you can eat looking down on the original press, surrounded by bare stone walls and candles burning in sconces. You could easily be in a vineyard restaurant in California, and the chef and co-owner, Sean Gerrard, does have a passion for the Napa Valley. Posters from Napa vineyards adorn the walls and the wine list is full of Californian wines that you don't see anywhere else.

The cooking is modern brasserie rather than complex restaurant. There is a pie, but it's filled with wild mushrooms, sautéed leeks and melting blue cheese. There's a perfectly seasoned pink duck breast on a luscious creamy parsnip purée, a mozzarella-and-mushroom-stuffed chicken breast with grilled polenta and, for afters, a rustic compote of mulled winter fruits with cinnamon ice-cream. Though there are dishes from Turkey, Italy and France, Gerrard is obviously not bothered about fashion; he lets the excellent produce, most of which is local or home-grown, speak for itself.

The menu is the same throughout. There are guest beers as well as Marston's Pedigree, Brains SA and Buckley's IPA and micro-ciders. The staff are all touchingly proud of the place.

Bluestockings and bearded poets make pilgrimages from Hay-on-Wye to eat here during the literary festival. The rest of the time, it's well-off families out celebrating, men trying to impress their new girlfriends, and clusters of posh ladies complaining about their husbands *sotto voce*.

the salutation

Pontargothi
Carmarthenshire
01267 290336
serves lunch and dinner
mon to sun;
bookings advised;
children welcome; garden

It doesn't look like much from the outside – it's just a simple black and white roadside inn – but the 'Sal', as it's affectionately known, serves good, no-nonsense food. You can drink ales from the local Felinfoel Brewery in front of the fire in the bar, but meals are the important thing here.

The owners – Richard Potter is in charge of the kitchen while his wife, Sera, does front of house – were both trained at the Savoy, so the place is slickly run. There's plenty of traditional and homely stuff on the menu, including grilled steak and Pembrokeshire fish pie with a parsley and cheddar crust, plus some more modern dishes, such as Thai fishcakes and halibut in Parma ham with sauce vierge.

the queen's head

Glanwydden
Conwy
01492 546570
serves lunch and dinner
mon to sun;
bookings accepted;
children over 7 welcome;
patio

This cream-painted village local is just a short drive inland from the sea and there is a separate fish section on the menu, offering such dishes as moules marinière made with Conwy mussels and scallops with Llanrwst Cheddar. They take the trouble to source other good Welsh produce, such as the lamb cutlets, which are served with a plum and port sauce, and pork and leek sausages made in Conwy.

It's a great place if you're a sugar junkie, as they offer six cold and six hot puddings every day, including a sterling bread and butter pudding made with bara brith. If you just want to drink, you're also well catered for: there are guest ales, eight wines by the glass and ten malt whiskies.

The natural and the man-made meet head-on in the northwest. Kiss-me-quick Blackpool couldn't be more different from the Lake District, with its waterfalls and fellside tarns. In Lancashire, the odd brooding chimney or ruined mill, built during the Industrial Revolution, lends a note of sad grandeur to a landscape of woodland and rich grassland. In fact, industrialization has left its mark on the cooking of the whole region. Many Victorian families, in which women worked long hours outside the home, depended on cooked food shops in which they could buy potted and pressed meats, pies and sausages, fish and chips and dishes such as Lancashire hot-pot, which they could leave to cook all day.

In this era of fast food, slow-cooked dishes are dwindling, as are the well-liked cheap concoctions made from offal, such as cow-heel pie and tripe and onions. But a love of potted meats, sausages, black pudding and fish and chips remains. People here want food that is gutsy and earthy. Fashion and pretence aren't much tolerated, though the revitalization of Manchester has brought the usual parade of culinary accessories — wasabi, polenta et al — to the tables.

The good pubs in the area don't have to go far for great ingredients; some of the country's best small food producers are based in the northwest. Near Goosnargh, Ruth Kirkham makes her flowery, crumbly Lancashire cheese, while on the edge of the village Reg Johnson breeds ducks and chickens that the Roux brothers even use in their restaurants in France. Richard Woodall in

cumbria and the northwest

Waberthwaite produces superb air-dried ham and the best Cumberland sausages you'll ever taste. And small outfits are making such products as gins and fruit liqueurs flavoured with local sloes and damsons.

The northwest isn't teeming with great dining pubs, but the best are top-notch, turning out unpretentious food touched by modern and foreign influences, but with their feet on local ground. At the Mulberry Tree in Wrightington in Lancashire, chef Mark Prescott serves a just-cooked fillet of salmon with a crust of basil and Lancashire cheese. At the White Hart in Lydgate near Oldham, John Rudden updates fish and chips by serving light beer-battered haddock with a caper butter sauce and fried potatoes. At the Punch Bowl in Crosthwaite in Cumbria, Steven Doherty make pâtés, terrines and potted meats and serves them with British pickles and chutneys. And they all serve fantastic British cheeses.

Crosthwaite

Cumbria

015395 68237

www.punchbowl.fsnet.co.uk

serves lunch and dinner

tues to sun lunch;

bookings advised;

children welcome; garden

the punch bowl inn

The next time you crave comforting country cooking — rabbit in a piquant mustard sauce, succulent duck confit, melting shank of lamb with braised white beans — don't assume that you need to book a flight to Lyons or Bordeaux; just get on a train to the Lake District. Here, on the edge of a quiet valley filled with damson trees, you'll find an unassuming dining pub serving the kind of earthy, deeply flavoured dishes you dream of.

The Punch Bowl Inn looks pretty ordinary; it's built of local slate, with modern timbered windows. But the framed menus on the walls give the game away. These pay homage to some of the greatest restaurant chefs in the world — Alain Chapel, Michel Bras, Paul Bocuse — as well as Le Gavroche, The Waterside Inn, and various outposts of the Roux brothers' empire where The Punch Bowl's Steven Doherty was a star chef for more than 13 years.

Steven soaked up the Roux brothers' attitude to cooking, what he describes as their 'attention to detail, utter respect for ingredients, ceaseless perfectionism', and has applied it to rustic dishes. The result is superbly wrought bourgeois cooking that carefully mixes French and British traditions. There are pâtés and terrines with very British relishes such as quince chutney or tomato pickle, baked ham with mash, creamy cider sauce and black pudding, and a compote of sweet-tart damsons with cinnamon ice-cream and shortbread.

Doherty's desire to apply a French finesse that takes dishes to a higher plane is a passion nurtured under Albert Roux, with whom he perfected the recipe for lemon tart and made it a classic. This quest makes him wrestle with the simplest of dishes. Shank of lamb with beans, for example, always bothered him. The shank was slow-cooked to mouth-watering tenderness, but the skin around it was always flabby. So he now double-cooks the lamb shanks, braising them until the meat is almost falling off the bone, then scattering them with parsley and garlic crumbs and grilling them to get a crispy finish. Every dish shows this desire to maximize flavour, to improve texture.

Doherty left London, and his stellar career, because he was sick of city life. He decided to cook in a pub, rather than a restaurant, because, as he puts it: 'I wanted to cook in a place where the car park would have Nissans beside Mercedes, where people could afford to eat good food regularly.' At the Punch Bowl, you can eat something as simple as a great ham sandwich at lunchtime, and saddle of rabbit with wild mushrooms in the evening. And it'll cost you less than eating at many of the chain restaurants up and down the country.

Tell anyone in Cumbria that you're interested in good places to eat and they'll say, 'Oh you'll want Steven Doherty's then — the Punch Bowl. Best place to eat in the Lakes.' And they're right: it's the best place to eat in the Lakes, and way, way beyond.

salad of baked goat's cheese with roast beetroot and a walnut oil dressing

Goat's cheese and beetroot is a marriage made in heaven. If you don't want to be bothered with pastry, you could just put the bread on warm circles of toasted bread.

serves 4

2 medium beetroot

50g (1¾oz) unsalted butter, melted

2 sheets filo pastry (Steven likes to use Jus Rol)

1/2 goat's cheese log, rind scraped off and cut into 4 x 2cm (3/4 inch) slices

black pepper

olive oil

24 button onions, peeled

a little peanut oil

generous handful of frisée, watercress or lamb's lettuce

15ml (1tbsp) walnut oil dressing

1 Preheat the oven to 200°C/400°F/gas mark 6. Scrub the beetroots, wrap tightly in aluminium foil and bake for 2½ hours, or until tender, in the hot oven.

2 Leave to cool, then peel and cut into thick wedges. (The beetroots are best baked a day ahead – they will keep for up to a week in the refrigerator.)

3 Brush the melted butter on a sheet of filo pastry and lay another sheet on top. Cut out 4 x 7cm (2¾ inch) circles, and place on a greased baking sheet and bake in the preheated oven for about 5 minutes, until golden brown.

4 Turn up the oven to 240°C/475°F/gas mark 9. Put the goat's cheese on top of the pastry, season with freshly ground black pepper, drizzle with olive oil and bake in the very hot oven, or under a hot grill, for about 5 minutes, until the cheese is golden and melting.

5 Put the beetroot wedges on a baking sheet, pour on a little olive oil and season with black pepper, then roast for 5 minutes. Meanwhile, fry the onions in the peanut oil until they are golden on the outside and tender in the middle.

6 Toss the watercress, lamb's lettuce or frisée with the walnut oil dressing. Arrange on 4 plates or in deep bowls, place the goat's cheese pastry on top and the beetroot and onions around it.

walnut oil dressing

5ml (1tsp) Dijon mustard

salt and pepper

25ml (1½tbsp) walnut oil

45ml (3tbsp) sunflower oil

12.5ml (2½tsp) white wine vinegar

1 Whisk the mustard with the salt and pepper in a medium-sized bowl.

2 Gradually add the oils and wine vinegar, whisking continuously until combined.

smoked haddock and mash with grain mustard sauce and poached egg

The ultimate in comfort food, this is typical of the northwest's love of honest, down-to-earth dishes with a modern twist.

serves 4

1kg (2lb 3oz) potatoes, Maris Piper or Ratte, peeled

sea salt

255g (9oz) unsalted butter, softened

ground white pepper

freshly grated nutmeg

2 large naturally smoked, undyed haddock fillets, halved

full-fat milk

for the grain-mustard sauce

255ml (9fl oz) double cream

10ml (2tsp) grain mustard

5ml (1tsp) Dijon mustard

15ml (1tbsp) white wine vinegar

4 medium eggs, very fresh

1 Cut the potatoes into large dice and cook in boiling, salted water until soft. Drain well and put through a sieve or a *mouli-légume*.

2 Beat in the softened butter, then season with white pepper and a grating of nutmeg to taste. Keep warm.

3 In a shallow pan, poach the fish in water with a splash of milk to cover and simmer for 8 minutes. (Do not add salt.)

4 While the fish is poaching, bring the cream to the boil in a heavy-bottomed pan, whisk in the grain and Dijon mustards and add a pinch of salt. Keep warm.

5 Remove the fish from the poaching liquid and peel off the skin. Neatly spoon some mashed potato onto 4 warmed plates, place the haddock on top, coat with the sauce and gently place a soft-poached egg on top of the fish.

soft-poached eggs

1 Fill a deep saucepan with water, bring to the boil and add the vinegar.

2 Break an egg into a teacup and tip very gently into the water at the point when it is bubbling. Quickly add the other 3 eggs, one at a time, and poach for 3–4 minutes with the water at a rolling boil.

3 Using a slotted spoon, remove the first egg and press with your fingertip to check that is properly cooked – the white should be set but soft to the touch.

'good eating shouldn't just be for a special occasion. i hoped that by cooking in a pub more people would get great food more often.' steven

pan-fried breast of chicken on creamy leeks with black pudding

They use Woodall's Cumbrian pancetta for this at The Punch Bowl, but you can use Italian stuff if you can't get hold of that.

serves 4

2 large leeks

4 x 200g (7oz) chicken breasts with wing attached, skin on and partly boned

plain flour

salt and pepper

sunflower oil

100g (3¾oz) unsalted butter

125g (4½oz) or 8 strips of Woodall's Cumbrian pancetta

200g (7oz) black pudding, cut into roughly 1.5cm (½ inch) dice

½ garlic clove, chopped

75g (2¾oz) Parmesan cheese, freshly grated

255ml (9fl oz) whipping cream

1 Preheat the oven to 240°C/475°F/gas mark 9. Trim the leeks, top and bottom, and split each one into 4 lengthways. Cut into 1cm (⅜ inch) dice. Wash well and drain. Remove any excess skin around the edges of the chicken breasts and wing.

2 Lightly dust the chicken with flour and season with salt and pepper. In a heavy-bottomed frying pan, heat a splash of sunflower oil and half the butter. When hot, add the chicken breasts, flesh side down, and quickly fry on both sides until golden brown. Put the chicken on a baking tray and bake for about 10 minutes. Remove from the oven and keep warm.

3 Turn the oven down to 220°C/425°F/gas mark 7. Bake the pancetta on a baking sheet for 10–15 minutes, until it's crispy. Brush the black pudding with a little oil and bake in a baking dish for 5 minutes. Remove and blot on kitchen paper.

4 Melt the remaining butter in a large heavy-bottomed saucepan. Add the leeks, season, and sweat over a medium heat until soft – the leeks must not fry or colour. Make some béchamel sauce (recipe below) and mix this together with the leeks, garlic and two-thirds of the Parmesan cheese. Add the cream and bring back to the boil. Simmer for 5 minutes, then remove from the heat and keep warm.

5 To serve, slice the chicken breasts in half. Spoon the leek béchamel into a gratin dish, place the chicken on top and arrange the black pudding around it. Sprinkle with the remaining Parmesan cheese and cook under a hot grill until golden brown. Scatter the pancetta on top of the chicken and serve.

béchamel sauce

50g (1¾oz) butter

50g (1¾oz) plain flour

565ml (1 pint) full-fat milk

salt and white pepper

freshly grated nutmeg

1 Melt the butter in a pan. Combine the flour with the butter and cook, stirring, for 4 minutes. Remove from the heat, gradually whisk in the milk, blending well after each addition, and season with salt, a pinch of white pepper and nutmeg. Bring to the boil, whisking continuously. Simmer for 5 minutes. Pour the sauce into a clean bowl, cover with clingfilm and keep warm.

seared duck breast with braised red cabbage and damson-fig sauce

Steven is fond of using the damsons from the valley below the pub, but he suggests using soaked dried apricots instead if you can't get hold of damsons. The red cabbage is also great with venison, pheasant, or even a good meaty pork chop.

serves 4

1kg (2lb 3oz) damsons

1kg (2lb 3oz) granulated sugar

4 fresh figs, quartered

balsamic vinegar

255ml (9fl oz) beef stock

4 x 180g (6½oz) Barbary duck breasts

salt and pepper

to serve

4 fresh figs (optional)

Demerara sugar

1 Put the damsons, sugar and 500ml (18fl oz) water into a heavy-bottomed pan and bring to the boil, then simmer for 10 minutes. Strain into a clean bowl. (This will keep for about 2 weeks in the refrigerator.) Return the damson syrup to the pan, add the figs and boil until it has reduced by half. Add a splash of vinegar and the stock and reduce by half again. Strain through a fine sieve.

2 Preheat the oven to 220°C/425°F/gas mark 7. Trim the excess fat from the duck breasts and lightly season. Put the duck breasts into a very hot frying pan, fat side down, and quickly sear on both sides for about 5 minutes, until golden brown. Put into a roasting tin and finish off in the preheated oven for 5 minutes, if you want pink meat, or 10 minutes if you want it well done.

3 Quarter the remaining figs, if using, sprinkle with demerara sugar and gently grill for about 3 minutes. Arrange the braised red cabbage on 4 warmed plates. Thickly slice each duck breast and place on the cabbage, then pour over the damson fig sauce and garnish with the grilled figs.

braised red cabbage

200ml (7fl oz) duck fat

3 red onions, finely sliced

1 small red cabbage, finely shredded

salt and pepper

150ml (5½fl oz) red wine

10ml (2tsp) each ground cumin and ground coriander

1 clove garlic, minced

10ml (2tsp) demerara sugar

1 large Bramley apple, peeled, cored and cut into chunks

1 Preheat the oven to 150°C/300°F/gas mark 2. Heat a heavy-bottomed pan, then add the duck fat, sliced onions and cabbage and mix well. Season lightly with salt and pepper and sweat with the lid on for 15 minutes.

2 Add the red wine, spices, garlic, sugar and apple and again mix well. Replace the lid and braise in the slow oven for 1 hour.

toffee apple ice-cream

Steven started to make this with the caramelized apples from left-over bits of tarte tatin. It's not the kind of thing you have hanging round all the time, so this is a version where you caramelize the apples specially for the ice-cream.

serves 4–8

125g (4½oz) unsalted butter

125g (4½oz) caster sugar

4 large Cox's apples, peeled, halved and cored

for the custard base

10 medium egg yolks

225g (8oz) caster sugar

1 vanilla pod, split

565ml (1 pint) full-fat milk

bowl of ice

1 Put the butter into an aluminium or copper sauté pan, then add the sugar and apples, rounded side down. Place over a moderate heat and caramelize gently until the apples are golden and soft. This will take up to 25 minutes. (Take great care as this mixture is extremely hot and could burn you badly.)

2 Place the cooked apples in a bowl, mash with a whisk and allow to cool.

3 Make the custard for the ice-cream by whisking together the egg yolks, sugar and scraped out insides of the vanilla pod.

4 In a heavy-bottomed pan, bring the milk to the boil with the split vanilla pod. Remove the vanilla pod and pour the milk into the egg mixture, whisking continuously. Pour this custard into a clean pan and stir over a moderate heat for about 5 minutes, until it just coats the back of a wooden spoon – do not boil or it will curdle.

5 Remove immediately from the heat, strain through a fine sieve into a clean bowl, using the back of a ladle to push the custard through. Whisk, over a bowl of ice, until the mixture is cool.

6 Whisk the apples into the cooled custard and churn in an ice-cream maker.

the best
of the
rest

the mulberry tree

9 Wrightington Bar
Wrightington
Lancashire
01257 451400
serves lunch and dinner
mon to sun lunch;
bookings advised;
children welcome; terrace

The cooking here, as you might expect from a Roux brothers' alumnus, is ace. Mark Prescott, chef and co-owner, turns out terrific renditions of pub classics such as steak and kidney pudding and fish and chips with tartare sauce, which here comes wrapped in pages of the *FT*, as well as refined French dishes, such as lobster with Champagne and herb sauce, and more modern brasserie food, such as teriyaki-glazed sea-bass.

Puddings are a mix of British old-timers, such as apple and blackberry crumble or bitter marmalade bread and butter pudding, and classic French sweets, such as rhum baba with raspberries and Chantilly cream. Whatever your mood, you're spoilt for choice, and even though the menu is long, every dish is well executed.

You can eat either in the restaurant, which has white linen and a menu made up of the more complicated, luxurious dishes, or in the big, open, brasserie-style bar, where you're just as welcome to have a drink as to dine. The only downside here is the decor, which is expensive but has the corporate feel of a hotel bar. A makeover costing a fraction of the money could have produced a place with more character. But the cooking's the thing at the Mulberry Tree: go for the food.

drunken duck inn

Barngates
Ambleside
Cumbria
015394 36347
www.drunkenduckinn.co.uk
serves lunch and dinner
mon to sun;
bookings accepted
(dining room only);
children welcome; garden

A 17th-century hostelry, surrounded by craggy fells and with Lake Windermere in its sights, the Drunken Duck is one of the loveliest destinations in this part of the world. The small, relaxed bar, with settles and spindle-backed chairs, has been refurbished but is still cosily pubby, with hops hanging from the ceiling and old prints on the walls. You can eat here, or in the smart, simple dining rooms.

The talented chef, Nick Spencer, is at his best with the simpler dishes served at lunchtime, such as Cumberland sausages with chilli roast potatoes or lemon sole with prawns and leeks. The evening is more risky, as the kitchen goes into ambitious over-drive. Some dishes, such as 'venison marinated in espresso on sautéed greens and chestnuts with a fig and vanilla confit', are just too complicated to pull off.

But the simpler dinner dishes, such as roast monkfish with wild mushrooms, leeks and a mussel butter sauce, are very good and the basic ingredients are high quality. Desserts, such as tarte tatin of Granny Smith apples with clotted cream ice-cream, are much more restrained, and well done.

The inn's own brewery, Barngates, makes some really good ales (they even make an ice-cream from the hoppiest one, which is called Taglag), and there's a very interesting wine list too.

the mill bank

Mill Bank

near Sowerby Bridge

West Yorkshire

01422 825588

www.themillbank.com

serves lunch and dinner

tues dinner to sun lunch;

bookings accepted

(dining room only);

children welcome; garden

Anyone who wants to open a modern gastropub should come and look at the Mill Bank, because owners Paul and Christine Halsey really know how to do it.

The Halseys bought this old stone pub in a pretty village near Sowerby Bridge, gutted it, filled the garden with bits of funky iron sculpture and added a wooden verandah at the back where you can dine looking out over the brooding West Yorkshire countryside. Christine Halsey is an architect, and the space she has created is clean-lined but feels as cosy and warm as any old-fashioned country pub. There's a smaller 'snug' room to one side of the bar, with low tables, a flagstone floor and a fire, and a large open dining room round the rest of the bar. The furniture is cherry wood, the walls are either bare stone or painted in mauve, rust and burnt orange. The Halsey's really have created a modern boozer.

Bar snacks run to beer-battered cod on pea purée and fried egg and chorizo sandwich, and there's a longer menu with slightly more fancy food for the dining room. The cooking is modern European with a few Yorkshire touches: black pudding with roasted red onions and mustard dressing, and belly of local pork braised with honey and cloves. Sourcing is important here. Both the chicken and the duck come from Reg Johnson in Goosnargh, Lancashire, and there's a top-class, constantly changing range of Yorkshire cheeses, such as Swaledale with Theakston's Old Peculiar, Ribblesdale goat's cheese and a gorgeous mature Wensleydale called King Richard III.

The cooking is slick and not too fussy, the operation is professional and caring (endless patience is shown to difficult children), and punters from every age group seem to have a whale of a time.

the white hart

51 Stockport Road,

Lydgate

Greater Manchester

01457 872566

www.thewhitehart.co.uk

serves lunch and dinner

mon to sun;

bookings advised;

children welcome; garden

When the White Hart, a 200-year-old stone inn on the edge of Saddleworth Moor, was refurbished and re-launched in 1995, it quickly established itself as a place worth travelling to, and has gone from strength to strength.

The White Hart tries to please everyone. There's a proper drinking bar with small tables and banquettes around the walls, and two cosy dining rooms with wine-coloured walls, velvet curtains and dark polished tables. The owners describe these as 'pub/brasserie' but the big fireplace, beams and country prints make it feel more pub than brasserie, even if the china is smart and the chairs upholstered. There's also a cool, contemporary dining room – wood block floor and walls covered in modern art. The menu is the same throughout.

This pub is a real good-time place, absolutely brimming at the weekends, and anything goes. Walkers come in wearing t-shirts and trainers, gaggles of girls on a good night out sport sequins and tiaras. You'll rarely see such a varied clientele, and they'll all be enjoying themselves – noisily.

The food, cooked by chef and co-owner John Rudden, is terrific. It's mostly modern brasserie fare – Caesar salad, crab-stuffed chicken with noodles – but there are a few clever spins on British dishes, like a 'full English breakfast terrine' (sausage, bacon, mushroom, black pudding and egg with tomato relish), and calves' liver with black pudding fritters and pickled red cabbage. Sausages are made on the premises – everything from chicken and smoked bacon to wild boar and apple – and offered with no fewer than four different types of mash, including Dijon mustard and spring onion and garlic.

yorkshire and the northeast

This is a vast area. The poet, Simon Armitage, has described Yorkshire as 'the county with more acres than there are letters in the bible'. The landscape is certainly more varied than that of many countries. Standing on a flat-topped, heather-carpeted moor, you can turn 360 degrees and see the landscape disappear over the horizon on all sides. The Yorkshire dales can feel as harsh as the limestone with which they are scattered, but in the greenness of summer they become softer, a place to drink a pint listening to the bleating of sheep. In Northumberland, there are long stretches of empty white beach. This region is a world in itself.

Perhaps that's why the food in pubs here tends to be more distinctly regional than in many other areas of Britain. Some of the very best chefs here are cooking in pubs, and many of them — Andrew Pern at the Star in Harome, Frances Atkins at the Yorke Arms in Ramsgill, Bruce Elsworth at the Angel in Hetton — were born here and have returned. This connection has a profound affect on their food: they want to cook with the ingredients they grew up with; to rediscover the produce of a place they have reclaimed. You

only have to look at Andrew Pern's menu — fillet of beef with stock-pot carrots and dark ale, black pudding with foie gras and scrumpy, ginger parkin with rhubarb ripple ice-cream — to see that he isn't just using local produce; he, and chefs like him, are looking anew at familiar ingredients and British dishes.

Using local produce is worn as a badge of honour here. Maybe this is because pride in regionalism is not considered unseemly. Particular ingredients turn up again and again. Black pudding is used in more ways than you could imagine: with scallops, in salad, in cassoulet, in stuffings. Pork, particularly belly of pork, is on nearly every menu: slow-roasted and served with mustard mash and wild mushrooms, or cut into chunks and tossed in a salad with bacon, sauté potatoes and poached egg. Fish comes from Whitby, game is shot on the moors and sweet lamb is farmed on the dales. But among the most abundant and adored foods here are the local cheeses: you'll find them in such dishes as Yorkshire blue and spinach risotto, an omelette filled with Cotherstone and summer herbs, a tart of tomatoes and Ribblesdale goat's cheese.

Outstanding dining pubs, such as the Star, the Yorke Arms and the Angel, are sending out ripples. New dining pubs are opening all the time, and this is hardly surprising when you think of the region's role in their evolution. The first dining pub in Britain was the Walnut Tree Inn in Wales, but the next landmark establishment was the Angel in Hetton, opened by Denis Watkins in 1983. Denis thought the combination of great beer and good food in a pub — the place in which the British, and particularly Yorkshire people, feel most at ease — was a winner. He could never have imagined quite how far that simple idea would go.

High Street
Harome
North Yorkshire
01439 770397
www.thestaratharome.co.uk
serves lunch and dinner
tues to sun lunch;
bookings accepted
(dining room only);
children welcome; garden

the star inn

Three years before they bestowed a star here, the Michelin inspector told the chef and owner, Andrew Pern, that he had to decide what he was running: The Star Inn could either be a pub or a restaurant, but it couldn't be both. The star, when it came, was vindication of Andrew's insistence that it could.

Andrew Pern is an exceptional cook. He could work anywhere, but he has never wanted to own a restaurant. He loves pubs, and he saw running a pub not just as a job, but as a way of life. He wanted to open a place where the dominoes team could play a game over a decent pork pie, where cricketers could tuck into a top-notch ploughman's, and those who wanted to splash out could eat foie gras. He's as proud of the fact that you might find 30 locals in his bar on a Sunday night, boogying to old Rolling Stones hits, as he is of the rave reviews and accolades for his cooking.

The same food is served in the bar – with its warm fires and organically shaped wooden tables carved by Yorkshireman 'Mousey' Thompson – and the dining room – an elegant, cosy place with homely corner cupboards, occasional tables and piles of books. The wine labels on the ceiling, the cheese trolley, and the sideboard groaning with liqueurs, make the place feel like a French auberge, and France was a potent influence in Andrew's upbringing. His mother, a French teacher, made the family speak in French on Sunday evenings, and with his father, a farmer, he used to forage for wild mushrooms, go shooting and make liqueurs from local fruits.

This has resulted in a cooking style that is an English version of 'cuisine terroir'. But Andrew's food is not stuck in the past. He has the ability to look at familiar ingredients and old-fashioned dishes and, with skill, imagination and taste, create something new. He turns the old pub classic of gammon and pineapple on its head by serving a ham terrine with a fried quail's egg and pineapple pickle, and he gives Yorkshire baking a new spin by serving old-fashioned ginger parkin with rhubarb ripple ice-cream.

Andrew sources locally because the produce is good and he likes the circular wholeness of chatting to the farmer who raises his beef over a pint in the bar. Whatever he can't get locally he has encouraged farmers to produce – he helped one set up a business raising free-range chickens – and he grows some of his own vegetables. He's proud of the fact that the pink fir apple potatoes that end up on your plate in the evening were still in the ground at five o'clock.

The food at The Star is individual, generous, exuberant and cooked with consummate skill. But it isn't the whole story. When you eat here, you feel that the place, the food, the cook and the customers are all connected. You do leave The Star feeling well-fed – but you also leave it feeling that life is great. And you can't wait to come back.

terrine of yorkshire gammon with fried quail's egg and spiced pineapple pickle

This is a great spin on the old pub standard, grilled gammon steak and pineapple. It takes less effort than you'd think — all the stages are easy — and it looks stunning.

serves 10

3 ham knuckles

6 bay leaves, 6 cloves and 6 black peppercorns

1 large onion, halved

2 medium carrots, halved

6-8 thin slices York ham

olive oil

1 shallot, finely chopped

salt and pepper

20g (3/4oz) flat-leaf parsley, finely chopped

2 gelatine leaves

pinch of ground mixed spice

10 quail's eggs

olive oil, for frying

55g (2oz) mixed leaves and herbs, eg chervil, wild rocket

for the pineapple pickle

1 pineapple, skinned, cored and finely chopped

1 clove garlic, crushed

5ml (1tsp) grain mustard

60ml (4tbsp) white wine vinegar

pinch of saffron strands

150g (5 1/2oz) demerara sugar

for the dressing

75ml (5tbsp) each of Pommery mustard, extra virgin olive oil and cider vinegar

1 Put the ham knuckles, bay leaves, cloves, peppercorns, onion and carrots in a large saucepan. Cover with cold water, bring to the boil and simmer for 2½–3 hours, until the meat is tender.

2 Meanwhile, line a 20 x 8cm (8 x 3½ inch) terrine mould with clingfilm, then line with the York ham. Heat a little olive oil in a small pan and gently sweat the shallot.

3 Remove the cooked ham knuckles from the pan, leave to cool slightly, then, while warm, remove the meat in pieces from the bone. Place in a small bowl with the shallots, seasoning and parsley. Mix thoroughly, then pack into the terrine mould. Soak the gelatine in cold water for 5 minutes, until soft.

4 Strain the ham stock. Taste and, if it is too salty, dilute with water. Pour 500ml (18fl oz) into a pan and add the mixed spice. Warm gently and add the soaked gelatine; leave for 2–3 minutes for the gelatine to dissolve before stirring. Pour into the terrine. Overlap the edges of York ham to cover the roughly torn ham pieces.

5 Cover with clingfilm; the terrine needs to be quite solid and 'packed'. Put a uniform weight on the terrine to press it down and leave overnight in the fridge.

6 To make the spiced pineapple pickle, put all the ingredients into a heavy-bottomed pan. Simmer gently for 1½ hours, stirring occasionally, until it's golden yellow and the consistency of runny honey. Spoon into an airtight jar and leave to cool. (It will keep for 3–4 weeks in a cool place.)

7 To make the mustard seed dressing, simply whisk all the ingredients together.

8 To serve, turn out the terrine, unwrap the clingfilm, then, using a sharp knife, cut into 2cm (⁴⁄5 inch) slices and place each in the centre of a cold dinner plate.

9 Shallow fry the quails' eggs in olive oil. On each plate, spoon 3 piles of pineapple pickle around the terrine, placing a few leaves between each. Put a fried egg on top, grind over a little black pepper and drizzle with dressing. Serve immediately.

risotto of fadmoor beetroot with a deep-fried blue wensleydale beignet and wild garlic pesto

Fadmoor is a village 5 miles from Harome, where Newfield Organics, run by the Wass family, produces all sorts of root and leaf vegetables. Andrew loves this risotto as the beetroot, blue Wensleydale and garlic are all earthy ingredients but still make an elegant dish with great colours. If you can't find wild garlic, then make the pesto with baby spinach leaves and extra garlic.

serves 4

870ml (31fl oz) vegetable stock

310g (11oz) arborio rice

425g (15oz) beetroot

255ml (9fl oz) full-bodied fruity red wine, eg Shiraz

50ml (1³/₄tbsp) whipping cream

50g (1³/₄oz) blue Wensleydale cheese, finely grated

50g (1³/₄oz) baby spinach, shredded

salt and pepper

sprigs of chervil or dill

for the beignets

olive oil

1 small shallot, finely diced

100g (3³/₄oz) blue Wensleydale cheese

15g (1tbsp) finely chopped fresh sage

1 medium egg, beaten

50g (1³/₄oz) fine white breadcrumbs

vegetable oil, for deep-frying

30g (1oz) pine nuts, toasted

155ml (5¹/₂fl oz) extra virgin olive oil

2 cloves garlic, crushed

2 handfuls wild garlic leaves

50g (1³/₄oz) Parmesan cheese, finely grated

1 To make the beignets, heat a drop of olive oil in a small pan and sweat the shallot. Blend this with the cheese and sage and form 3cm (1¼ inch) balls. Chill for 20 minutes. Dip each ball in beaten egg, then coat with breadcrumbs. Set aside.

2 To make the risotto, put the stock in a small saucepan and simmer over a low heat. Heat a heavy bottomed-pan and add the rice and a ladleful of hot stock. Stir until all the liquid has been absorbed. Continue adding the stock, a ladleful at a time, stirring constantly, until the rice is *al dente* and all the liquid has been absorbed. Remove from the heat and spread it out on a tray to cool.

3 Boil the beetroot in a deep pan, with 200ml (7fl oz) of the red wine and enough water to cover, for 15–20 minutes, until tender. Peel and purée.

4 Put the cooked rice into a heavy-bottomed pan, add the beetroot purée, cream, cheese and the remaining red wine. Bind together and simmer for 4–5 minutes, season, then add the spinach. Season to taste. Spoon the risotto onto 4 warmed plates.

5 Heat the vegetable oil for the beignets and, when hot, deep-fry them for 20 seconds, until golden brown. Drain on kitchen paper and place on the risotto. Garnish with a sprig of chervil or dill and drizzle the pesto around the base of the risotto. Serve immediately.

garlic pesto

1 Liquidize everything together. Check seasoning.

2 Store in an airtight tub in the refrigerator. Use within 1–2 weeks.

roast loin of ryedale lamb with asparagus, goat's cheese and lavender

This, says Andrew, is summer on a plate. He presents it in quite a cheffy way, but you may prefer to just put the asparagus and creamed cheese beside the salad and lamb when cooking this at home. The goat's cheese he uses is made by Mr and Mrs Newton in the Esk Valley, which is where Andrew comes from.

serves 4

4 x 115g (4oz) lamb loins from the saddle

10ml (2tsp) Pommery mustard

2 sprigs of lavender, leaves, roughly chopped

2 x Grosmont goat's cheeses or any fresh, soft variety of goat's cheese, each weighing approximately 100g (3¾oz)

5ml (1tsp) whipping cream

5g (1tsp) black peppercorns, cracked

15g (1tbsp) finely chopped fresh chives

olive oil, for frying

200g (7oz) wild rocket leaves and soft garden herbs, such as oregano and flat-leaf parsley

12 medium asparagus spears, trimmed and blanched

for the garlic croutons

2 slices wholemeal bread, 1cm (3/8 inch) thick

115g (4oz) butter, softened

1/2 clove garlic, crushed

for the vinaigrette

45ml (3tbsp) each of Pommery mustard, extra virgin olive oil and cider vinegar

5ml (1tsp) runny honey

1 Trim the lamb loins, then roll in the grain mustard and then the chopped lavender leaves. Wrap tightly in clingfilm and chill until ready to cook.

2 For the garlic croûtons, preheat the oven to 190°C/375°F/gas mark 5. Remove the crusts from the bread and cut it into 1cm (⅜ inch) cubes. Melt the butter in a small pan with the garlic – do not let it boil. Then add the bread cubes and stir until thoroughly coated with butter. Place on a small baking sheet and bake in the preheated oven for 8 minutes, until crisp and golden. Leave to cool.

3 For the mustard and honey vinaigrette, simply whisk all the ingredients together.

4 Cream the goat's cheese in a blender for 2–3 minutes, adding a touch of cream to slacken if necessary – the mixture should stand in peaks. Season with cracked black peppercorns and chives.

5 Unwrap the lamb. Heat a little olive oil in a frying pan and fry the meat for 2–3 minutes on each side, until an even crust forms. Lift out of the pan and rest.

6 Pipe or spoon 3 pyramids of goat's cheese at triangular points on 4 plates. Arrange the wild rocket, garden herbs and croûtons in the centre of the plate, and 1 asparagus spear between each pyramid. Cut each lamb loin into 5 slices and arrange on top of the salad.

7 Drizzle some vinaigrette around the plate and over the lamb to give it a little shine and serve immediately.

caramelized rice pudding with somerset apple brandy and boozy prunes

Andrew rather modestly describes this dish as 'autumn fuel at its comforting best'.
Actually, it propels humble rice pudding into the stellar league. Cracking stuff.

serves 4

255g (9oz) arborio rice

1/2 vanilla pod, split and seeds scraped out

5ml (1tsp) vanilla extract

5ml (1tsp) ground mixed spice

45ml (3tbsp) Somerset apple brandy

pinch of grated nutmeg

300ml (10 1/2fl oz) double cream

700ml (24fl oz) full-fat milk

200g (7oz) caster sugar, or to taste

20g (4tsp) demerara sugar, for caramelizing

1 Place all the rice pudding ingredients, except the milk and sugars, in a heavy-bottomed pan over a medium heat. Stir for 2–3 minutes, then add the milk. Bring to the boil, cover with buttered greaseproof paper, then simmer for ¾–1 hour, until the rice is soft and tender. Sweeten to taste with caster sugar.

2 Spoon into 4 x 7.5cm (3inch) copper pans or ramekins, sprinkle with demerara sugar and caramelize with a blow-torch, or place as high as possible under a very hot grill, until the sugar melts and blisters.

3 Serve immediately on 4 warmed plates, with 3 mulled prunes on each.

boozy prunes

150g (5 1/2oz) caster sugar

45ml (3tbsp) cooking brandy

12 Agen prunes, pitted

1 Put the sugar and brandy in a small heavy-bottomed pan with 150ml (5½fl oz) water. Bring to the boil, stirring to dissolve the sugar, then boil vigorously to reduce by half.

2 Add the prunes and warm through.

'the michelin inspector told me that we couldn't be both a restaurant and a pub. i said that maybe we were just unique.' andrew

baked ginger parkin with rhubarb ripple ice-cream and hot spiced syrup

This is the dish for which The Star has become most famous. It's also Andrew's favourite. The cake itself is a Yorkshire favourite on bonfire night. The rhubarb comes from the 'Yorkshire triangle', home of English forced rhubarb. Andrew is very proud that the *Guardian's* restaurant critic, Matthew Fort, made it his dish of the year, describing it as 'a brilliant addition to the roll of honour of British puddings, tarty, tasty, spicy, racy and plum duff delicious'.

serves 8

100g (3³/₄oz) self-raising flour

10g (2tsp) ground ginger

2.5g (¹/₂tsp) each of ground nutmeg and mixed spice

80g (2³/₄oz) oatflakes

175g (6¹/₄oz) golden syrup

50g (1³/₄oz) black treacle

100g (3³/₄oz) unsalted butter

100g (3³/₄oz) soft brown sugar

1 medium egg, beaten

10ml (2tsp) full-fat milk

8 chunks cooked rhubarb, to serve (optional)

for the hot spiced syrup

200g (7oz) golden syrup

10ml (2tsp) dry cider

21/2g (1/2tsp) ground mixed spice

for the ice cream

6 medium egg yolks

100g (3³/₄oz) caster sugar

¹/₂ vanilla pod, split

200ml (7fl oz) full-fat milk

250ml (9fl oz) double cream

255g (9oz) rhubarb, in 1cm (3/8 inch) lengths

50g (1³/₄oz) caster sugar

1 Preheat the oven to 140°C/275°F/gas mark 1. Butter a 20cm (8 inch) square cake tin.

2 Sieve the flour, a pinch of salt, the ginger, nutmeg and mixed spice together into a large bowl. Mix in the oatflakes.

3 Warm the tins of syrup and treacle in hot water to make it easier to measure them out accurately. Put the syrup, treacle, butter and soft brown sugar into a small saucepan and melt over a gentle heat – bring up to a simmer but do not boil. Stir into the flour mixture.

4 Mix in the beaten egg and milk to create a soft, almost pouring, consistency. Pour into the buttered tin. Bake for 1¼ hours, until firm in the centre. Remove from the oven and leave in the tin for 5–10 minutes before turning out and cutting into squares.

5 For the hot spiced syrup, simply whisk all the ingredients together in a small pan and warm, but don't boil.

6 Serve the parkin immediately with a scoop of ice-cream and the hot spiced syrup, garnished with cooked rhubarb if you wish. Alternatively, leave to cool on a wire rack, then store in an airtight container. For the best flavour, leave for 3 weeks.

rhubarb ripple ice-cream

1 Use the first five ingredients to make the custard (follow method on page 163, but add the cream with the milk). Leave to cool.

2 Stew the rhubarb with a splash of water and the sugar until tender. Coax through a sieve into a saucepan. Bring to the boil and reduce by three-quarters.

3 Pour the cold custard into an ice-cream machine and churn. Alternatively pour into a freezerproof container, put in the freezer and beat every 20 minutes, until set. When nearly frozen, add the purée to give a ripple effect, then turn off the machine.

Hetton
North Yorkshire
01756 730263
www.angelhetton.co.uk
serves lunch and dinner
mon to sun; bookings accepted
for early tables in bar (weekends
only) and for restaurant;
children welcome; terrace

the angel inn

Back in the 1980s, when the buzz was all celebrity chefs and gold card dining, Denis Watkins, who had trained as a chef and worked in hotel management, had the foresight to buy a run-down pub in the Yorkshire Dales. 'Everyone was obsessed with fine dining,' says Denis, 'and we had a love-hate relationship with pubs: we loved the idea of them, but were often disappointed with the reality. I thought if I could put really good food into a characterful pub it would be the perfect combination, our equivalent of the French bistro or *auberge*, a place where everyone could drink and eat without needing a special occasion.'

So he restored the Angel, revealing its beams, stone walls and fireplaces, and opened its doors in 1983. Before long, punters could sit with a pint of Black Sheep and a dish of top-notch cassoulet or Lancashire hot-pot. The Angel became a standard bearer for dining pubs, and it's still one of the best in the country.

The food is a mixture of robust country stuff and modern brasserie fare, all slickly executed. Sourcing is as local as possible and everything – even their delicious, fruity black pudding – is made in-house. There are now plans to produce more *charcuterie*. The Angel may have been at the top for more than 20 years, but it's not resting on its laurels.

seared tuna salad niçoise

No, it isn't authentic, as in Nice they don't make salad niçoise with seared tuna –
or quail's eggs, come to that. But I think this is even better than the original. If
you can't find anchovies packed in salt, then use anchovies tinned in olive oil,
drained, soaked in a little milk, drained again and patted dry.

serves 4

8 medium new potatoes

90g (3½oz) extra fine green
beans, topped and tailed

12 quail's eggs

olive oil

8 anchovies in salt, rinsed

20 black olives, pitted

12 vine-ripened cherry
tomatoes, halved

255g (9oz) lamb's lettuce

Maldon sea salt and pepper

4 x 170g (6oz) tuna loin steaks

lemon juice

for the vinaigrette

makes 285ml (½ pint)

1 clove garlic

1 small shallot

5ml (1tsp) Dijon mustard

15ml (1tbsp) runny honey

sea salt and pepper, to taste

juice of ½ lemon

70ml (2½fl oz) white wine
vinegar

70ml (2½fl oz) extra virgin
olive oil

140ml (5fl oz) vegetable oil

caster sugar, to taste

1 Cook the potatoes until tender, drain and leave to cool. Skin.

2 Plunge the green beans into a pan of boiling, salted water. Cook for 4 minutes,
until *al dente*, then drain and refresh in very cold water.

3 Place the quail's eggs in a pan of boiling water. Bring back to the boil and cook
for 2 minutes. Refresh in cold water, shell and cut in half.

4 Slice the new potatoes into small wedges or cut in half lengthways, brush with
olive oil and chargrill.

5 For the vinaigrette (which makes more than you need for this recipe), blend all
the ingredients together in a food processor. Season to taste. Alternatively, crush
the garlic and finely chop the shallot and place in a small bowl. Add the mustard,
honey, salt and pepper, lemon juice and white wine vinegar. Whisk together and
slowly add the olive oil and vegetable oil. Add sugar to taste. Keep for up to a week
in the refrigerator.

6 Mix together the beans, potatoes, anchovies, olives, tomatoes and lamb's
lettuce in a large bowl with 30ml (2tbsp) vinaigrette and seasoning. Divide between
4 bowls. Add the quail's eggs.

7 Season the tuna steaks. Heat a little olive oil in a large heavy-bottomed frying
pan. Sear the steaks for approximately 2 minutes on each side (for medium rare).

8 Squeeze the lemon juice over the tuna and place on top of the salad. Add more
vinaigrette, if you want to.

chargrilled aberdeen angus rib-eye steak with béarnaise sauce

A bistro classic that is turning up on gastropub menus everywhere.

serves 4

4 x 285g (10oz) Aberdeen Angus rib-eye steaks

20 small new potatoes, boiled and allowed to cool

15ml (1tbsp) vegetable oil

Maldon sea salt and pepper

3 medium shallots, sliced

55g (2oz) unsalted butter, diced

handful of flat-leaf parsley, roughly chopped

to serve

4 small handfuls rocket or watercress

Parmesan shavings (optional)

1 Season the rib-eye steaks, then chargrill for about 4 minutes on each side. Rest for 5 minutes on a warm plate.

2 Cut the potatoes into 6mm (¼ inch) slices. Heat a little vegetable oil in a hot sauté pan, then place the potato slices flat in the pan with some seasoning.

3 Slowly cook the potatoes for about 4 minutes, until they start to colour on both sides. At this point add the sliced shallots.

4 Continue cooking until evenly golden brown, and stir in the butter.

5 Check the seasoning and fold in the chopped parsley. Serve the steaks with some béarnaise sauce, the sauté potatoes and rocket or watercress topped with Parmesan shavings, or left plain.

béarnaise sauce

255g (9oz) unsalted butter

30ml (2tbsp) water

15ml (1tbsp) white wine vinegar

15ml (1tbsp) white wine

6 white peppercorns, crushed

1 bay leaf

2 tarragon sprigs, stalks and leaves separated and roughly chopped

1 shallot, finely sliced

4 medium egg yolks

salt and pepper, to taste

juice of ½ lemon

1 Melt the butter slowly over a very low heat. Skim any scum off the surface of the butter. When a milky sediment has settled, carefully pour off the clear butter – not the white solids – through a fine sieve and keep warm.

2 Put the water, vinegar, white wine, peppercorns, bay leaf, tarragon stalks and shallot in a small saucepan. Boil until the liquid has reduced by a third. Strain through a fine sieve lined with kitchen paper.

3 Pour the liquid into a round-bottomed Pyrex bowl set over a pan of simmering water (the bowl shouldn't touch the water). Add the egg yolks and whisk continuously for 7–9 minutes, until the mixture emulsifies and becomes smooth and creamy.

4 Remove the bowl from the heat and slowly whisk in the clarified butter, a little at a time. Season and add lemon juice to taste. Fold in the tarragon leaves.

crisp belly of pork with the angel's black pudding and mustard mash

The Angel's black pudding is sensational — spicy and very fruity. Use other good quality black pudding if you don't want to make your own. Buttered spinach is good with this.

serves 6

1 pork belly, about 1.5kg (3½lb), skin and bones left on

3 medium onions, roughly diced

3 medium carrots, roughly diced

4 celery sticks, roughly diced

1 medium bulb fennel, roughly diced

2 bulbs garlic

bunch of thyme

10 white peppercorns

2 bay leaves

8 whole star anise

½ red chilli, deseeded and diced

115g (4oz) cold unsalted butter, diced

for the black pudding

155ml (5½fl oz) white wine vinegar

115g (4oz) caster sugar

1 small onion, finely diced

140g (5oz) pork back fat, cut into small dice

90g (3½oz) sultanas

55g (2oz) smoked pancetta, cut into very fine strips

200g (7oz) baked ham, sliced

small handful of oats, ground

425g (15oz) black pudding mix (dried blood mixture)

1 Preheat the oven to 140°C/275°F/gas mark 1.

2 Place all the pork belly ingredients except the butter in a deep roasting tin. Cover the pork well with water. Cover the tray with a double thickness of foil and slowly braise in the preheated oven for 3½ hours, until a knife point goes into the flesh very easily.

3 Allow the pork to cool in the liquid for 20 minutes before transferring it to a cooling rack. Then remove the skin, bones and cartilage while still warm.

4 Strain the pork liquor through a fine sieve into a saucepan. Bring to the boil and reduce by a good half.

5 Spread out 4 layers of wide clingfilm and slowly roll the pork up into a cylinder along its widest side. Tie both ends with knots.

6 Place in the fridge for 2 hours, then unwrap and slice into 3.75cm (1½ inch) pieces.

7 In a medium-hot frying pan, slowly crisp the pork for 2–3 minutes each side before serving.

8 Finish the sauce by reheating the reduced pork liquor, then whisking in the diced butter.

9 To serve, place the mash in the centre of 6 warmed bowls. Top with the grilled black pudding, followed by buttered spinach, if using. Place the crispy pork belly on top to finish and spoon over the sauce.

1 sprig each of rosemary and thyme, finely chopped

unsalted butter, melted

for the Pommery mash

4 medium floury potatoes, peeled and cut into chunks

55g (2oz) unsalted butter

7.5ml (1½tsp) Pommery mustard

Maldon sea salt, to taste

black pudding

1 Bring the vinegar, sugar and 375ml (13fl oz) water to the boil in a pan. Add the onion, pork fat and sultanas. Return to the boil, lower the heat and simmer for 5 minutes. Add the pancetta, ham, oats, black pudding mix, rosemary and thyme. Combine well, adding more water if it looks a bit dry. Allow to cool slightly.

2 Shape into a sausage. Wrap tightly in 4 layers of clingfilm. Knot the ends and boil for 30 minutes. Refresh in iced water. To serve, cut the black pudding into 1.5cm (½ inch) slices, brush with melted butter and warm, but don't crisp, under the grill.

pommery mash

1 Boil the potatoes until tender, then mash with butter and mustard. Salt to taste.

sticky toffee pudding

No pudding appears on pub menus more often than this one. Even those who usually find it too sweet and rich will like The Angel's, which is lighter than most versions.

serves 6

55g (2oz) unsalted butter, plus a knob for greasing tin

170g (6oz) caster sugar, plus extra for coating tin

1 medium egg

170g (6oz) stoned dates, chopped

225g (8oz) self-raising flour

5g (1tsp) bicarbonate of soda

285ml (½ pint) boiling water

5g (1tsp) baking powder

for the caramel sauce

115g (4oz) unsalted butter

115g (4oz) caster sugar

55ml (2fl oz) single cream

1 Preheat the oven to 190°C/375°F/gas mark 5. Grease a 20 x 10 x 3.75cm (8 x 4 x 1½ inch) baking tin with butter, then coat evenly with caster sugar. Tip out any excess.

2 In a large bowl, cream the butter and sugar until the mixture is light and fluffy, then beat in the egg. Dust the dates with a little flour. Put them in a small bowl. Stir the bicarbonate of soda into the boiling water and pour over the dates. Mash.

3 Sift the flour with the baking powder. Mix the flour into the creamed butter, then add the date mash. Stir thoroughly and pour into the prepared baking tin. Bake in the preheated oven for 40 minutes, until dark brown and a skewer pushed into the pudding comes out clean. Leave in the tin.

4 While the pudding is cooking, make the caramel sauce by heating the butter and sugar together in a small heavy-bottomed saucepan. Bring slowly to the boil, then carefully stir in the cream (don't let the cream boil). Take off the heat.

5 Prick the surface of the cooked pudding, pour over some of the caramel sauce and leave to sink in for 2–3 minutes before serving. Cut into 6 and serve with the remaining caramel sauce and double cream or vanilla ice-cream.

the best of the rest

the durham ox

Westway

Crayke

North Yorkshire

01347 821506

www.thedurhamox.com

serves lunch and dinner

mon to sun;

bookings accepted; children

welcome; garden

The Fosse Way runs through the village of Crayke, but ramblers beware: stop at the Durham Ox and you'll probably give up for the day.

The bar has a gracious, slightly arty feel: rust-coloured walls, a huge red-brick fireplace, old dark wooden panels (copies of a collection from an Irish cathedral) and a big oak sideboard bearing ceramic lamps, flowers and pottery. The proprietor, Michael Ibbotson, has involved his whole family – his mum made the curtains and cushions and his brother took the black-and-white photos on the walls. There is a separate dining room – primrose-coloured with oak beams and damask napery – but the same menu is served throughout, and it's the bar that has real character.

Michael has put a lot of thought into the kind of food he should serve. He wants the place to be a pub that serves good food, not a restaurant that has a bar, and judging from the clientele – the cricket team, local business people, girls on a good night out – he has succeeded. Chef Jason Moore offers straightforward dishes that are spot on: home-cured gravadlax, wild mushroom and goat's cheese tart with onion marmalade, roast bacon with mash, homemade black pudding and a poached egg with grain mustard sauce. They also offer superb chargrilled steaks with either pepper or mushroom sauce, and an exemplary selection of British cheeses.

the red lion

Burnsall

North Yorkshire

01756 720204

www.redlion.co.uk

serves lunch and dinner

mon to sun;

no bookings; children

welcome; garden

Alan Bennett would have a field day here. The Red Lion is frequented by all sorts – gussied-up grannies, leather-jacketed bikers, screaming babies in high-chairs and tweedy old fogies – and is gloriously undesigned and chaotic. A little plastic Union Jack, bunches of keys and a fluorescent pink calendar from a commercial supplier decorate one corner of the copper-topped bar. The bar room is big, with wooden floors, faded rugs, leafy wallpaper and curtains made from a fabric depicting technicolor hunting scenes, which was popular in the 1950s. The flying ducks on the wall are not in the least bit ironic.

The barman and his red-haired consort tell jokes – loudly – and give each other high fives. It seems as though confusion reins, but everything gets done and service is friendly and caring.

The cooking is straightforward and unpretentious – no towers, no drizzles. It roams around a bit. There are modern brasserie dishes, such as Moroccan-spiced sardines and duck with soy sauce and spring onions, alongside British classics such as grouse with game chips or treacle tart. The ingredients are fresh and high quality and the cooking, by the owners' son-in-law, is very able.

The pub itself is made up of a string of terraced stone cottages and is in a pretty-as-a-picture location, beside the arched bridge that crosses the River Wharfe. There are bedrooms and a restaurant here as well, and you'll find something to make you smile at every turn.

the yorke arms

Ramsgill

North Yorkshire

01423 755243

www.yorke-arms.co.uk

serves lunch and dinner

mon to sun lunch;

bookings advised;

no children; garden

You expect bliss here, and you get it – not just because the chef and owner, Frances Atkins, has a formidable reputation as a cook, but also because the place and its location have an easy beauty.

The Yorke Arms is a creeper-covered, 18th-century shooting lodge, situated just by the village green in Nidderdale, which is in one of the most gentle and lush areas of Yorkshire. Inside there are polished flagstones, wooden floors and oak beams. A small bar, with jewel-like stained glass and several ancient settles, stocks a well-kept Black Sheep Special from nearby Masham, and here they offer a few lunchtime pubby dishes, such as steak sandwich or potato pancakes with smoked bacon.

The dining room is a model of simple, elegant country style: highly polished tables, sparkling cut glass, a huge dresser and pewter plates on the wall. You know you are in the hands of someone with impeccable taste, an impression that carries through to the food.

The cooking scales the heights. The pasta for various ravioli is fine and silken. The fish cookery, in particular, is outstanding, with dishes such as smoked haddock and black pudding in brioche with mustard hollandaise, and lemon sole with asparagus, peas and artichokes. Every dish is light and considered, and there's no showing off.

This is undoubtedly restaurant food, but Frances insists on keeping the pubby element of the Yorke Arms alive. She believes the pub has a special place in Yorkshire life and that people are more inclined to come out to a pub than to a restaurant – and she likes the laidback atmosphere this brings to the place. Locals do use the bar for drinking, but you can't roll up and get a ham sandwich, or even classics from the gastropub vernacular, such as sausages and mash or sticky toffee pudding. You will be served sophisticated, highly crafted fare. The style and standard of cooking offered here would, in a restaurant environment, engender reverential behaviour, the kind of hallowed atmosphere, which Frances abhors. Keeping the Yorke Arms as a pub means you get to eat some of the most exquisite cooking in Britain in a state of joyful ease.

the rose and crown

Romaldkirk

Co. Durham

01833 650213

www.rose-and-crown.co.uk

serves lunch and dinner

mon to sun lunch;

bookings accepted;

children welcome; terrace

As soon as you see the Rose and Crown you have high expectations. It's a plain but beautiful 18th-century stone coaching inn right by the village green. Geraniums in terracotta pots adorn the outside tables; primary-coloured parasols shade them. All is neat, well kept and tasteful, and you find the same inside.

There's a traditional bar with plenty of exposed stone, an imposing inglenook, lush red velvet curtains and a richly coloured carpet. A small dining room on the other side of the bar is smarter: big oak tables, contemporary chairs and bright, humorous prints of chefs.

The kitchen makes good use of local ingredients to produce first-class dishes such as smoked haddock soufflé, Yorkshire blue, mushroom and spinach risotto, steak and kidney pie with Theakstons ale gravy and an omelette of summer herbs and Cotherstone cheese. It's unfussy but refined; simple but skilfully done.

The clientele are smart and tend to be older, though not yet in possession of bus passes. The staff are warm and professional, and Romaldkirk, a lovely unspoilt village of stone houses and cottages in deepest Teesside, is a good place to linger.

the three acres

Roydhouse
West Yorkshire
01484 602606
www.3acres.com
serves lunch and dinner
mon to sun;
bookings accepted
(restaurant only);
children welcome; terrace

A stone roadside inn right by the Emley Moor TV tower, The Three Acres is totally distinctive. Enter through the Grocer – the Three Acres' deli, which sells their own pies and preserves as well as every recherché ingredient you could ever want – and you are immediately enveloped by warmth and easy-going luxury.

Apart from the bar, which runs the length of the room and is hung with pewter tankards, The Three Acres is not particularly pubby. The tables have cloths protected by glass tops, under which are displayed an eccentric collection of cuttings from magazines and interiors brochures, wine labels and postcards. There are comfy tub chairs, some of them in leather, and the room is broken up by alcoves and a big brick column right in the centre, which houses a glowing fire. Each small window is swagged with acres of fabric and has a miniature tree sitting in it.

There's a seafood bar with fresh oysters, smoked salmon and bottles of Moët & Chandon on display, and the whole place, which serves as café, pub and restaurant, is more like a Parisian watering hole than anything you might expect to find in the Yorkshire moors.

The bar food is brasserie stuff with lots of British touches: cassoulet, lobster thermidore (made with lobster from Whitby), and Peking duck with egg noodles and Chinese greens, sit comfortably alongside smashing renditions of fish and chips with mushy peas and tartare sauce and steak and kidney pie under a mustard and onion crust. There are also some well-sourced assemblies such as Bobby Baxter's famous potted shrimps with buttered soldiers and platters of *charcuterie*.

Sandwiches, served at lunch time, are so fabulous and original that they take the snack into another league. Try steak with caramelized onions and melting blue cheese or Jack Scaife's roast ham with Pendle Forest smoked cheese and mustard mayo. Soups are delicious and properly seasoned, puddings, such as brown bread ice cream with butterscotch sauce, are scrumptious.

There are two gorgeous dining rooms, with bottle-green walls, tartan fabric, big fires and ironwork candleabras, if you fancy something more formal. Service is delightful. The product of 30 years of nurturing by owners, Neil Truelove and Brian Orme, the Three Acres is a cracking place.

the general tarleton

Boroughbridge Road
Ferrensby
North Yorkshire
01423 340284
www.generaltarleton.co.uk
serves lunch and dinner
mon to sun;
bookings accepted;
children welcome; garden

This 250-year-old coaching inn has the same owners as The Angel at Hetton, and is run with the same savvy professionalism. It has a restaurant and some pretty luxurious bedrooms in a handsome stone extension, as well as a bar. The bar itself is big, divided into various areas by exposed stone pillars, and has prints of food on lobster-coloured walls and a rich, dark carpet. It's brasserie-like in feel.

The food is also brasserie-style, with dishes such as sausages with onion gravy and mash, pea and ham risotto, tomato tart, steaks and duck confit, and the cooking is fresh, polished and slick. The only downside is that the place feels a bit too slick; the bar has a newly refurbished feel. It has been 'done up' rather than being allowed to evolve, and consequently lacks the character of less pristine places.

You'll eat very well, mind you, among a dapper crowd of ladies-who-lunch, businessmen and smart mums with well-behaved children, and there are no fewer than 22 wines by the glass and beer from Yorkshire breweries Timothy Taylor and Black Sheep.

the black bull inn

Moulton

North Yorkshire

01325 377289

serves lunch and dinner

mon to sat;

bookings accepted;

no children; terrace

The Black Bull Inn is endearingly old-fashioned. The outside is cottagey; the bar, with its wood panelling, velour-covered banquettes and cartoons of Victorian politicians, is traditional. The dining room, though, is the real treat: it's in a converted ex-Brighton Belle Pullman carriage and on a sunny day you feel you should roll up in your most dapper old-fashioned clothes with a matching parasol.

The menu, too, harks back to the past. There are dishes you rarely see nowadays, such as lobster Newburg and seafood crêpes, and plenty of timeless classics such as châteaubriand with béarnaise, duck confit, salmon with hollandaise and crab bisque. Chef Paul Grundy also does contemporary dishes such as saffron-roast chicken with coriander couscous, and seared scallops with sweet chilli sauce and crème fraîche – but it's great to find an eating place that values the star dishes of the 1960s and 1970s, and he does them well. Simpler bar food – sandwiches, sticky ribs, platters of gigas oysters and smoked salmon – is served too. The Pagendam family, who own the place, have been at the helm since the 1960s, and they know how to do it. Service is warm.

the appletree inn

Marton

near Pickering

North Yorkshire

01751 431457

www.appletreeinn.co.uk

serves lunch and dinner

weds to mon;

bookings advised;

children welcome; garden

You have to hand it to the owners here: to open a dining pub just 10 miles from that glittering heavenly body, The Star at Harome, is a brave move. But chef T.J. Drew and his partner, Melanie Thornton, are running this inn well, putting in herbs and a vegetable garden, tending their orchard, and making the goods – chutneys and flavoured vinegars – that are sold on the premises under the Appletree's own label. The inn, a lovely old stone house, is pleasingly unfussy and spick and span. A fire lights the bar. The dining room is a traditional country affair, with dark, plain furniture and warm terracotta-coloured walls. In the evening it's lit by no fewer than 130 flickering candles.

The food is big on flavour and ranges from country dishes such as venison suet pudding with red onion marmalade, Yorkshire game terrine with chutney, and confit of belly pork with apple sauce and sage *jus*, to more contemporary, exotic offerings, such as spiced duck breast with black rice. It's strongest when on home ground. There are also good sarnies, such as smoked bacon and egg, at lunch time. As much of the food as possible is sourced locally and service goes the extra mile.

the crab and lobster

Dishforth Road

Asenby

North Yorkshire

01845 577286

www.crabandlobster.com

serves lunch and dinner

mon to sun;

bookings accepted

(dining room only);

children welcome; garden

Coming here is like visiting a fun-fair. The Crab and Lobster's originators, David and Jackie Barnard, threw weird and wonderful junk-shop finds together to create a place that makes you feel as if you are simultaneously in your Granny's front room (circa 1935) and in a surrealist painting. There are antique mannequins in worn fox furs, faded standard lamps draped in lace mantillas, battered old suitcases, yellowing musical scores and even an old copper diving suit. Musical instruments and over-the-top crystal chandeliers hang from the ceiling. And it works: the place is truly eccentric.

The menu goes on a whistle-stop tour, both of the world and of cooking styles. There's classically French herb-crusted salmon with asparagus and pea velouté, a very British platter of smoked haddock and black pudding on bubble and squeak and, in the exotic corner, jalfrezi sweet potato curry and Thai fish cakes with oriental salad. The cooking is good most of the time, but beware of dishes which are trying to be too clever. The waiting staff have flair and try to live up to the camp surroundings, and everyone seems to have a rip-roaring time.

scotland

Scotland is a rare beast. There aren't many areas of Europe that seem undiscovered, but there are parts of Scotland that feel almost as though they have never been seen; the mountains of Sutherland might only just have been created, hewn from some raw shoulder of rock.

Scotland is a massive landscape, both lovely and harsh, and the best Scottish food is steeped in this ruggedness: whisky smelling of peat; shellfish as fresh and briny as the sea; salmon and venison infused with wood-smoke; game that has fed on heather. Travelling around the country, stocking up at local shops – smokeries, cheesemakers and distilleries – you soon find you have your own deli-on-wheels, stuffed with Dundee cake, tawny marmalade, heather honey, wild chanterelles, raspberries, haggis, kippers and shortbread, plus oatcakes and Lanark Blue, Crowdie and Caboc cheeses.

These foods make for a cuisine that is both solidly hearty (barley, oats and broth) and luxurious (smoked salmon, oysters, game and wild mushrooms). It's just the kind of food that's right for pubs and inns. Much of the produce doesn't even need cooking, and the most clued-up pubs take advantage of this by offering dish upon dish of 'assemblies': platters of cold- or hot-smoked fish, dill-cured salmon and fresh oysters, dressed crab salad or a ploughman's with Scottish cheeses. Beyond that you'll find poached

salmon, chowder and the smoked fish soup, cullen skink, herrings in oatmeal, smoked haddock with mash, crab cakes, Highland venison and great steaks.

Like some of the landscape, Scottish food is still waiting to be explored. Her raw ingredients have famously been more revered abroad than in Scotland itself. It's sad to sit in a Scottish coastal pub perusing a menu that lists frozen scampi, while watching articulated lorries take most of the shellfish landed there to Spain or France.

But Scotland, like Ireland, increasingly appreciates what is on its doorstep. Chefs such as Nick Nairn have spearheaded a new respect for Scottish food that has given birth to great restaurants. With pubs, this is happening more slowly. Those that are doing good food, like the pubs in this chapter, are doing it well. They haven't fallen into the trap of turning out dishes that are merely fashionable, but are producing a mix of well-executed Scottish home cooking, such as the gratin of smokies and Scottish Cheddar served at the Plockton Hotel, and more sophisticated dishes that have roots in both Scotland and France, such as the guinea fowl with Stornaway black pudding and Savoy cabbage served at The Harbour Inn on Islay.

The good news is that this food is being served in some of the most spectacular locations in the world. Nearly every pub in this chapter will make you stare at your surroundings before you've even looked at a menu. Fancy a pint of squat lobster and mayo while you look out to the Hebridean islands? Or savouring a single malt while you watch the sunlight move over the surface of a Highland loch? Delight in your surroundings increases your enjoyment of food, and vice-versa. Nowhere is this truer than in Scotland.

The Square
Bowmore
Islay
01496 810330
www.harbour-inn.com
serves lunch and dinner
mon to sat
(dinner in restaurant only);
bookings advised;
children welcome

the harbour inn

Chef Scott Chance doesn't come from Islay – he moved here less than 10 years ago – but listen to him slipping into a Scottish lilt as he chats to local fishermen, or peruse his menu, and you'll see how Scotland has burrowed into his soul.

The dishes he serves at his white-washed pub on Islay are firmly built on the island's produce: oysters gratinéed with leeks and cream, baked crab with a soufflé topping, wild venison with rosehip jelly. A 'less is more' attitude is central to the food and the result is unfussy, modern Scottish cooking.

The shellfish, which you can see being unloaded at the harbour from the pub's dining room, are the star of the show, but the local game and meat are also superb. 'I couldn't believe the meat when I came here,' says Scott. 'Because it's reasonably mild, the cattle stay outdoors in every season, grazing on grass and wild herbs, and even eating the seaweed and drinking the seawater at the beach. It has an astonishing effect on the flavour.'

The Harbour was what you might call a 'grotty boozer' when Scott bought it, so it had to be revamped and now has a little pine bar, where you can eat at lunch time, with bare stone walls, an old porthole window in the door and about 30 whiskies. The new, more restauranty dining room juts out over the rocks of the harbour and you can practically smell the fresh fish as it arrives.

islay crab fishcakes

You can use good-quality shop-bought mayonnaise to make the tartare sauce, instead of making your own, if you prefer.

serves 4

500g (1lb 2oz) floury potatoes

255g (9oz) fresh crabmeat, a mix of brown and white meat

125g (4¹/₂oz) very fine white breadcrumbs

1 medium onion, finely chopped

15g (1tbsp) each of finely chopped dill and parsley

salt and pepper

¹/₂tsp paprika

2 medium eggs, beaten

50g (1³/₄oz) unsalted butter

30ml (2tbsp) olive oil

salad leaves, to serve

extra virgin olive oil, to serve

lemon wedges, to serve

for the tartare sauce

100ml (3¹/₂fl oz) mayonnaise

30ml (2tbsp) white wine

15g (1tbsp) chopped parsley

25g (1oz) gherkins, chopped

25g (1oz) capers, chopped

25g (1oz) shallots, chopped

for the mayonnaise

2 medium egg yolks

5ml (1tsp) English mustard

75ml (5tbsp) white wine vinegar

100ml (3¹/₂floz) sunflower oil

salt and pepper

dash of Tabasco sauce

dash of Worcestershire sauce

1 Peel the potatoes and chop them into even-sized chunks. Bring a pan of water to the boil and cook the potatoes until just tender, then mash them.

2 Put the mashed potatoes in a large bowl with the crabmeat, breadcrumbs, onion, herbs, seasoning, paprika and beaten eggs and mix together. Using your hands, form the mixture into 8 circular patties, all the same size.

3 Heat the butter and oil together in a large heavy-bottomed frying pan and, when hot, fry each fishcake on both sides for approximately 4 minutes, until golden brown. If necessary, cook the fishcakes in batches rather than cramming too many into the pan. Keep warm.

4 Lightly dress the salad leaves with extra virgin olive oil.

5 Serve 2 fishcakes per person with a dollop of tartare sauce, some dressed green salad leaves and wedges of lemon.

tartare sauce

1 Blend the ingredients for the tartare sauce together well and chill.

mayonnaise

1 Put the egg yolks and mustard in a food processor and whizz, then add the white wine vinegar and mix. Drizzle in the oil extremely slowly while the motor is running so that the mixture emulsifies.

2 Alternatively, whisk together the egg yolks and mustard, then add the white wine vinegar and whisk until a thick emulsion has formed. Add the oil slowly, whisking continuously to incorporate all the oil before the next trickle is added.

3 Once all the oil has been added, season and add Tabasco and Worcestershire sauce to taste. Chill.

halibut with loch etive mussels in saffron cream

You can use other white fish for this, such as turbot, brill or bass — and your mussels, of course, don't have to be from Loch Etive.

serves 4

4 x 150g (5¹/₂oz) halibut steaks or fillets

2 plum tomatoes

coarse sea salt

500ml (18fl oz) fish stock

255ml (9fl oz) dry white wine

50g (1³/₄oz) shallots, finely chopped

pinch of saffron threads

255g (9oz) fresh mussels, cleaned

255ml (9fl oz) double cream

a sprig of dill or wild fennel or 30g (2tbsp) snipped chives, to serve

1 Season the halibut with sea salt.

2 Immerse the tomatoes in boiling water for 15 seconds. Refresh in cold water. Slip the skins off, halve, remove the seeds and dice the remaining flesh. Set aside.

3 Place a rack or trivet in a large frying pan. Pour in the fish stock and white wine and add the shallots. Bring to the boil.

4 Gently steam the fish over the simmering liquid for 7 minutes. Remove the fish from the steam, cover with foil and keep warm.

5 Bring the liquid to a full boil and add the saffron and mussels to it (the colour of the saffron will intensify as it cooks, so do not be tempted to add more).

6 After 3–4 minutes, remove the mussels. Discard any that haven't opened and cover the rest with foil. Keep warm. Stir the cream into the cooking liquor. Boil rapidly to reduce by half, so that the sauce will coat the back of a spoon. Add the diced tomato flesh.

7 Place the halibut on 4 warmed plates, scatter the mussels around the fish and spoon the saffron cream around the mussels; do not spoon the saffron cream onto the white flesh of the fish. Garnish with a sprig of dill, wild fennel or snipped chives, and serve.

'i would love to see more growers, food producers and an enterprising cheesemaker on islay. i'd rather source here than go to the mainland.' scott

BROWN WOOL

FLAT F

MUSKRAT STRIP

GOLDEN STONE
NYMPH

BOWMORE

collops of venison with wild mushrooms and rosehip jelly

Scott gets his rosehips from a neighbour. Look for them in November and make enough of this jelly to keep you going for the rest of the year – it's brilliant with rice pudding. If you can't get hold of any rosehips, or don't want to make the jelly, use shop-bought redcurrant or rowanberry jelly instead.

serves 4

2 x 255g (9oz) venison saddle, boned and trimmed

salt and pepper

15ml (1tbsp) vegetable oil

1 clove garlic, unpeeled

3 sprigs thyme, plus extra for serving

small knob of butter

30g (1oz) shallots, finely chopped

125g (4¹/₂oz) wild mushrooms (or 55g/2oz dried wild mushrooms soaked in water for 2 hours), roughly sliced

255ml (9fl oz) full-bodied red wine

255ml (9fl oz) venison or beef stock

50g (1³/₄oz) cold unsalted butter, diced

30ml (2tbsp) rosehip jelly

750g (1lb 10oz) ripe rosehips, washed well

juice of ¹/₂ lemon

1kg (2lb 3oz) Bramley apples or tart green apples, roughly chopped

granulated sugar

jam jar, washed in hot soapy water, rinsed and dried in a warm oven

1 Preheat the oven to 220°C/425°F/gas mark 7. Season the meat.

2 Heat the vegetable oil a large frying pan and seal the venison. Place in a roasting tin and add the garlic and thyme. Roast in the preheated oven for 10 minutes. Transfer the meat to a plate, cover loosely with foil and rest in a warm place.

3 Remove the garlic and thyme from the roasting pan and discard. Add the butter, shallots and mushrooms. Gently cook on a low heat for 5 minutes. Increase the heat, add the wine and boil rapidly to reduce the liquid by half.

4 Add the stock, bring back to the boil and again reduce by half. Whisk in the cold, unsalted butter in small pieces to enrich the sauce.

5 To serve, either thinly slice the venison or cut into thicker medallions. Divide between 4 warmed plates. Stir the rosehip jelly into the sauce and spoon over the meat; some of the jelly will still be visible. Do not add the rosehip jelly too early or it will all melt. Garnish with small sprigs of thyme.

rosehip jelly

1 Place the rosehips in a pan with the lemon juice, cover with water and simmer until very soft, then mash. Place the apples and a splash of water in another pan and simmer until soft. Mix the 2 ingredients together, then strain through a jelly bag or jam strainer overnight to get a clear liquid.

2 Measure the liquid, then pour it into a pan. Add 150g (5¹/₂oz) sugar for every 200ml (7fl oz) liquid and bring to the boil, stirring. Boil rapidly until setting point is reached – to test, cool 5ml (1tsp) of jelly on a saucer; if it forms a skin when pushed with a finger it is ready. Pour into the jam jar and cover. Leave to cool.

islay whisky parfait with plum grits

If you aren't a big oatmeal fan, serve the parfait with plums that have been poached until tender in a mixture of sugar and red wine or orange juice. You'll then need to remove the plums and reduce the cooking liquid until it's syrupy.

serves 4

2 medium eggs, separated

50g (1³/₄oz) granulated sugar

255ml (9fl oz) full-fat milk

50g (1³/₄oz) caster sugar

255ml (9fl oz) double cream.

45ml (3tbsp) Islay malt

4 sprigs mint, to serve

1 Whisk the egg yolks and granulated sugar together in a bowl until the mixture is thick and creamy.

2 In a small saucepan, bring the milk to the boil, then whisk it into the yolks and sugar. Pour the mixture back into the saucepan and heat gently, stirring constantly until just below boiling point (you musn't let it boil or the yolks will scramble). Pour into a bowl and allow to go cold.

3 In a large bowl, whisk the egg whites until stiff. Put the caster sugar and 15ml (1tbsp) water in a small saucepan. Place over a gentle heat to dissolve the sugar, stirring all the time. Turn the heat up and reduce the liquid until syrupy but not coloured. Take off the heat.

4 Add the sugar and water mixture to the stiff egg whites, whisking all the time. Keep whisking for about 5 minutes, until cool. Stir a couple of spoonfuls of this mixture into the cold custard to loosen it, then fold the remaining egg whites into the custard in 2 halves.

5 Semi-whip the double cream so that it is starting to hold, but is not stiff, and fold into the custard mixture. Stir in the whisky. Pour into a freezer-proof mould, such as a loaf tin, and place in the freezer overnight.

6 To serve, briefly immerse the outside of the mould in hot water, then invert the parfait onto a board; it should slide out easily. Slice with a hot knife and serve with some warm plum grits, garnished with a sprig of mint.

plum grits

500g (1lb 2oz) ripe plums (English Victoria are best), halved and stoned

125ml (4¹/₂fl oz) red wine

125g (4¹/₂oz) granulated sugar

50g (1³/₄oz) medium oatmeal

1 Put the plums, red wine and sugar in a heavy-bottomed pan and bring gently to the boil, stirring to dissolve the sugar. Simmer for 5–10 minutes, until the plums are soft.

2 Thicken with the oatmeal and gently simmer for another 10 minutes.

the best of the rest

the glenelg inn

Glenelg
Highland
01599 522273
www.glenelg-inn.com
serves lunch and dinner
mon to sun lunch, but
closed October to Easter;
bookings advised
(dining room only);
children welcome

This highland pub and restaurant is tucked away at the end of a long, winding road that takes you down to the water's edge at Glenelg Bay, right opposite the Isle of Skye. You'll probably find the owner, the charming Christopher Main, in his kilt, and local fishermen, farmers and holidaymakers might be chatting together to the sound of pipes and fiddles, as a good ceilidh is not an unusual event here. This is one of the loveliest, most unfussy bars in Scotland. Dark wooden panelling, a bare stone floor, a huge blazing fire, barrels, settles and old crates to sit on, green candles in wine bottles, collections of rocks and shells: it all makes you want to linger, and you'll end up booking a bed for the night.

The bar menu is limited but good: big, well-dressed salads such as feta and vine tomatoes or smoked chicken, homemade soup with warm bread, venison casserole, and sandwiches of Orkney Cheddar and pickle. Lest things sound too idyllic, be warned that frozen scampi, mandatory on most Scottish bar menus, is found here too, and some of the bar desserts are bought in.

In the evening you can opt for the four-course set menu served in the small dining room. Chef Yvonne Winn's food shows a love of Scottish ingredients and exotic spices, so you'll find carrot, coconut and coriander soup alongside roast haunch of venison with shallots and chestnuts. Winn's strength is in turning out big flavours rather than fussy dishes, and the whole event has a party atmosphere.

the old inn

Gairloch
Highland
0800 542544
www.theoldinn.co.uk
serves lunch and dinner
mon to sun;
bookings accepted;
children welcome; garden

White beaches, lush woods, lighthouses and great mirrored stretches of blue water, Wester Ross seems to have everything, and the Old Inn at Gairloch is one of many Scottish watering holes in a breathtaking location. It's situated at the foot of the Flowerdale Valley and has views over Gairloch harbour, with its fishing boats and yachts, Skye and the Outer Isles beyond. Alistair Pearson, who owns the Old Inn, is one of the most helpful and amenable hosts anywhere and he can advise you – in fact you'll have trouble stopping him – on the best walks and climbs.

The inn is an old, white-washed building with several traditional, pubby bars, partly exposed stone walls, wood-burning stoves, standard-issue furniture, and a huge range of whiskies and decent beer. The fish and shellfish caught around here are unsurpassable and the Old Inn makes the best of them. Loch Torridon mussels are served three ways – marinière, Provençal or Thai – and lobster is grilled, served cold with mayonnaise, or cooked with brandy, cream and cheese for that fantastic old classic, lobster thermidor. There's also grilled langoustines with garlic butter, a platter of Wester Ross smoked fish and dressed crab. More complicated dishes, such as grilled halibut with sun-dried tomato pesto, are more hit and miss (and a few don't whet the appetite at all – cod wrapped in smoked salmon with rhubarb compote, anyone?). Go for the simple classics.

babbity bowster's

16-18 Blackfriars Street
Glasgow
0141 552 5055
serves lunch and dinner
mon to sun;
bookings accepted
(dining room only);
children accepted; terrace

Babbity's, a pub-restaurant in an 18th-century townhouse in Glasgow's revamped Merchant City area, is a bit of an institution. You can get a pint, a cappuccino or a velvety bowl of cullen skink at any time of the day, plus a good breakfast on a Sunday morning. It strikes a good balance between being a pub and a café: the place seems both Scottish and French, a feeling reinforced by the blackboard menu, which always has a 'Scotch Corner' and a 'French Quarter' on it.

The ground floor is one large open room. In the corner is a big handsome bar, on which there is always a vase of flowers, and there are tables covered in check oilcloths, and contemporary black-and-white photos of Glasgow on the walls. The owner, Fraser Laurie, is a character – you might see him sporting his eye-patch and running round after the chef – and his personality seems to be stamped on the place. It is nearly always noisy, exudes warmth and attracts an interesting crowd of students, architects, designers and the generally loquacious.

The chef, Jean-Claude Marccosio, is from Lyons and refuses to put chips on the menu. Everything, except the bread and ice-cream, is made on the premises, and there's a good range of unfussy food. Scottish classics include haggis, neeps and tatties, and West Coast mussels with white wine and cream, plus dishes that you rarely see, such as potted hough – a pâté made with shin of beef. Jean-Claude gives vent to his Frenchness by serving duck confit and Toulouse sausages with mash. There are also superior sandwiches, such as pastrami, plus various croques.

A separate dining room upstairs, the Scottische, serves more sophisticated fare, such as rack of lamb with red wine and thyme *jus*, in a lovely plain dining room with tall windows. It's not ambitious cooking, and some dishes can be hit-and-miss, but Babbity's is a great, convivial place to sit and chat, over a plate of oysters or a platter of Loch Fyne smoked salmon.

applecross inn

Shore Street
Applecross
Highland
01520 744262
serves lunch and dinner
mon to sun, but in bad
weather check whether it
can be reached;
bookings accepted;
children welcome; garden

The modernist Spanish chef, Ferran Adrià, once said that a great meal should begin with a long journey. Well, the journey to the Applecross Inn, along the highest mountain pass in Britain, Bealnach-na-Ba, with a 50-mile sweep of mountains, sea and sky around you, would be difficult to beat, either in its beauty or for the thrill of driving on roads that skirt sheer drops.

At the end, you'll find a plain white inn by a beach. The inside is perfectly simple: pine tongue-and-groove walls, a few potted plants and framed photographs of the local lifeboat crew. A blackboard lists an enormous menu, which includes the usual pub staples such as ham and eggs or sausages and mash. They're done fine, but the fish, which is all local or from the West Coast, is the thing to go for. Simple dishes, such as dressed crab, mussels and chips or Applecross Bay prawns with mayonnaise, are fresh and faultless, but it's the more adventurous assemblies that really surprise. Pan-fried salmon on crushed pesto potatoes with roast tomatoes, and sole with fennel and squat lobster are brinily fresh and zingily flavoured – better than you'd find in many a top-notch fish restaurant charging three times the price.

Puddings, such as raspberry cranachan or fruit crumble, or a choice of Scottish cheeses all from the same dairy in Achmore, are a fitting end.

Bag a table by one of the big uncluttered windows so that you can look out over the sands to Rassay and Skye and you'll soon be chatting to the locals: the inn is the hub of village life here.

the ceilidh place

14 West Argyle St
Ullapool
Highland
01854 612103
www.theceilidhplace.com
serves lunch and dinner
mon to sun;
bookings advised;
children welcome; garden

There's nowhere quite like The Ceilidh Place. It started life in 1970 in an old Ullapool boatshed, where the poet Robert Urquhart and his wife Jean served modest refreshments to accompany the poetry readings, concerts and exhibitions they put on. A bar-cum-café gradually developed, and The Ceilidh Place now occupies several whitewashed cottages and consists of a small, traditional bar, complete with a peat fire and cosy sofas, a large bar-cum-café, a restaurant, a bookshop, a small poetry library and bedrooms.

The Ceilidh Place's conception as an arts venue has set the tone, and it has an earnest, happy, liberal feel. It isn't just used by students and would-be writers, though: there are plenty of kids having ice-cream with their mums, grannies chatting over scones, and teenage girls drinking lattes and texting their boyfriends.

Feeding time starts with breakfast. Then there's cake, coffee and tea, served in all varieties, great sandwiches such as Argyll ham with home-made chutney, and more substantial dishes, from smoked haddock soup to lamb braised in heather ale or garlic-roasted monkfish. Main courses aren't cheap, but the food here has great purity, and for that you need good ingredients. Don't go looking for fancy restaurant food though; this is simple cooking, very well done.

The dining room, in a spacious, sunny conservatory by the bar, has the same menu as the rest of the place, but it's still worth reserving a table here, as it's an uplifting place to sit, with its pine tables, stone floor, curtains in time-warp 1970s fabric and contemporary art and photographs on the wall. Poetry readings, plays and concerts now take place in a small hall across the road; there's usually something going on if you feel like food for the mind as well as the body.

the wheatsheaf

Main Street
Swinton
Borders
01890 860257
www.wheatsheaf-
swinton.com
serves lunch and dinner
tues to sun in summer,
tues to sun lunch in winter;
bookings advised;
children accepted; garden

The Wheatsheaf, a no-nonsense stone inn opposite the green in the dour town of Swinton, is one of the few really good places to eat in the Scottish borders. Chef and owner Alan Reid cooks with prime Scottish ingredients (he's a stickler for the best materials) to produce food that is a careful blend of modern Scottish and classical French, with a touch of the Med thrown in.

Reid is a keen shooter and fisherman, so it's likely that he will have done more than just cook the fish on your plate. From the River Tweed there's salmon that might be seared and served with salsa verde or cooked in a toasted oatmeal crust and served with lemon butter sauce – and it's a million miles away from the farmed stuff. There are good renditions of pub classics (beer-battered haddock; liver with onions, bacon and Madeira) alongside more sophisticated dishes, and Reid regularly offers 'Taste of Scotland' dinners: his creamed smoked haddock with St Andrews cheese or Highland venison with juniper and sloe gin are hymns to Scottish produce.

Two small dining rooms are furnished with traditional dark furniture and so much bottle green you'd think it was Christmas. A third, in a conservatory extension, is pine-lined and furnished with cane furniture. The bar is filled with settles, low tables and winged chairs and is very much a place for a civilized drink before dinner rather than a boozy evening.

The Wheatsheaf is definitely a dining destination rather than a boisterous local and herein lies the only problem: it can lack atmosphere, even when busy, and tends to be rather staid. It's not a place for a swinging evening, but if that suits you, you'll enjoy an exceptional meal.

crinan hotel

Crinan
Argyll and Bute
01546 830261
www.crinanhotel.com
serves lunch and dinner
mon to sun;
bookings advised;
children welcome; terrace

The road to Crinan is breathtaking. Travelling along beside sea lochs and silver inlets on the edge of Argyll, you already feel like you're in some kind of Eden – and then you reach Crinan itself, where the boats, the canal, the lighthouse and the Crinan Hotel make everything perfect.

The Crinan Hotel is quietly stylish and individual. The walls are covered with Scottish art – both the owner's wife and his son are artists – and the place is full of interesting pieces of old furniture, ethnic and antique lamps and *objets*. There's not a hint of chintz or corporate blandness.

The bar, which has its own entrance, is oak-panelled, and furnished with antique tables and tartan-covered banquettes. It feels smart and old-fashioned, though the big contemporary canvas on the wall and checked cotton napkins give it a touch of modern simplicity. The first-class food is in similar vein: the chef, Ben Tish, uses fine raw materials and does very little to them. There's Loch Etive mussels with white wine and garlic, and high-quality sausages with a rich, silky mash and an intense onion gravy. Fish with hollandaise sauce or Aberdeen Angus rib-eye with salsa verde and roast tomatoes is as fancy as it gets. Chips and bread are homemade and couldn't be better. There's usually only a couple of puddings, but they're part of the same class act – dishes like Valrhona bitter chocolate tart or nougat parfait with berries.

The punters are yachties – mostly in big groups with hungry, well-behaved children – and moneyed elderly couples, and there's a smattering of dapper city types who like the civility of the place. There are two restaurants at the Crinan, overseen by the same chef, serving much more sophisticated food, but you'll eat just as well, though more simply, in the bar, with the advantage of a view over the lighthouse and a prime position from which to watch boats negotiate the lock system on the Crinan Canal before sailing away on the Sound of Jura.

the plockton hotel

Harbour
Plockton
Highland
01599 544274
www.plocktonhotel.co.uk
serves lunch and dinner
mon to sun;
bookings accepted;
children welcome;
garden (for drinking only)

A vast stretch of sea loch, tree-covered mountains, clusters of Highland cottages and not a shred of tourist tat: Plockton is the kind of Scottish village that you long to find. No wonder it's where they filmed the television drama *Hamish Macbeth*.

The stone-built Plockton Hotel, which has been painted glossy black, has adopted the rather un-Scottish emblem of a palm tree against the moon as its logo. It's entirely appropriate, however; it's so balmy in Plockton that palm trees do grow along the seafront right by the hotel.

The Plockton's owners, Tom and Dorothy Pearson, have created something rare here: a hotel bar that serves traditional pubby food – steaks, fish and chips and stews – well. There's no skimping on the standard of ingredients used and no short-cuts are taken in their preparation. Steaks are from the Highlands and sourced from their favourite butcher in Dingwall, as is the venison, which might be braised with red wine and juniper. The fish is all caught off the West Coast, and there's a smattering of simple dishes based on what's right on their doorstep: Plockton prawns, landed at the harbour every afternoon, served with mayo; Lochcarron salmon, either smoked or poached; hand-dived scallops with lime and ginger; and, their signature dish, 'Plockton Smokies', which consist of flakes of smoked mackerel layered with cheese and cream and baked.

The Pearsons take great care of you, and the views from the hotel and it's little outside tables are stunning.

northern ireland
and eire

Rock, earth, water and light: you are always aware of the elements in Ireland. Dublin may now be one of the hippest cities in Europe, and Galway may be humming with youth and energy, but wherever you are the land is still pre-eminent. There's inky lakes and glittering pools, bogs that can be cut into big square sods, and all that stone — mountains, mammoth boulders, cairns, tumbling walls, shale and scree. The Irish have always been proud of this landscape, but they've had trouble knowing what to do with its produce. The potato famine of the mid-19th-century fostered a culture that appreciated food but was wary of asking for more than its presence. Irish wild salmon, native oysters, Dublin Bay prawns, lamb, beef, butter and cheese: they've all been exported and valued worldwide, but in Ireland — although folk were glad to have reasonable food on their plates — they didn't make too much of a fuss about them.

Now all that's changed. The Celtic tiger came into the kitchen with a roar in the early 1990s. People didn't just have more money, they had confidence in all things Irish. Instead of leaving the country, young

people returned, bringing with them tastes from New York, San Francisco and London. People from other nationalities, who loved food and the countryside, started to settle here too. It seems that every other person you meet in County Cork is a cheesemaker, and they're as likely to be German or English as Irish.

What is so remarkable about this revolution is that it hasn't produced a 'modern Irish cuisine' littered with sun-dried tomatoes and doused in Asian fish sauce. The cooking that has emerged – fuelled by such influential people as chefs Myrtle and Darina Allen at Ballymaloe House in County Cork and John and Sally McKenna with their exemplary Bridgestone food guides – is more a confident return to traditional ingredients and dishes than an espousal of innovation.

This style of cooking, in which the watchwords are 'simple' and 'local', is well-suited to pubs. Many of the pubs in this chapter serve top-notch versions of Irish classics alongside more individual dishes based on good Irish ingredients. That's not to say things haven't moved on – you'll find crab cakes with smoked chilli mayonnaise and thin scorched pizza topped with caramelized onions and Cashel Blue cheese. But influences from abroad have been incorporated with so much taste and skill that you start to think dishes like pizza must have been Irish all along. That is the mark of a culture that's confident about its cooking.

Irish pubs have always been great, partly because they're great levellers (everybody goes to them), partly because they can be both stages for the loquacious and refuges where the thoughtful can sup a pint unbothered, and partly because impromptu music sessions seem to erupt at any time. Put all this together with good food and you have an unbeatable combination.

Ballymore Eustace

Co. Kildare

Eire

045 864585

serves lunch and dinner

tues to mon lunch;

bookings accepted

(dining room only);

children welcome; garden

the ballymore inn

Roll up at The Ballymore Inn at four in the afternoon and you'll find it still humming from lunch. Punters who've had a win at the race-course will be swigging Champagne and smart County Kildare ladies – this is a well-heeled area, home to Ireland's greatest stud farms – will be having coffee and pastries. Chef and owner Georgina O'Sullivan has created a modern country pub and everybody loves it.

The food isn't fancy; it's modern café style. Georgina would describe it as 'home-food', and it smacks of Californian casualness, though there's nothing ad-hoc about the standard of cooking. As much of the produce as possible is organic. Chicken is free-range, beef is hung until it tastes like beef, and fish is delivered daily. Georgina takes inspiration from everywhere – there's Moroccan lamb couscous, Thai fish broth with coconut milk, and beef and wild mushrooms in Guinness – and she is true to the roots of all of these dishes.

The food in the bar is simpler than that in the dining room, but both rooms have similar decor: modern Irish art on cream walls, green canvas blinds and a mixture of furniture. When The Ballymore Inn opened, there wasn't a pub in Ireland doing this kind of cooking. At first local people thought it was mad to go out to eat dishes like sausages and mash; now they're queueing up for it.

pizza with caramelized onions, walnuts and cashel blue

This is a good example of how to use regional produce – in this case Cashel Blue cheese – in a dish from another country in a way which enhances the produce. Cashel Blue is a great cheese, with undertones of smoky bacon. There's really nothing like it, but if you can't find it, use dolcelatte or a creamy Gorgonzola instead.

serves 4

450g (1lb) pizza dough (see recipe)

for the topping

30ml (2tbsp) olive oil

4 large onions, thinly sliced

30ml (2tbsp) granulated sugar

30ml (2tbsp) sherry vinegar

salt and pepper

115g (4oz) Cashel Blue cheese, crumbled

55g (2oz) shelled walnuts, broken

for the dough

1.5kg strong white flour

15ml (1tbsp) sea salt

30g (1oz) fresh yeast or 2 sachets fast-acting dried

5ml (1tsp) honey (optional)

30ml (2tbsp) olive oil

1 Preheat the oven to 240°C/475°F/gas mark 9.

2 Heat the olive oil in a large heavy-bottomed pan. Add the onions and a dash of water, cover and sweat them over a very low heat until soft – it will take 30–40 minutes. Turn the heat up so that the onions begin to brown, then add the sugar and cook, stirring, to caramelize them. Add the vinegar, season and set aside to cool.

3 Grease a baking sheet with a little extra olive oil. On a floured surface, roll the dough out in as thin a circle as possible. Carefully place on the baking sheet.

4 Spread the onion mixture over the dough and sprinkle over the cheese. Bake for 15–20 minutes, until crisp and fully cooked, adding the walnuts about 5 minutes before the end. Don't add them too soon or they will burn.

pizza dough

1 Sift the flour and salt together in a large bowl.

2 If using fresh yeast, blend it with the honey and a little warm water. Allow to stand in a warm place until dissolved and foamy on top. Alternatively, the fast-acting dried yeast can be added directly into the flour.

3 Mix 900ml (32fl oz) water and the olive oil with the fresh yeast and stir into the dry ingredients. Continue to mix until it forms a manageable dough.

4 Turn out onto a floured surface and knead for 10 minutes, until really smooth. Put it back in the bowl, cover with a damp tea-towel and leave in a warm place to rise for a couple of hours, until doubled in volume. (The dough can be kept at this stage, covered in clingfilm, in the refrigerator for 2 days.)

5 Knock back the dough and shape or roll it to the size and thickness you want.

chargrilled aubergine salad with mature ardrahan cheese

If you can't find mature Ardrahan but want to stick to an Irish cheese, try Milleens or Gubbeen. If you can't get any of these, try Italian taleggio. Serve this salad as soon as you've cooked the vegetables, as their warmth slightly melts the cheese.

serves 4

75ml (5tbsp) balsamic vinegar

2 medium aubergines

olive oil

salt and pepper

10 cherry tomatoes

2 handfuls of salad leaves – rocket, watercress and lamb's lettuce

55g (2oz) Ardrahan cheese, cut into small chunks

for the dressing

2.5g (1/2tsp) cumin seeds

60ml (4tbsp) extra virgin olive oil

juice of 1/2 small lemon

1 clove garlic, very finely chopped

1 To make the dressing, heat the cumin seeds in a dry pan and toast them for about 30 seconds. Grind. Mix with the other dressing ingredients.

2 For the salad, in a small saucepan bring the balsamic vinegar to the boil and reduce by half. Set aside.

3 Cut the aubergines into 1cm (⅜ inch) slices. Brush with olive oil and season well. Heat a cast-iron griddle pan and cook the aubergines on both sides until they are coloured and quite soft. Put them in a bowl.

4 Halve the tomatoes and place them, cut side down, on the hot pan for 1–2 minutes to slightly soften and heat them. Add these to the aubergine.

5 Pour half of the dressing onto the vegetables. Dress the salad leaves with the other half.

6 To serve, place the salad leaves on a large plate (or divide between 4 smaller ones), and top with the aubergines and tomatoes. Scatter the Ardrahan cheese over this and drizzle on the reduced balsamic vinegar.

'peoples' concerns have changed a lot over the last five years. now they want to know where their food comes from and who produced it.' georgina

beef and wild mushrooms in guinness with champ

Champ is a great dish when made with plenty of butter and seasoned well, so don't stint on either. Serve it in a mound with a little hollow in the middle, in which you should melt yet another good knob of butter. Dip each forkful of champ in the resulting puddle of butter before you eat it. Not healthy, but wonderful!

serves 4–6

30ml (2tbsp) olive oil

1kg (2lb 3oz) chuck steak, cut into thin slices

2 large leeks, white and lower green parts only, roughly chopped

2 medium carrots, roughly chopped

2 celery sticks, roughly chopped

2 cloves garlic, finely sliced

250ml (9fl oz) Guinness

130ml (4½fl oz) beef stock

salt and pepper

approx. 30g (1oz) butter

50g (1¾oz) streaky bacon, diced

100g (3¾oz) wild mushrooms, roughly sliced

1 large Spanish onion, finely chopped

10g (2tsp) plain flour

to serve

small handful of flat-leaf parsley, finely chopped

1 Heat the olive oil in a large heavy-bottomed pan and quickly brown the meat on all sides. Put the meat into a casserole dish.

2 Sauté the leeks, carrots and celery in the same pan in which you browned the meat, then add to the meat with the garlic. Pour in the Guinness and beef stock and season. Turn the heat down low, cover and simmer gently for about 1½ hours.

3 Remove the meat from the casserole and strain off the liquid, discarding the vegetables. Place the meat back in a clean casserole dish with the liquid.

4 Melt a knob of butter in a frying pan and briskly sauté the bacon, mushrooms and onion. Add to the pot.

5 Make a *beurre manié* by mashing another knob of butter with an equal quantity of flour, until you have a soft paste. Reheat the casserole and whisk small bits of the *beurre manié* into the boiling liquid – this will slightly thicken it. Simmer for a few minutes more and taste for seasoning. Scatter with parsley and serve with buttery champ.

champ

1kg (2lb 3oz) floury potatoes, peeled

6 spring onions, finely chopped

55ml (2fl oz) full-fat milk

55g (2oz) butter, plus extra to serve

salt and pepper

1 Cut the potatoes into even-sized chunks. Bring a large saucepan of water to the boil and cook the potatoes till tender.

2 Put the spring onions and the milk in a small saucepan and heat until just boiling. This softens the spring onions and flavours the milk.

3 Mash the potatoes, stirring in the milk, onions and butter as you do so. Season well. Serve with extra butter on the side.

almond and apricot cake

This is one of the most delicious cakes I have ever tasted. The secret is the light soaking in lemon syrup – this makes it gorgeously moist. At the Ballymore Inn, they sometimes serve this cake with oranges in caramel.

serves 8

225g (8oz) butter, plus extra for buttering

100g (3¾oz) dried apricots (the no-need-to-soak variety)

225g (8oz) caster sugar

juice of 1 lemon

80g (2¾oz) ground almonds

3 large eggs, beaten

100g (3¾oz) plain flour, sifted

for the lemon syrup

15ml (1tbsp) caster sugar

juice of 1 lemon

to serve

whipped cream or crème fraîche

1 Preheat the oven to 180°C/350°F/gas mark 4. Lightly butter a shallow 23cm (10 inch) round cake tin and then line it with 2 layers of baking parchment.

2 Roughly chop the apricots in a food processor or with a sharp knife.

3 In a large bowl, beat the butter and sugar together until light and fluffy. Add the lemon juice, ground almonds and beaten eggs and mix thoroughly. Fold in the flour and the apricots.

4 Put the mixture into the lined tin and bake for about 35 minutes, until the cake is firm and golden and leaving the sides of the tin. Leave in the tin for a few minutes, then lift out onto a plate and remove the baking parchment.

5 To make the lemon syrup, in a small saucepan gently heat the sugar and lemon juice together until the sugar has dissolved. Pour this syrup over the cake while it is still warm.

6 Serve warm or cold, with whipped cream or crème fraîche.

'i serve home food. every dish that we do here is cooked first in my own kitchen.' georgina

Glencairn

near Lismore

Co. Waterford

Eire

058 56232

www.lismore.com

serves dinner only mon to sun

in high season, weds to sun

for the rest of the year;

bookings advised;

children welcome by special

arrangement

buggy's glencairn inn

Buggy's isn't just worth a detour; it is worth getting on a plane for. Even from the outside, the place enchants. A pink cottage with small-paned windows, its white picket fence just about contains an anarchic garden of herbs, flowers and creepers. Inside, three cottagey dining rooms are done up in the idiosyncratic style that is Ken and Cathleen Buggy's. There are red and white checked cloths on the tables and pots of wild flowers dotted around. A profusion of objects – old taps, binoculars, a milking stool and an antique model plane – hang from the beamed ceilings. Shelves are lined with poetry books and old recordings of musicals, and the walls are covered with bits of Irish art and sketches and cartoons by Ken Buggy himself.

None of this seems contrived. The place has obviously been put together in the haphazard, maverick way in which Ken Buggy operates. He just does what he fancies, and this approach is evident in his cooking. Read the short menu and you think you'll get some good, country home-cooking: tomato and wild herb soup; baked salmon with Buggy's chips; Sicilian braised rabbit; rhubarb and ginger crumble. When the food arrives, you see that it's domestic cooking taken to the highest level. Everything you taste, from a salad leaf to a mouthful of wild salmon, sings with flavour and is presented without fussy adornment. Fish comes with a wedge of lemon and a sprig of dill or wild fennel. Irish stew comes in a broad soup plate with a scattering of parsley. Chips, which are so finely cut that some of them frizzle into golden curls, are scattered with sea salt and served in a huge white bowl.

Ken Buggy seems to muse over the cooker, improvising as he goes. I saw him making the day's bread, thinking aloud about what he'd cook or what herbs were doing well in the garden, and I wondered how he'd manage to feed 30 people later on. But he works from an inner compulsion to simply serve a good meal, rather than to any grand plan. He chooses his organic veg, grown just up the road, before they're even pulled from the ground. The daily fish delivery doesn't arrive till seven in the evening, so he has to keep an open mind about what to do with it. Every menu is dictated by what he can get hold of, what he still has to use up from the previous day and what's in the garden, and the effort he makes – in choosing just the right herb for a summery tomato soup, say – translates through to the plate. The food is full of creativity, simplicity and joy.

The Buggy's experience is very much like being entertained by a friend who wants to give you the very best meal he can, in a place that you'll never cease to find interesting. There's just nowhere like it.

salmon baked in herbs with buggy's chips

Sounds ordinary? Not a bit of it. Ken's chips are thin and golden, some cooked into light little curls. You'd think angels had made them. Cook them exactly as he says. The secret is using plenty of fresh water for soaking, and then cooking the chips in good oil – twice – at *exactly* the right temperature. If you can get your hands on wild salmon, it doesn't need any fancier treatment than the method below. This dish is pure bliss.

serves 8–12

a few big bunches of herbs, wild if possible, such as chervil, dill, parsley, fennel or tarragon and nettle tops

salt and pepper

1 medium fennel bulb, finely sliced

225g (8oz) unsalted butter

1 x 3.6kg (8lb) wild salmon, gutted

juice of 1 lemon

1 Preheat the oven to 180°C/350°F/gas mark 4. Lay the herbs on a large sheet of tin foil, folded so that it's double thickness. Season.

2 Put the fennel and some big knobs of butter into the salmon and season inside and out. Lay the salmon on the herbs and squeeze over the lemon juice.

3 Generously cover the upper side of the salmon with slices of butter. Fold the sheet of foil over the salmon and seal tightly. Carefully place on a large baking tray, and bake on the middle shelf of the preheated oven for about 1½ hours.

4 Remove from the oven and open up the foil package. Serve warm with chips.

buggy's chips

1½ large potatoes, such as Maris Piper or Golden Wonder, per person

vegetable oil, for deep-frying

to serve

sea salt

cider or white wine vinegar (optional)

fresh parsley, finely chopped

1 Slice the end off each potato and peel them evenly. Cut them into thin lengths the width of a Bic Biro, putting them immediately into a large sink of fresh cold water to rinse off the starch.

2 To cook the chips, blanch them (ie half-cook them) in vegetable oil heated to 160°C for a few minutes, until the chips are tender but not coloured. Fry in batches if necessary, as it's important not to overfill the chip basket. Put the 'blanched' chips onto a tray lined with newspaper or kitchen paper.

3 Line a big bowl with kitchen paper. To finish the chips, cook them in oil heated to 185°C, then put them in the bowl to drain. Again, don't overfill the basket. Sprinkle the cooked chips with plenty of sea salt, vinegar if using, and parsley. Serve immediately.

irish stew

This is a refined version of Irish stew, as it's made with good chops rather than scrag end of lamb. Make sure the chops are good and fatty, or ask your butcher for extra lamb fat. If you can't get a decent amount of lamb fat, do the initial browning in unsalted butter. Traditionally Irish stew is served with a pint of Guinness which, as Ken says, is a disgusting habit...

serves 4

8 x 115g (4oz) chunky lamb chops, with fat

6 medium onions, thickly sliced

6 large carrots, cut into 6mm (1/4 inch) slices

12 medium potatoes, cut into 1.5cm (1/2 inch) slices

handful of parsley, chopped

salt and white pepper

3 sprigs fresh thyme leaves

15ml (1tbsp) plain flour

15g (1/2oz) unsalted butter

15g (1tbsp) finely chopped parsley

1 Put a large casserole dish to warm in an oven preheated to 150°C/300°F/gas mark 2.

2 Cut the fat off the lamb and melt it in a large heavy-bottomed pan over a high heat, then quickly brown the chops for about 30 seconds on each side. Remove and set aside on a plate.

3 Sweat the onions in the same pan until they're shiny and coated with fat but not cooked through. Remove and set aside. Sauté the carrots briskly in the lamb fat.

4 Layer the chops, onions, carrots and potatoes in the warm casserole dish, adding generous amounts of parsley, salt, pepper and thyme to each layer. The last 'layer' should be potatoes. Pour over enough cold water to just cover.

5 Put the casserole back into the oven (without a lid) and cook for 2 hours. Half an hour before the end of the cooking time, remove the casserole and carefully drain off all the 'stock' into a saucepan.

6 Make a little *beurre manié* by mashing the flour with an equal amount of butter until you have a soft paste. Bring the stock to the boil and whisk in small bits of the *beurre manié*. This should slightly thicken it. Pour the stock back over the stew and return to the oven to warm through.

7 Preheat the grill. Just before serving, brown the top under the grill for a moment. Sprinkle with the finely chopped parsley.

stuffed loin of pork cooked over hickory chips

This recipe is pure Ken Buggy – born of improvisation, unusual but simple, and fantastic home food. It has been on and off the menu at Buggy's for quite a few years. Serve with boiled potatoes and buttered cabbage.

serves 4

900g (2lb) pork loin

55g (2oz) mixed dried fruit

5ml (1tsp) demerara sugar

ground cinnamon

salt and pepper

bunch of herbs, wild if possible, such as thyme and sage

1 medium carrot, roughly chopped

1 small onion, roughly chopped

1/2 bag hickory chips

approx. 40ml (2½tbsp) plain flour

140ml (1/4 pint) dry cider

1 Ensure the butcher does not trim off too much of the 'belly' from the pork loin, or there won't be enough meat to place the stuffing on and then turn over on to the 'eye' of the loin. Ask the butcher to cut back the eye almost clear of the flap, and cut back the meat at the 'thin' end so that it opens up like two pages in a book.

2 Soak the dried fruit in water with the sugar and a small pinch of cinnamon for at least 2 hours, but ideally overnight. (Dice any large fruits, such as apricots or prunes, first.)

3 Preheat the oven to 180°C/350°F/gas mark 4. Spread the dried fruit onto the meat 'pages' and season, then roll up so as the 'eye' is innermost.

4 Tie up the loin with cotton string at 5cm (2 inch) intervals. Tie each loop individually. Spread the herbs, chopped vegetables and hickory chips in the bottom of a cast-iron pan. Place the loin on top and season with salt, pepper and 10g (2tsp) cinnamon. Cook in the oven for about 2 hours, until the juices run clear when the meat is pierced with a sharp knife. Lift the loin from the casserole dish and carefully wrap it in foil to rest.

5 Strain off the liquid into a jug and discard the vegetables, herbs and hickory chips. Return the liquid to the casserole.

6 Off the heat, add enough flour to the mixture that's left in the bottom of the casserole to make a small roux (use roughly the same amount of flour as oil left in the dish.) Stir the roux for a couple of minutes to brown – there will be enough heat in the pan to cook it.

7 Place the casserole over a gentle heat and very slowly add the cider and juices from the resting meat, whisking continuously. Bring to the boil and reduce to a thick, rich gravy, then strain. Keep warm.

8 Cut the loin into 1cm (⅜ inch) slices and serve with the gravy.

chocolate and rum cake

This, like many of Ken's recipes, sounds perfectly ordinary, but it is a stunning cake – rich yet very, very light. I suspect he adds rather more alcohol than the amount given here, so feel free to up the quantity.

serves 6–8

sunflower oil, for greasing

3 large eggs, separated

225g (8oz) caster sugar

225g (8oz) plain flour

5ml (1tsp) baking powder

65g (2¹/₄oz) cocoa powder

¹/₂ teacup Lamb's Navy Rum or Tia Maria

for the topping

100g (3³/₄oz) plain chocolate, with 55% cocoa solids

55g (2oz) unsalted butter, diced

60ml (4tbsp) runny honey

125ml (4¹/₂fl oz) double cream

to serve

whipped cream

vanilla ice-cream

1 Preheat the oven to 190°C/375°F/gas mark 5. Grease a 20 x 30cm (8 x 12 inch) cake tin with sunflower oil, then line with foil, leaving at least 5cm (2 inch) overhanging at the sides

2 In a large bowl, whisk the egg yolks and caster sugar together for 2 minutes. Add 75ml (5tbsp) cold water, and whisk for about 10 minutes, until creamy.

3 Whisk the egg whites in another large bowl, until firm.

4 Sift together the flour, baking powder and cocoa. Fold the dry ingredients into the egg yolk mixture, then gently fold in the whisked egg whites. Pour into the greased cake tin and bake in the preheated oven for about 20 minutes, until a metal skewer inserted in the cake comes out clean. Invert the cake out onto a wire rack and carefully peel off the foil. Leave to cool.

5 Once cool, cut the sponge in half horizontally and then cut each half in half again horizontally.

6 Lay flat, with the cut sides up, and soak each layer of cake with rum.

7 For the topping, melt the chocolate in a small bowl over a pan of simmering water. Add the butter, honey and cream. Mix together, but do not let it boil.

8 Just before serving, spread each layer with warm chocolate sauce and stack together. Pour the remaining sauce over and serve with whipped cream or vanilla ice-cream, or both.

'i suppose i cook irish food, though i do the odd dish like sicilian rabbit. even when it's Irish, i take a kind of provençal approach – it's rustic, unfussy, local.' ken

the best of the rest

blair's inn

Blarney

Co. Cork

Eire

021 4381470

www.blairsinn.ie

serves lunch and dinner

mon to sun;

bookings accepted;

children welcome; garden

If you'd like the chance to catch a nun approaching a plate of corned beef, cabbage and parsley sauce with the same degree of reverence she usually reserves for communion wine, pitch up at Blair's Inn. I saw three, munching their way through huge plates in silent, shared enjoyment.

Everyone comes to Blair's for the good, no-nonsense Irish home cooking: lamb braised in Murphy's stout, baked ham with cabbage and champ, Irish stew, roast stuffed loin of pork with apples and cider. All these recipes were passed down to the owner, Anne Blair, by her mother. Anne, a pharmacist-turned-cook, also offers more modern Irish dishes, such as a tart of leeks and Co. Clare goat's cheese, and simple French dishes made using good Irish ingredients, such as escalopes of wild salmon with grain mustard sauce.

The pub's exterior – a white-washed cottage with red paint work and baskets of flowers – is rural Irish, but there's a touch of provincial France inside. A big table weighed down with brandies and liqueurs and a jug of country flowers sets the tone in the two small dining rooms. A stone fireplace piled high with books, and storm lanterns glowing with candles, make you want to settle down for the evening, and the service, with Anne's husband John at the helm, is full of banter.

the purple heather

Henry Street

Kenmare

Co. Kerry

Eire

064 41016

serves food 11.45am-5pm mon

to sat; no bookings;

children welcome

The Purple Heather is the model for a new kind of eating place – a seamless blend of pub and café – that is gradually evolving in Ireland, particularly in locations with culinary reputations, such as Kenmare and towns and villages in County Cork. It works so well that you wish one would open everywhere.

Tall, arched windows with plants silhouetted against their panes, ox-blood coloured walls, Irish ceramic lamps and a mixture of old posters and contemporary Irish art make the place feel comforting and elegant at the same time, and more than a little bohemian. A handsome old bar, running almost the length of the room, dispenses coffee and rich, fruity Guinness cake, as well as pints and crab sandwiches, while ladies who lunch, lone readers of poetry books and groups of giggly girls squeeze around the dark antique chairs and tables that fill the rest of the place.

The pub is owned by Grainne O'Connell, sister of Maura O'Connell Foley, one of the foremost restaurateurs in the area (the Foley family owns Packie's restaurant just up the street), and the food is as good as you'd expect, made with the freshest ingredients and the utmost care. There's organic salad leaves dressed with perfectly seasoned vinaigrette; roasted peppers with black olives and pesto; Irish farmhouse cheeses with wheaten bread and apple chutney, and a 'Purple Heather' omelette: light, creamy and oozing with cheese, onions, potatoes and thyme. Everything tastes homemade or freshly baked and the place is so friendly and civilized that you'll want to borrow a copy of *The Irish Times*, order another pint or a pot of tea and while away the afternoon.

moran's of the weir

The Weir

Kilcolgan

Co. Galway

Eire

091 796113

www.moransoystercottage.com

serves lunch and dinner

mon to sun;

bookings accepted;

children welcome; terrace

Slurping oysters and supping Guinness outside Moran's on a warm spring or autumn day must be one of the great, simple pleasures in life. Sure, it's a kind of Ireland that the cynical might scorn as twee and unreal: a white-washed thatched cottage a dozen miles outside Galway town, by a weir where swans glide and cattle graze. But it's real. Moran's is a family business going back more than 250 years. The food is tasty and unpretentious, there are more locals than tourists, and the buzz is terrific.

Hardly any cooking goes on at all. Apart from grilled oysters and lobster or *moules marinière*, everything is cold and simply assembled: great platters of wild smoked salmon, locally grown oysters or superb crab. And don't be too snobbish to order the prawn cocktail: the sweet, meaty prawns you get here are a million miles away from the water-logged morsels you often find.

You can eat in the cosy little front bar, with a snug that you can have all to yourself, or in any of the interconnecting dining rooms at the back, with their rough-hewn walls, stone floors, 1930s lamps and old dressers. The walls are covered in black-and-white photos of all the celebrities who've ever visited (they make quite a song and dance about their celebrity strike rate). But don't worry, in 15 years of visiting Moran's I haven't spotted a single one. You're more likely to find yourself surrounded by sprawling family groups, courting couples, people having a jar on the way home from work, serious drinkers and the odd priest.

Desserts aren't really worth bothering with unless you want a shot of sugar. Just order more Guinness or Chablis and forget about the rest of the day.

o'sullivan's

Crookhaven

Co. Cork

Eire

028 35319

serves food 11am-8pm

mon to sun;

no bookings;

children welcome;

outside dining by the pier

Unlike a number of the gastropubs in this book, O'Sullivans hasn't been refurbished or newly designed, and it doesn't have a stellar chef who used to work in a country house hotel. In fact, there's very little cooking done here at all. But if you're in this part of the world, go, for it's a genuine, unpretentious, uniquely hospitable place that serves simple, good food.

The journey's worth it for a start. You travel out to near Mizzen Head, the most south-westerly point of Ireland, along a coastline shredded by tiny inlets. O'Sullivans, a big, weather-beaten white house, is a stone's throw from the water's edge. Inside, everything is just as it has evolved, with stone walls and floors, a collection of black-and-white photos of the townsfolk, taken in the 1960s and now yellowing behind glass, framed obituaries of local fishermen, and a huge stuffed lobster.

It's all overseen by the charming Dermot, whose family bought the place in the 1930s, and his mum, Angela, who does the cooking. The menu runs to seafood chowder, platters of poached salmon, smoked salmon or crab salad and baskets of tiny shrimps with mayonnaise. It's some of the freshest fish you'll ever taste. The desserts are comforting: rhubarb crumble, chocolate biscuit cake and bread-and-butter pudding. It's the kind of place you're more likely to find in coastal Brittany than in Ireland or Britain: simple décor and food from just outside the front door.

Yachties, fishermen, tourists and locals all chatter together, and it seems like there are as many children as adults in the mix. Irish music sessions take place most nights, making the great atmosphere even better, and Dermot – who tends to everyone with a gentle friendliness – will probably escort you to the door and wave you good-bye. You'll leave glowing.

mary ann's

Castletownshend
Co. Cork
Eire
028 36146
serves lunch and dinner
mon to sun in summer,
tues to sun in winter;
bookings accepted
(dining room only);
children welcome; garden

You don't go to Mary Ann's just for the food, you go for the whole experience. An old, dusky-pink terraced house in the beautiful village of Castletownsend, it embodies what people dream of when they think of an Irish pub: a clientele that has turned enjoyment into an art form, great banter with the barman (and everybody else, for that matter), and a lived-in, authentic interior.

You can eat in several different areas, but the bar-rooms – usually crammed, and you can't book tables – are where the action is. With their slate floors, sea-grass chairs, ships' paraphernalia and antique clocks, they're lovely places to sit, and completely unstudied in their charm; witness the two bottles of sun-tan lotion beside the coffee machine (this part of Ireland is warmed by the Gulf Stream, so you could get lucky).

All human life is here – children, grannies, teenagers, guys out on the razzle – ably presided over by owner Fergus O'Mahony, a smiling bear of a man who hurries about dispensing warmth and good humour while keeping his finger firmly on the pulse. He's a great publican.

The cooking is straightforward and based on good ingredients. There's smoked salmon from nearby Union Hall, rack of West Cork lamb with rosemary, a gargantuan and spankingly fresh seafood platter, and some more contemporary dishes such as John Dory with sun-blush tomatoes and black olives. The raspberry crème brûlée, with a glassy surface that you could skate on, is one of the best you'll ever taste. And you won't be able to stop ordering the wildly potent Irish coffees. You can find more polished cooking in other West Cork venues – there's no shortage of decent restaurants in this part of the world – but Mary Ann's combination of good food and great *craic* is unique.

kealy's

Greencastle
Co. Donegal
Eire
077 81010
serves lunch and dinner
tues to sun in summer,
thurs to sun in winter;
bookings advised;
children welcome lunch
and early evening only;
garden

At Kealy's you get both romance and reality. Open the door and, as soon as you smell the garlic and fish frying in olive oil, you feel as though you're on holiday. You'll be glad you have booked a table in this bustling room full of paint-washed furniture, seascapes and wooden fish. It's just the kind of watering hole that you hope will be tucked away in every seaside town.

On the other hand, Kealy's doesn't look like much on the outside. It's a plain, four-square Irish pub in a working port, where there are trawlers and ice plants down at the harbour as well as little boats in primary colours. The lights that twinkle so prettily at night across the bay are actually from Magilligan prison.

So the Kealy's experience is not twee, and neither is the food. The starters are no-nonsense: smoked salmon, *moules marinière* and seafood chowder. These are well done, but they give no hint of the standard of fish cookery to come. Main courses – John Dory with anchovy butter; salmon with grain mustard sauce on cabbage and bacon; hake with tomatoes and saffron butter sauce – are all blissful celebrations of the sea, cooked with flair and precision. The vegetables, unfortunately, aren't; if they gave you less than five, they might have more chance of cooking them well.

Owner and chef James Kealy has established quite a reputation over the last decade, and people drive from as far away as Co. Antrim to eat here. In summer you can take a car ferry from Magilligan, which makes the visit all the more fun. In good weather it's thronged, so reserve well in advance.

the john hewitt

Donegall Street

Belfast

Northern Ireland

028 9023 3768

serves food noon to 6pm

mon to sat;

bookings accepted

(except for fri lunch);

children welcome at

lunch time only; garden

Named after the late Ulster poet and socialist, this pub is owned and run by the Belfast Unemployment Resource Centre. But banish from your mind all notions of worthy brown food served by earnest young politicos. You get gutsy stuff here, far beyond normal pub grub in execution, but true to the origins of pub food: homely, restorative, unfussy stuff.

Lamb pie with Savoy cabbage, chicken with leeks, barley and black pudding, fruit crumbles, tarts and platters of Irish cheeses with home-made chutney: it's the kind of food you wish someone would do for you every day. Would that it were the norm for pub food everywhere! The prices also make it one of the best bargains in this book, and an additional glow comes from the knowledge that the money you hand over is going to a good cause.

The John Hewitt was refurbished before it opened at the end of the 1990s, but there's nothing faux about it. It still feels like a genuine pub, complete with a marble-topped bar, open fire and dark wood panelling. There are black-and-white photos of contemporary Irish poets on the walls and the beautiful exterior, with its panels of etched and stained glass, is pure pub vernacular. The punters, mostly students, journalists and arty types, give the place vitality. It's the kind of pub where you're likely to fall into an interesting conversation.

There are traditional Irish music sessions most nights, and jazz on Fridays but – as befits a pub named after a poet - it also has its quiet periods when you often see lone diners with novels or collections of poetry propped up against their pints.

the cross of cloyne

Cloyne

near Midleton

Co. Cork

Eire

021 465 2401

serves dinner only, weds to

sun; bookings advised;

children welcome

The Cross of Cloyne, with its lilac and deep purple painted frontage, is a pub in the modern mould. There's a bar-room with pine fittings, a contemporary stone fireplace and blanket-thick woollen curtains flung over iron poles, where you eat at small, low tables. Then across the hallway is a sleek dining room with a mirror-backed bar, bright abstract paintings, black ash furniture and a slate-grey floor. If this room sounds too restauranty, rest assured that the fact it's part of a pub makes all the difference to the atmosphere: it's laidback and informal, and you're just as welcome to have one dish and a pint in here as three courses and a bottle of wine. The same menu is served throughout.

Chef and owner Colm Falvey trained in the neighbouring village, at Ballymaloe House, the country house hotel that really put Irish cooking on the map. His background shows in everything he does, with dishes that have not a single extraneous flavour or bit of frippery; just the very best ingredients cooked with flair and restraint. Classic French cooking, Mediterranean influences and modern Irish cooking are all deftly blended. There's a salad of grilled Ardsallagh goat's cheese with Italian black olives, hake from Ballycotton with a crab and herb crust, and poached wild Blackwater salmon with broad bean hollandaise. The food is so fresh and clean-edged that it makes you feel as though you've been swimming in the sea.

Simple plates of pasta or fishcakes are just as good, and puddings such as blackcurrant fool with shortbread are delicate yet homely. You could easily be eating at Ballymaloe House, except that it's a fraction of the cost. The place is full of savvy diners who know they've discovered a gem. Get there before the prices go up.

quarterdeck @ fiddler's green

The Square
Portaferry
Co. Down
Northern Ireland
028 4272 8393
www.fiddlersgreenportaferry.com
pub serves lunch and dinner
mon to sun, Quarterdeck serves
dinner only thurs to sat;
bookings advised;
children welcome; garden

Portaferry is an unspoilt little coastal town on the Ards Peninsula. As you drive out to it, you enjoy sweeping views over Strangford Lough. Fiddler's Green is a real old Irish pub and a great local. Everyone goes there, and they all talk loudly, discussing everything from the fishing quota to *Blind Date*. The bar, with its collection of hats and eccentric junk-shop finds, is bursting with character.

They've always served pub standards such as scampi or ham and eggs here, but now the owners' sons, the McCarthy brothers, have opened a dining room, the Quarterdeck, at the back of the building. In a big, high-ceilinged room, surrounded by a seascape mural, you can eat modern brasserie food such as Thai fishcakes with noodles or – even better – updated Irish classics such as shank of lamb in ale with champ, and cod with cabbage and bacon. It's admirably unpretentious stuff, done just right. Desserts, including chocolate brownies, fruit crumble and steamed sponge, are indulgent, comforting finales.

The folk sessions in the bar, with the McCarthys on guitar, bass and accordion, are feel-good, family affairs and make a great end to the evening.

lennon's

121 Tullow St
Carlow
Co. Carlow
Eire
0503 31575
serves lunch only,
mon to sun;
bookings accepted;
children welcome

Lennon's is typical of the kind of modern watering hole that has evolved in the small, gourmet town of Kenmare in Co. Kerry: a pub that turns seamlessly into a café-restaurant at the back. Here, leather armchairs give way to modern cherry furniture and contemporary Irish art (constantly changing and always on sale). It's stylish without being in-your-face and attracts a clientele to match. 20-somethings sup Guinness at the front; trendy mums with toddlers fill the back (tea, coffee and cakes are served all day).

The staff are proud of the place and eager to please, and the food is a vibrant mix of modern and old-fashioned dishes based on sound Irish produce: courgette, bacon and Cashel Blue soup; deep-fried fritters of Irish goat's cheese with salad; and lamb shanks in Guinness. The breads are among the best you'll find in a country where good baking is valued. Lennon's is a great contemporary pub.

an sugan

41 Wolfe Tone Street
Clonakilty
Co. Cork
Eire
023 33498
serves lunch and dinner
mon to sun;
bookings accepted;
children welcome

An Sugan is a handsome-looking place on the outside, but the inside is more of a mish-mash. Two dining rooms sport furniture for giants – big, chunky pine tables and chairs – and the bar-room is a cross between a steak house and an old-fashioned Irish boozer. But it is a genuine place, a million miles away from an Irish theme pub, and the food is unpretentious and delicious.

Chef Sinead O'Crowley gets the freshest fish and she knows how to cook it. You think scampi is a dish of reconstituted fish flakes in leaden batter? Not here. O'Crowley's scampi is to die for: fresh, fat, sweet prawns, with the lightest coating of breadcrumbs, accompanied by homemade tartare sauce. Then there are such dishes as a deeply savoury and satisfying crab gratin, buttery grilled lobster, simple cod with a herb crust, and wild salmon with mayonnaise. The accompanying potatoes are big and floury and the carrots taste as though they've just been pulled from the ground, while side salads are some of the best you'll find. Puds are copious, down-home affairs like apple pie. The meat dishes, however, aren't nearly as good as the fish.

the derg inn

Terryglass

Co. Tipperary

Eire

067 22037

serves breakfast, lunch
and dinner mon to sun;

bookings accepted;

children welcome; garden

The Derg Inn is the hub of village life in lakeside Terryglass. A large, deep-pink house with duck-egg-blue shutters and Swiss chalet trims on the eaves, it dominates the main street physically and socially, serving as boozer, café, breakfast bar, restaurant, post office and grocery store.

Boating types from the nearby marina pitch up early for big bowls of cappuccino. Those with more robust constitutions come a bit later for a full Irish breakfast washed down with a pint of Guinness. By lunchtime, the place is buzzing with locals and holidaymakers of all ages and types, reading papers, playing cards over plates of beer-battered fish, or shooting pool between mouthfuls of steak sandwich.

All this happens in several rooms, both large and small, which range in style from smart modern country – bottle-green tongue-and-groove, ironwork lamps, big chunky tables, black-and-white landscapes on the walls – to basic roadside bar, with rickety tables and red-and-white check paper tablecloths. Sawdust gets scattered on the stone floor in wet weather and the pub labrador snuggles up to whoever will stroke him.

The Derg is full of life and diversity and has evolved to suit everyone's needs. It also serves some delicious, unfussy food. The chef, a six-foot-blonde Dane with a pony-tail or, as one local woman puts it, 'a pure Viking vision', is famed in these parts for his renditions of solid Irish dishes. People come from miles around to eat his Irish stew and corned beef with cabbage, but if your appetite is smaller and your tastes more modern, you can try the brasserie fare on offer instead, such as crab with guacamole or duck with sweet and sour cabbage.

grace neill's

33 High Street

Donaghadee

Co. Down

Northern Ireland

028 9188 4595

www.graceneills.com

serves lunch and dinner
mon dinner to sun lunch;

bookings advised
(dining room only);

children welcome

This is supposed to be the oldest pub in Ireland, established in 1611. Friendly staff will regale you with stories of sightings of Grace Neill's ghost (she owned the place in the 19th-century and evidently did not want to leave), whether you want to hear them or not. The front bar hasn't been changed for decades: it's dark and snug, with low ceilings made of wood from an old ship and walls covered in aged painted Anaglypta. The room beyond that, which they call 'The Library', has been modernized, but is meant to feel old: lots of mahogany, green leather sofas, highly polished flagstones, marble-topped tables and a gorgeous copper-topped bar. A further room, right at the back, is done in French brasserie style.

Co. Down is bursting with good restaurants, but chef-owner Steven Jeffers still manages to make Grace's a destination dining address. George Best, who used to live nearby, likes the food here so much that it's said he even had it delivered to him in hospital. Jeffers goes for big flavours in stunning dishes, such as a soup of Stangford mussels and pumpkin with Thai spices, as well as more traditional Irish offerings, such as honey-glazed loin of bacon with plums and cabbage. Some dishes suffer from having too many flavours on one plate, but Jeffers mostly pulls it off, and there's a simpler menu if you prefer less fancy fare, with offerings such as pork and leek sausages with champ, or superbly-flavoured rib-eye steak with garlic butter.

You'll have difficulty not striking up conversation with your fellow diners – Grace's is an ebullient place – and if you come for Sunday lunch, when there's live jazz all afternoon, just plan on writing off the rest of the day.

index